THE HUMANITIES

Λέγοιτο δ'ἂν ἱκανῶς, εἰ κατὰ τὴν ὑποκειμένην
ὕλην διασαφηθείη. τὸ γὰρ ἀκριβὲς οὐχ ὁμοίως ἐν
ἅπασι τοῖς λόγοις ἐπιζητητέον, ὥσπερ οὐδ' ἐν τοῖς
δημιουργουμένοις . . . ἀγαπητὸν οὖν περὶ τοιούτων
καὶ ἐκ τοιούτων λέγοντας παχυλῶς καὶ τύπῳ τἀληθὲς
ἐνδείκνυσθαι, καὶ περὶ τῶν ὡς ἐπὶ τὸ πολὺ καὶ ἐκ
τοιούτων λέγοντας τοιαῦτα καὶ συμπεραίνεθαι. τὸν
αὐτὸν δὴ τρόπον καὶ ἀποδέχεσθαι χρεὼν ἕκαστα
τῶν λεγομένων. πεπαιδευμένου γάρ ἐστιν ἐπὶ τοσοῦτον
τἀκριβὲς ἐπιζητεῖν καθ' ἕκαστον γένος, ἐφ' ὅσον
ἡ τοῦ πράγματος φύσις ἐπιδέχεται. παραπλήσιον
γὰρ φαίνεται μαθηματικοῦ τε πιθανολογοῦντος
ἀποδέχεσθαι καὶ ῥητορικὸν ἀποδείξεις ἀπαιτεῖν.

Our inquiry will be adequately pursued, if it is as clear
as the subject matter allows it to be. Precision is not to be
sought equally in all discussions any more than in all crafts.
We must be content in a study dealing with such subjects
and based on such premises to point out the truth approximately and in outline, and in dealing with things which are
only for the most part true to reach conclusions of the same
kind. In this spirit also should everything that we will have
occasion to say be received. For it is a mark of an educated
man to look for exactness in each class of things only so far
as the nature of the subject permits. It is quite manifestly
equally foolish to accept probable arguments from a mathe-
matician and to demand of a rhetorician scientific proofs.

—ARISTOTLE, *Nicomachean Ethics*, I, III

The Humanities

APPLIED AESTHETICS

Louise Dudley and Austin Faricy

THIRD EDITION

Revised by Louise Dudley

McGRAW-HILL BOOK COMPANY, INC.

New York   Toronto   London

1960

THE HUMANITIES

17968

Binding decoration made from a segment of a hieroglyphic papyrus, early Nineteenth Dynasty, showing detail of the Chapter of Offerings from the *Book of the Dead*. (Courtesy of the Metropolitan Museum of Art, gift of Edward S. Harkness, 1935.)

PREFACE

The traditional ways of presenting the humanities—literature, music, painting, sculpture, architecture, and the dance—are well established and are familiar to everyone. But that they have, or should have, different particular objectives is not so generally realized. All of them are trying to attain "appreciation," but each is striving for an appreciation of a different aspect of the field. Courses in practical painting are trying to instill an appreciation of the craft of the painter at the same time that they are trying to make painters of the students. Histories of art are concerned with an appreciation of the periods, influences, growths of techniques and expressional possibilities, and perhaps the lives of the principal artists. Surveys focus attention on the great examples of an art, and often, in a nontechnical way, its development. Histories of culture, as they are usually called, show the parallels, the influences, the reflections between works of art and the development of science, sociology, religion, politics, and philosophy. In these traditional approaches to the study of humanities, the work of art is nowhere treated for its own sake, and little if any attention is given to the relationship existing between the arts.

On the other hand, everyone wants to know how to study and enjoy a specific work of art for itself, and he would like to know how the same principles apply in more than one art. Accordingly, an experiment was set up at Stephens College to integrate the study of the arts and at the same time focus attention on an understanding and appreciation of the individual masterpiece. Throughout the years the basic content has remained essentially the same, but the organization of the material has varied. At first the work was divided into three sections,

v

one being devoted to the visual arts, one to music, and one to literature. This arrangement did not stress sufficiently the unifying principles of the separate arts. Later, the arts were united under a rather rigid philosophical scheme, with the concepts of time and space as the basis of organization. This arrangement proved too abstract. Still later, the plan was changed again, this time to the one used in the present volume, where the arts are united and the different aspects are studied as they are usually brought to one's attention in the consideration of any specific work.

In content, this study of the humanities differs from the traditional approaches in three major ways. First, it approaches the arts through their common principles: subject, function, medium, elements, organization, and style. Second, it tries to supply the vocabulary and equipment by means of which any individual can make his own criticism and his own analysis, and realize his own appreciation. (He has thus the opportunity to learn the language of art, the methods by which the artist expresses himself, and how such knowledge assists in an individual's understanding and appreciation.) Third, and most important, this approach uses the work of art as the beginning and end of its study. It starts with the surface and penetrates inward as far as the abilities of the teacher and the students can go. Its sole business is the examination and appreciation of the works of art it encounters, and to this end the entire effort of the book is bent.

Before the first edition of this text was published in 1940, two experimental versions had been printed for class use; I wrote the first, Mr. Faricy and I the second. For the first and second editions Mr. Faricy contributed the chapters on music. For the present revision I alone am responsible. I have, however, made extensive use of the illustrations selected and edited by Mr. Faricy.

Most of the chapters have been rewritten. The changes may in most cases be traced to the classroom. In twenty years of teaching one learns which passages are obscure and which are unnecessary. In the revision, as in the original text, I have tried to write simply and honestly, and to avoid the temptation to be learned or subtle or "modern." It is a great corrective to keep in mind the young person of about eighteen and to write only what he or she will be interested in and can understand.

In the text, the footnotes, and the bibliography, I have recorded, as far as possible, my indebtedness to specific authors. I regret that I have not been able to do so in every case. In an enterprise which has extended over a period of years, I have in some cases forgotten whether an idea or an illustration is original or borrowed. In other cases, I know the idea is not original but I am not able now to indicate the exact source.

In recording obligations it is a pleasing duty to name the two men who, more than any others, helped in the development of this material: the late Dr. James M. Wood, formerly President of Stephens College, and the late Dr. W. W. Charters, formerly Educational Advisor of Stephens College. They gave the initial impetus for the study and stood by it through all its early failures and experiments.

For the present edition I am indebted to Thad Suits and Don Woolley of the Stephens staff for drawings and photographs, and to John Sewall, a former colleague, for help in the difficult business of finding materials.

My greatest obligations, however, are to those who have taught the course. In the years of its existence the class has grown from a single section of fifteen or twenty students to twenty-five sections enrolling over six hundred students. As a result I have had many associates in the work, and every one of them has given something of information and challenge.

Louise Dudley

CONTENTS

LIST OF ILLUSTRATIONS

FOREWORD TO THE TEACHER

This book is designed as a means, not an end. It should be a key whereby the teacher can open doors through which the student will see new fields to be explored, new waters to be crossed, and new mountains to be climbed. The danger for the student is that the mountains may seem too steep, the waves too high, and the fields too wide in extent for safe and comfortable passage. It is wise, therefore, to reassure him at the start and to go as slowly as need be for confidence and understanding. In other words, students are in the habit of thinking of the arts as belonging in separate compartments, each of which is difficult and intricate. When they are faced with the prospect of studying all of them together, they are often confused by the very multiplicity of detailed knowledge which they are afraid they may be asked to master. Therefore it is wise for the teacher to move cautiously at the start.

The plan used in this book has proved generally satisfactory over a period of about twenty years, beginning as it does with that point about art of which the student is most conscious and with which he is most concerned, the subject. However, there have been many different points of emphasis, and much valuable experience has been accumulated as the book has been used by different teachers. Some are mentioned here.

A Tour of the Text. Many teachers like to begin the course with a tour of the whole book. The table of contents and the outline in Chapter I may serve as a sort of itinerary.

A good first assignment might be to take an example from each of the arts and go over it with the students in class, formulating some statements which are to be included in each of the six areas of inquiry. The second step could be to let the student do an analysis, however simple and stumbling, of an example in each of the arts. It is a good plan to file this analysis away to be compared with another of the same work done at the end of the year.

Illustrations. There are two ways of handling the examples in a text of this kind. One is to have a very small number of illustrations which are used over and over. One poem and one painting and one song may be used to illustrate almost every point in the text. The disadvantages of this method are two: (1) Students and faculty both get bored with the same examples, no matter how excellent they are, and (2) the students are unnecessarily limited in the art with which they become familiar. Therefore a different way has been adopted for this text. A new illustration is given of each point made; thus the student is constantly being introduced to new examples of art. There are a few exceptions, but this plan is usually followed. Since, however, any example can be used to illustrate almost any point, each example may be used many times by the teacher or the student.

Intensive Study. Many teachers have found it wise to introduce units for intensive study from time to time. These units fall into two classes: (1) The study of a story which can be found in a number of different arts. Examples are the tales of Romeo and Juliet, Orpheus and Eurydice, Othello, Samson and Delilah, The Creation, The Nativity, and The Crucifixion. Such subjects are especially good at the beginning of the year when the student is learning to think in terms of more than one art. (2) Careful study of any single work. For the symphonies included in the bibliography, I have found the "Skeleton Scores" (published by Theodore Presser Company) to be of great value and of about the right degree of difficulty.

Materials. The course may be taught with many or with few additional materials. A minimum number of records and slides is necessary. Usually the class is asked to buy additional material in literature. Some teachers prefer a large anthology; others buy separate volumes for specific works: individual editions of the plays and novels read, a small anthology for lyric poetry, etc. With the inexpensive editions of classics on the market now, an adequate number can be purchased at a nominal cost.

Motion pictures for class study are frequently very useful. Those we have found most valuable fall into three classes: (1) Films showing techniques. Frequently the movie shows a technique more clearly than it could be shown in real life. Examples are demonstrations of techniques of painting, print making, or playing musical instruments. (2) Films which illustrate works of art; for example, *Matisse,* or *French Tapestries.* (3) Films for comparison with other mediums; for example, the movie version of a play or novel, to be studied with the play or the novel.

Teacher's Choice. For all phases of the course it is essential that each teacher choose his own materials. The teacher who feels little or no enthusiasm for the examples he is teaching is handicapped from the start.

Creative Work. The humanities course is not designed primarily for creative work, and yet there are many ways in which the student will learn better by doing creative work. Sometimes it is wise to assign creative work; usually it is wiser to suggest that those who wish may try their hands at such work. In every case emphasis should be put on the idea presented, rather than on the technical skill displayed. Students like to attempt abstractions, soap carvings, poetic forms, or original tunes.

Applications. Dedicated as it is to the proposition that art is experience, this book has failed if it is used solely as a text which the student is supposed to master as it stands. Instead, it should be the starting point for him to go out and find examples and experiences of his own. From the beginning of the course he should be encouraged to apply the facts and principles learned to other illustrations besides those given in the text. If, for instance, he is learning about subject, he can study the next concert he hears for the pieces which have subject and those which have not. For this purpose it does not matter whether it is a program on the radio or a "live" concert. Such illustrations should be from as many different sources as possible. At the end of each chapter are questions or suggested applications that may be made; however, the student should be encouraged to go on to new explorations of his own.

As the student learns to work independently, he gains confidence in his ability to perceive and to make judgments; then he loses his fear of the high mountains, the wide plains, and the perilous seas. No one text and no one teacher could ever help the student climb all the mountains or cross all the plains and seas. The purpose of this text will have been accomplished if the beginner learns the first steps, and discovers that in the world of art there lie adventure and a source of rich, full living open to everyone.

THE HUMANITIES

CHAPTER 1

INTRODUCTION: THREE BASIC ASSUMPTIONS

THE PURPOSE AND PLAN OF THE BOOK

This book has to do with the appreciation of the humanities. It is a subject which concerns everyone, for every day everyone makes decisions that are determined by his knowledge and appreciation of art. A young man chooses his handkerchief with reference to his socks and his tie; a child listens for his favorite radio serial; a teacher waits for a certain musical program on the radio. Even a hardheaded businessman who would deny emphatically any interest in art will trade in his automobile for one with better lines or will pay an extra hundred dollars for a special paint job! These are not examples of great art, it is true, but they show concern for art values.

Most of these people know that they are not getting all the pleasure they could from art. They know other persons who are getting greater pleasure from concerts, from paintings, from plays, and from poetry than they are. And whether or not they realize it, they themselves would like to be getting more. In the realm of art they feel like the inhabitants of the world before Prometheus brought them the divine fire:

Though they had eyes to see, they saw to no avail; they had ears, but understood not; but, like to shapes in dreams, throughout their length of days, without purpose they wrought all things in confusion.
—AESCHYLUS (fifth century B.C., Greek dramatist),
Prometheus Bound, 11, 447–451, tr. by Herbert Weir Smyth [1]

[1] The Loeb Classical Library, published by Harvard University Press.

This book is written for those people; its purpose is to guide them toward the light, where they may see and judge for themselves. It cannot and it does not pretend to teach appreciation. Appreciation cannot be taught. Appreciation, like any other pleasure, is an experience, and experience can only be had. A book like this can, however, show some of the bases of appreciation, some of the qualities that others have enjoyed, and some of the basic principles that underlie all the arts. In short, this book tries to open the eyes and ears to art in order that, seeing and hearing, men may understand and enjoy.

The plan of the book is to start with the more nearly obvious principles of art and proceed to the more abstruse. The first two questions asked of any work are usually: "What is it about?" and "What is it for?" The first question concerns the *subject,* the second the *function* of a work of art. Accordingly, subject and function are discussed first. Subject and function, however, are not essential to all art, for there are works without subject and works without function. For this reason subject and function are grouped together as background.

The next question asked of a work of art is: "What is it made of?" The answer is a *medium.* Medium, of course, is essential, since any work of art can be known only as it is presented in some medium.

The fourth question is: "How is it put together?" This question is extremely important because it has to do with *organization.* The elements of an art, whether they be tones, colors, or words, must be arranged according to some pattern to express some meaning; in brief, they must be organized before we can have a work of art.

The two remaining questions are in the nature of a comment on the finished creation. One asks: "What is the personality, the individuality of this work?" This is the matter of *style.* The other asks: "How good is it?" This is *judgment.*

If these items are put in order we have the outline of the book:
1. Background
    a. Subject. What is it about?
    b. Function. What is it for?
2. Medium. What is it made of?
3. Organization. How is it put together?
4. Style. What is its temper? Its mood? Its personality?
5. Judgment. How good is it?

Before we begin on the formal presentation of these points, however, there are certain assumptions about the nature of art which we need to clarify. They will determine our attitudes and our basic premises.

THE AGE AND IMPORTANCE OF ART

The humanities constitute one of the oldest and most important means of expression developed by man. Even if we go back to those eras called prehistoric because they are older than any periods of which we have written records, we find works to which we give an important place in the roster of the humanities. About eighty years ago, in 1879, a Spaniard, accompanied by his little daughter, was exploring a cave. Suddenly she began to cry, "Bulls! Bulls!" He turned his lantern so that the light fell on the ceiling of the cave, and there he saw the pictures of wild boar, hind, and bison which we now know as the Altamira cave paintings (Figure 1). Since that time similar paintings have been found in other caves, and the experts have given their judgment that these belong to the Upper Paleolithic Age, ten to twenty thousand years before Christ.

Great age is also found in poetry. The Greek epics the *Iliad* and the *Odyssey* date back to a time before the beginning of recorded history. These poems may have been put together between the twelfth

FIG. 1. *Galloping Wild Boar.* (Found in the cave of Altamira, Spain. Photograph, courtesy of the American Museum of Natural History.)

and the ninth centuries B.C., but it is generally believed that they are collections of earlier tales which had been known and sung for many years before that time.

No matter what age or what country we consider, there is always art. And this art is not good because it is old, but old because it is good! Songs and stories, pictures and statues are preserved because they are alive, because they meet the needs of people, because they are liked. There is a timelessness and universality about art which makes us feel it is not old, that is, it does not grow old. The girl who says,

> Mother, I cannot mind my web today
> All for a lad who has stolen my heart away.

is not thinking that she ought to brush up on Sappho and the other Greek lyric poets. The chances are that she is having trouble doing her own work, all for a lad who has stolen her heart away. When we recite the Psalms, "The Lord is my shepherd I shall not want," or "By the waters of Babylon, we sat down and wept, yea we wept when we remembered Zion," we do so because we find in them something that fits our needs.

When we sing folk songs or tell tall tales of Paul Bunyan, we do so because we like them. Another old favorite is the tune to which we sing both "We won't go home until morning," and "For he's a jolly good fellow." Early French words of the song began "Malbrouk s'en va-t-en guerre" ("Marlborough is off to the wars"), and it is dated about 1709, when the Duke of Marlborough was fighting in Flanders. And it is said to have been a favorite of Marie Antoinette about 1780. It was introduced into the comedy of Beaumarchais, *Le Mariage de Figaro*, in 1784. The tune itself, however, is much older. It was well known in Egypt and the East, and is said to have been sung by the Crusaders. But none of us who sing it today are thinking of these aspects of the song. We sing it because we like the song, because it fits our mood when we want a jolly, rollicking air.

Suppose it is a poem we are thinking about.

> Márgarét, are you grieving
> Over Goldengrove unleaving?
> Leáves, líke the things of man, you
> With your fresh thoughts care for, can you?
> Áh! ás the heart grows older
> It will come to such sights colder

By and by, nor spare a sigh
Though worlds of wanwood leafmeal lie;
And yet you will weep and know why.
Now no matter, child, the name:
Sórrow's spríngs aŕe the same.
Nor mouth had, no nor mind, expressed
What heart heard of, ghost guessed:
It ís the blight man was born for,
It is Margaret you mourn for.
—GERARD MANLEY HOPKINS (1844–1889, British poet),
Spring and Fall: To a Young Child (1876–1889) [2]

Homer's epics are prehistoric, Hopkins's little lyric seems written almost yesterday. But each is judged by itself, for its own qualities, without regard to age.

In the final evaluation of any work of art, age and nationality are matters of comparative indifference. Bach, Beethoven, and Brahms lived in different centuries and all composed great music; but the final evaluation depends on the music alone. Epstein's *Portrait of Oriel Ross* (Figure 2) was made in 1933, over three thousand years after the head of Queen Nefertiti of Egypt (Figure 3). There are differences that tell of the country and the date, but our judgment is determined by the faces themselves.

The first point then about the humanities is that art has been created by all people, at all times, in all countries, and it lives because it is liked and enjoyed. A great work of art is never out of date. This point has been stated in many different ways by different people. Some speak of the intrinsic worth of art: its value is in itself. Berenson, the art critic and historian, talks of the "life-enhancing" value of art. Whatever the words used, the fact remains that we like art for itself, and the value of art like all spiritual values is not exhausted. It is used but it is not used up. It does not grow old.

ART AND EXPERIENCE

Our second point in this study begins to ask the question, "What is art?" To this an immediate answer is that art is experience.

When we say that art is experience, we mean by experience just

[2] From *Collected Poems* by Gerard Manley Hopkins, Oxford University Press.

what we always mean by the word: the actual doing of something. If
you have talked on television you know what that experience is. If you
have never ridden a horse or fallen in love you do not know those
experiences. You have always wanted to see the home of Washington
at Mount Vernon; you have read much about it and have seen pictures
of it, but you do not have the experience until you see it for yourself.
It is one experience to sing a song and it is a different experience to
hear it. It is an experience to read a story or see a play just as it is an
experience to write the story or act in the play. But it is not an experience of the story, the song, or the play just to hear *about* it.

Once you have had an experience you know what it is as no imagin-
ing can tell you. It may not be as accurate, as detailed, or even as clear
as the information you can get from reading or secondhand reports,
but it has a different quality. Experience is thus a kind of knowledge,

Fig. 2. Jacob Epstein
(1880–1959), British
sculptor, born in U.S.A.
Portrait of Oriel Ross
(1933). (Bronze.
Height: 26½ inches.
New York, Museum of
Modern Art; gift of
Edward M. M. Warburg.
Photograph, courtesy of
Museum of Modern
Art.)

but it is not the kind you get in geometry or history. And there is no proof of this knowledge except the individual's consciousness of what he has experienced. All art depends on experience, and if one is to know art, he must know it not as fact or information but as experience.

On the lowest level, this means that since a work of art is always something to be seen or heard, we must see it or hear it, or see *and* hear it, if we are to know what it is. We must hear the music and see the painting if we are to know them. Years ago, Gertrude Stein was asked why she bought the pictures of the then unknown artist Picasso. "I like to look at them," said Miss Stein. After all, what can you do with a picture except to look at it? A painting is something to be looked at, a poem or a piece of music is to be heard. Many of the people who say they do not like poetry have never heard it; they read a poem as they would a stock market report, or a telephone directory.

Fig. 3. *Nefertiti.* Queen of Egypt, Eighteenth Dynasty (ca. 1375 B.C.). (Plaster cast of a painted limestone original now in Berlin, New Museum. Life-size. New York, courtesy of the Metropolitan Museum of Art; Rogers Fund, 1925.)

It is interesting and valuable to learn about any work, to know what the critics have said, or what were the conditions under which it was produced. But unless one knows the work itself, has experience of it, he knows little. The first and last demand of art is *experience*.

It is because of this physical appeal of art that we like to dwell on individual works. We look at a painting or a statue though we have seen it a thousand times. We drive a block out of the way every morning to see a building we admire. We continue to get pleasure from looking at Queen Nefertiti even though we have known this statue for years. In music we wear out a record playing it over and over, and if we are alone or among good friends we hum little bits of the melody. When we have heard Bach's great aria "My heart ever faithful, rejoices, rejoices," the chances are that we will be singing it all the next day. We quote poetry to ourselves and to others:

> If thou didst ever hold me in thy heart,
> Absent thee from felicity a while
> And in this harsh world draw thy breath in pain
> To tell my story.
>> —SHAKESPEARE,
>> *Hamlet,* V, ii, 356–359

> It ís the blight man was born for,
> It is Margaret you mourn for.
>> —HOPKINS,
>> *Spring and Fall: To a Young Child*

The scientist has no such love for the manner in which a scientific idea is expressed. He does not walk down the street repeating happily to himself, "The square of the hypotenuse is equal to the sum of the squares of the other two sides," or "The distance of the sun from the earth is some ninety millions of miles." Such ideas may be and are just as exciting as those of poetry, but the idea and the words are not the same; to the scientist the physical presentation of an idea is not important. To the poet the idea and the words are the same. Change a word and you have changed the poem.

It is this quality of experience that I think MacLeish had in mind when he said:

> A poem should not mean
> But be.[3]

[3] Concluding lines of *Ars Poetica,* from *Poems 1924–1935* by Archibald MacLeish. Used by permission of Houghton Mifflin Company.

In any of the arts the physical presentation is the art. All of the arts *are* more truly than they *mean*.

Before leaving this discussion we may note certain characteristics of experience. First, the experience of art is personal and individual; like all experience, it depends on what you are, what you have inside you. In the last analysis your experience will not be exactly the same as that of any other person. Do not expect to agree with everyone else; all you can do is to be as honest and straightforward as you can.

Second, every experience is accompanied by some emotion, or emotional reaction. You like it or you do not like it. As you react, you think it is "wonderful," "frustrating," "fine"; or you say "Lord, what fools these mortals be!" Your feeling may be changed markedly when you have closer acquaintance with that work or artist, but there is always some feeling that is a part of the experience.

ART AND NATURE

There have been many books written about art, and many learned theories to explain it. Some of these are good, some are poor; sometimes they agree, often they disagree. But on one point there is universal agreement. Art is *not* nature. Art is made by man. Art and nature are opposites. What is art is not nature; what is nature is not art.

There is a story that a woman looking at a painting by Matisse said, "I never saw a woman look like that!" and Matisse replied: "Madam, that is not a woman, that is a painting." A woman must be looked at as a woman, and a painting as a painting. We have just quoted the lines from *Hamlet*,

> If thou didst ever hold me in thy heart,
> Absent thee from felicity a while
> And in this harsh world draw thy breath in pain
> To tell my story.

No dying man ever said that. Art is made by man, nature is not made by man. Nature has been studied by man and variations have been made by him, but not even the most brilliant scientist can make a flower or an ear of corn.

Art is made by man, and no matter how close it is to nature, it always shows that it was made by man. Therefore we have a right to ask of any work of art, "Why did the artist make it?" "What did he want to show?" "What experience was he trying to make clear?"

"What had intrigued him so much that he wanted to share it with others?"

As children, probably most of us thought an artist learned how to paint very much as we learned to sew on buttons, to drive a car, or to write on a typewriter. We supposed that when he found a scene he wanted to paint, he sat down and painted it. In this view the artist was a kind of human camera to reproduce a scene. Poetry and music seemed about as easy, if one "knew how." The artist needed only to find words to rhyme or melodies to write and that was all. Such a view is of course nonsense.

The artist sees or learns something that impresses him, he wants to put it into some form that others may understand it too, and he starts to make a picture, a poem, or a piece of music according to his present inspiration and his previous training. He does not worry much about beauty, but he wants desperately to get it "right," to have it express just the point he has in mind.

Suppose for instance a poet is feeling the intoxication and freshness of spring, the very first day of spring, "just spring." The children are all on fire with the new life of the day, they are so eager they can't take time to say Betty and Isabel or Eddie and Bill; instead, the words come rushing out all run together, bettyandisbel, eddieandbill. And all this is tied up in the poet's mind with the little old balloon man who is lame, "goat-footed" like a satyr, and whose whistle can be heard "far and wee." To express all that the poet has only words on paper; he cannot even use voice or hands! No wonder he can't write as people do ordinarily, "Dear Mr. Balloon Man, Have just received your communication, etc." No wonder his words spill here and there over the page. No wonder he makes up new words—*puddle-wonderful, mud-luscious*—and spaces the words *far and wee* to try to make clear the faint sound of the whistle when it is first heard, and then the way the sound dies away in the distance. And when E. E. Cummings has finished, we feel he has captured the right flavor of the day.

> in Just-
> spring   when the world is mud-
> luscious the little
> lame balloonman
>
> whistles   far   and wee

and eddieand bill come
running from marbles and
piracies and it's
spring

when the world is puddle-wonderful

the queer
old balloonman whistles
far   and   wee
and bettyandisbel come dancing

from hop-scotch and jump-rope and

it's
spring
and
    the

      goat-footed

balloonMan   whistles
far
and
wee

    —E. E. CUMMINGS (1894——, American poet),
    in *Just spring* [4]

Cézanne painted a landscape which he called *Well and Grinding Wheel in the Forest of the Château Noir* (Figure 4). It looks very like scenes we have seen, and we would say Cézanne had copied nature. For this painting, however, we have a photograph of the exact scene, so that we can compare the actual appearance of the landscape with Cézanne's version (Figure 5). First we notice the amount of detail. Cézanne gains unity by paying no attention to the textures of the trees, the grass, or the stones; he paints them all in similar fashion. Next is the arrangement. The trees on the right are smaller, and there are more of them. The well and the grinding wheel in the center are made larger and more important. The path to the well is left out. And while he has kept the curling branches of the trees on the left, Cézanne has made them into a curved pattern which draws the eye to the trees on the

[4] From *Poems 1923–1954*, Harcourt, Brace and Company, Inc. Copyright 1923, 1926, 1944, 1951, 1954 by E. E. Cummings.

Fig. 4. Paul Cézanne (1839–1906), French painter. *Well and Grinding Wheel in the Forest of the Château Noir* (1895–1900). (Oil. Size: 25½ by 31½ inches. Merion, Pa., Barnes Foundation.)

Fig. 5. Photograph of location of *Well and Grinding Wheel.* (Courtesy of Erle Loran, *Cézanne's Composition,* University of California Press.)

right, and with them makes a circular movement which encloses the entire design. In the painting also he has made the contrasts between light and dark much less pronounced than in the photograph. In the painting we see what Cézanne has done with the landscape, or we can say that it is Cézanne's reaction to the landscape. Cézanne has changed details from the way they were in nature, and by doing so he has made a design that we want to look at and study. It is not nature, but art.

Our Perception of the World

When we say that art is not nature and that we should not expect to find in art exactly what we find in nature, we assume that all of us see the same things in nature and that our vision is accurate. But only a little study proves the opposite. We may look first at the statue of a bull that was found in front of an ancient Assyrian Palace (Figure 6), and is usually referred to as the "Guardian of the Palace." I think you will agree he is an important animal, large and stately. He should be capable of guarding anything that needed to be guarded. He is a very realistic bull, in fact. But if you look carefully, you can see that this bull is not like nature: he has five legs. There are four on the side, as you would see them if you were looking at him from the side. But come around in front. If you meet a quiet bull head on, you expect to see

Fig. 6. *Winged Bull with Five Legs* (ninth century B.C.), from the Palace of Ashurnasirpal II. (Limestone. Height: 11 feet 6 inches. New York, courtesy of the Metropolitan Museum of Art; gift of John D. Rockefeller, Jr., 1932.)

two legs; one leg would look queer by itself, and so another leg was added.

Or turn to the Egyptians. We are all familiar with the Egyptian paintings of men and women, the thin straight bodies, stiff but graceful (Figure 7). We like them but they do not follow nature. We will start with eyes. If you look straight in a person's face, you see his eyes roughly as oval. If you look at a face in profile, the shape is entirely different. But when drawing a face the Egyptians made the head in profile with the eyes as of a full face. Nor was that all. The body was presented facing you, but the arms and legs were in profile. In those cases, they were, of course, as were the makers of the Assyrian bull, portraying what they knew, what they thought of as the typical appearance instead of the actual look of things.

The same principles hold true in all aspects of life. The early works of Beethoven were thought to be the ravings of an upstart, and the orchestras of Wagner's time protested that his scores could not be played. We are all inclined to see and hear only what we know is there, what we have been taught to see and hear. The artist opens our eyes and ears so that we can see the world more clearly. But through the artist, we can open our eyes and ears to new visions of life. And it is amazing how quickly we do learn to see what the artist is trying to show us. A few years ago,

FIG. 7. Egyptian figure illustrating conventions in Egyptian painting. (Drawing by Thad Suits.)

Fig. 8. Vincent van Gogh (1853–1890), Dutch painter, etcher, and lithographer. *The Starry Night* (1889). (Oil on canvas. Size: 29 by 36¼ inches. New York, Museum of Modern Art; acquired through the Lillie P. Bliss Bequest.)

students looking at van Gogh's *Starry Night* (Figure 8) protested they never saw the sky look like that; now they sit back with a general purr of content: "Ah, van Gogh's *Starry Night*."

SUMMARY

The three basic assumptions of this study of the humanities are:

1. Art has been created by all people at all times; it lives because it is liked and enjoyed.

2. Art is experience.

3. Art is not nature.

FOR FURTHER EXPLORATION

1. Judge the last cinema you saw by the outline for this book, as given on page 2.

2. Do the same for a novel, a poem, a piece of music, a house, a chair, a suit or dress you **admire**.

3. Look up the history of some song or game you have known for a long time.

4. Do the same for a poem, or a painting.

5. Do you ever forget where you are in the experience of reading a novel? In listening to a symphony?

6. Read other poems by E. E. Cummings. How does the form help in getting the spirit of a poem?

7. Can you give from your own experience instances when you have lost the fun of a dance or a song because you were self-conscious? Can you give other instances when you forgot yourself?

8. What opportunities do you look forward to in the coming year in the way of

    a. Visits to art galleries

    b. Orchestra concerts

    c. Operas

    d. Plays

    e. Lectures or readings by artists, musicians, or writers

    f. Other art experiences

9. In which of the experiences listed in Question 8 do you already take pleasure? Which give you little pleasure at present?

10. Make a list of ten works of art you have enjoyed in the past year. Include music, movies, and houses, as well as stories, novels, poems, and paintings. What division do you find between new and older works?

11. Professor Loran has excellent analyses of Cézanne's paintings in his volume *Cézanne's Composition*. The student should look there for further study of Cézanne's distortions.

12. Have you ever had the experience of confusing art with life? What were your feelings?

PART ONE

BACKGROUND

CHAPTER 2

SUBJECT

I like to see it lap the miles,
And lick the valleys up,
And stop to feed itself at tanks;
And then, prodigious, step

Around a pile of mountains,
And, supercilious, peer
In shanties by the sides of roads;
And then a quarry pare

To fit its sides, and crawl between,
Complaining all the while
In horrid, hooting stanza;
Then chase itself down hill

And neigh like Boanerges;
Then, punctual as a star,
Stop—docile and omnipotent—
At its own stable door.
    —EMILY DICKINSON (1830–1886, American poet),
       I Like to See It Lap the Miles [1]

WHAT IS SUBJECT?

Subject is the term used for whatever is represented in a work of art. In the painting by Cézanne the subject is the landscape. In the poem at the beginning of this chapter the subject is a railroad train. The same

[1] From *The Poems of Emily Dickinson,* by Bianchi and Hampson, by permission of Little, Brown & Company.

19

subject is used in Honegger's music, called *Pacific 231*. Each of the
caryatids on the famous Porch of the Maidens on the Erechtheum
(Figure 9) represents a young woman. The short piano composition
by Ravel called *The Fountain* shows the rise and fall of the water in a
fountain. In brief the subject of a work of art answers the question,
"What is it about?"

Not all arts have subject. Those arts without subject do not represent
anything. They are what they are without reference to anything in the
natural world. The caryatids of the Erechtheum represent maidens,
but the other columns of the building do not represent anything at

Fɪɢ. 9. Erechtheum, Porch of the Maidens (420–393 ʙ.ᴄ.). (Pentelic marble.
Height of each caryatid: 7 feet 9 inches. Athens, Acropolis. Photograph, courtesy
of the Royal Greek Embassy.)

Fig. 10. Erechtheum, North Porch. (Pentelic marble. Height of columns: 21 feet 7 inches. Photograph, Clarence Kennedy.)

all. The columns of the North Porch (Figure 10) are tall and graceful; they are very beautiful, but they do not imitate or represent anything. Ravel imitated water in the *The Fountain,* but a Bach fugue has no subject. Subject is not essential to art.

Not only do some works of art have subject and some not, but in the matter of subject we find characteristic differences between one art and another. Architecture, for example, is essentially an art which is not representational. Occasionally we will see houses built to look like ice-cream freezers or coffeepots, if they are used for selling ice cream or coffee, but they are recognized as freak examples, and fortunately they are rare. A building is constructed for a certain purpose (a home, a factory, an office); and it may be in a definite style (a Greek temple or a Gothic cathedral); but usually it has no subject. A building will frequently show details that are representational, as are the caryatids of the Erechtheum, although the buildings themselves are not representational, and have no subject.

If architecture is the art with the least use of subject, literature is the one with the most. When we read words we expect them to be *about* something. There are so-called poems and bits of prose which have no subject, but they are rare. So important is subject in literature that we usually name any piece of writing by its content: novel, ballad, epic, biography, essay, etc. Moreover, we specify the particular contents by saying a "novel of adventure," a "psychological novel," a "literary essay," or a "political essay."

Sculpture and painting usually have subject. In looking at a painting or a statue, we expect to recognize the subject, to know what it is about: a man, a horse, a landscape, etc. And as in literature, painting and sculpture are classified according to the subjects employed. Paint-

Fig. 11. Henry Moore (1898——), English sculptor. *Two Forms* (1934). (Pynkado wood. Height: 11 inches. New York, Museum of Modern Art; gift of Sir Michael Adler.)

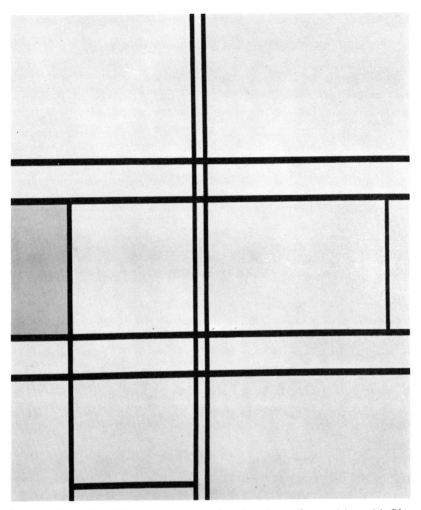

Fig. 12. Pieter Mondriaan (1872–1944), Dutch painter. *Composition with Blue and White* (1935). (Oil on canvas. Size: 41 by 38 inches. Hartford, Collection Wadsworth Atheneum.)

ings, for example, are identified as landscapes, seascapes, portraits, figure paintings, paintings of animals, etc. Statues are classified as portraits, single or group figures, animals, etc.

There is, however, a great deal of sculpture and painting without subject. The sculptor or the painter, like the architect, makes an arrangement of lines, shapes, and colors which is interesting in itself and which expresses his idea. Examples of this type are Henry Moore's sculpture *Two Forms* (Figure 11), and Mondriaan's painting *Com-*

position with Blue and White (Figure 12). In these cases the artists do not want or expect the critic to imagine any specific subject.

Of the combined arts the theater and the opera always have subject; the dance may or may not have subject. The minor arts, such as textiles, metalwork, and pottery, sometimes have subject and sometimes have not. Moreover, in these arts the subject may be a matter of complete indifference. One may eat with a certain spoon for months without ever noticing whether the design on the handle represents grapes or roses, or whether it has subject at all. Even in wallpaper and dress materials, where the design is more conspicuous, subject is of little importance. Choice is made on the basis of design and color rather than subject.

SUBJECT IN MUSIC

Music occupies a position about halfway between literature and architecture. A great deal of music has no subject: sonatas, études, fugues, etc. On the other hand, much music has subject; we had an example in *The Fountain.* Music without subject is called *pure music,* while music with subject is called *program music.*

Sometimes a distinction is made between program music which actually imitates the sounds in question and that which merely sets the mood and suggests the story or picture the composer had in mind. An example of the latter group is the composition called *Pictures at an Exhibition.* As the title indicates, Moussorgsky represents himself as visiting an art exhibit and looking at one picture after another. There are eleven pictures, with such different subjects as "The Old Castle," "Children in the Tuileries Gardens," and "Two Polish Jews." There is also a theme heard between each two pictures which represents the artist walking from one picture to the next. In this composition Moussorgsky tries to give the mood of each picture: romantic or gay, comic or quarrelsome, but he does not imitate the subject itself in the music. On the other hand, the sound of the music in *The Fountain* imitates the sound of the fountain, its ceaseless flow, its constant change, and

FIG. 13. (Right) El Greco (1541–1614), Spanish painter. *Resurrection* (ca. 1597–1604). (Oil on canvas. Size: 108¼ by 50 inches. Madrid, Prado. Photograph by Anderson.)

constant monotony. In *Pacific 231* the music imitates the sound of a train.

Music is unique among the arts in that it cannot make its subject clear. Even when the music is definitely imitative, as in Rimsky-Korsakov's *The Flight of the Bumblebee,* the subject is not always clear. If the music is played with no clue as to the subject, many people will not recognize what it is about. One person, hearing the piece about the bumblebee, realized that the music had subject, but decided that it represented a blizzard!

WAYS OF PRESENTING THE SUBJECT

Realism, Distortion, Abstraction

Realism. As we have said, no art is ever like nature. Even when he chooses a subject from nature, the artist changes, selects, and arranges details in order to express the idea he wants to make clear. Often the presentation of details and the organization of them in the work are so nearly obvious, and seem so natural, that we do not notice that the work is not like nature, as in Cézanne's painting. When this is the case, we say the work is *realistic.*

Fig. 14. Henry Moore (1898——), English sculptor. *Reclining Figure* (ca. 1935). (Elm wood. Dimensions: 19 inches high, 35 inches long, 17¼ inches wide. Buffalo, N. Y., Albright Art Gallery; Room of Contemporary Art Collection.)

Distortion. Distortion differs from realism only in degree. The word *distortion* is used when the change from nature is so great as to attract attention. We say the object is distorted when we notice that it is not like life.

In the *Resurrection* by El Greco (Figure 13), the bodies are unnaturally long. No natural bodies would ever be elongated in such a manner. El Greco was illustrating that part of the Creed which says of Christ that he

. . . was crucified, died and was buried. He descended into hell. The third day he rose again from the dead.

In his picture El Greco wanted the body of Christ to seem to rise, and it does seem to rise from the mass of writhing bodies around. A body of normal size would have seemed dumpy, stodgy, and still.

There are many degrees of distortion. Henry Moore's *Reclining Figure* (Figure 14) is much more distorted than the El Greco *Resurrection*.

Abstraction. Abstraction is a third way of presenting a subject. Sometimes an artist gets so interested in one phase of a scene or a situation that he does not show the subject at all as an objective reality, but only his idea of it, or his feeling about it. For example, Brancusi is impressed by the grace of a bird in flight, and by the sweep of its body as it flies through the air, so he tries to represent those qualities in his statue *Bird in Space* (Figure 15). It does not look like a bird, and it is not supposed to look

Fig. 15. Constantin Brancusi (1876–1957), Rumanian sculptor. *Bird in Space* (1919). (Bronze. Height: 54 inches. New York, Museum of Modern Art.)

like a bird. It is supposed only to convey an impression of the bird's grace.

Mondriaan has a painting which he calls *Broadway Boogie-Woogie* (Figure 16). Again, it does not look like Broadway, or boogie-woogie, yet it suggests many of the characteristics we associate with the dance: the disk of the piano player, monotony of beat, strong accent, improvisation, and the bright lights of the city. Probably no one would recognize the subject by himself, but once it has been suggested, he can see the connection. This painting looks very much like the Mondriaan painting we saw earlier, *Composition with Blue and White*. But that had no subject, and this has. Both types are commonly called *abstract*. A more distinctive term for the one without subject is *non-objective*.

The three terms, *realism, distortion,* and *abstraction,* must not be conceived as rigidly differentiated one from another, but rather as tendencies which merge one into the other, often in the work of a single artist. Picasso's *Old Guitarist* (Figure 18) seems more distorted, when compared with his realistic *Blue Boy* (Figure 17), than when compared with *Fernande* (Figure 19). And *Fernande* seems almost realistic when put by the side of *Ma Jolie* (Figure 20). In that picture the woman has disappeared into series of flat, or almost flat, straight-edged, transparent planes.

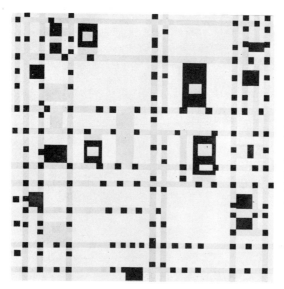

FIG. 16. Pieter Mondriaan (1872–1944), Dutch painter. *Broadway Boogie-Woogie* (ca. 1942–1943). (Oil on canvas. Size 50 by 50 inches. New York, Museum of Modern Art.)

Fig. 17. Pablo Picasso (1881——), Spanish painter. *Blue Boy* (1905). (*Gouache.*
Size: 40 by 22½ inches. Collection of Mr. and Mrs. Edward M. M. Warburg.
Photograph, courtesy Museum of Modern Art.)

Pure music and program music correspond exactly to the two types of abstraction in painting and sculpture. Pure music, like the nonobjective types, relies solely on its design. It is an arrangement of sounds, just as a nonobjective work is an arrangement of lines, colors, and masses. It conveys definite emotions—joy, gladness, sorrow, anticipation—but they are not connected with any particular events or situations. Program music is like those abstractions which have subject.

Fig. 18. Pablo Picasso. *The Old Guitarist* (1903). (Oil on wood. Size: 47¾ by 32½ inches. Courtesy, The Art Institute of Chicago. Helen Birch Bartlett Memorial Collection.)

You do not know what the subject is until you are told, but, being told, you understand.

Since the subject would not be known without the title, the question is often raised as to the advantage, or even the point, of giving a name to a picture or a musical composition, if it in no way bears any likeness to the object named. Would it not be better to count all such works nonobjective? Probably not. The title usually helps one to understand

FIG. 19. Pablo Picasso. *Fernande* (1909). (Oil on canvas. Size: 24¼ by 16¾ inches. Collection of Mrs. Henry H. Church. Photograph, courtesy Museum of Modern Art.)

Fig. 20. Pablo Picasso. *Ma Jolie* (*Woman with a Guitar*) (1911–1912). (Oil on canvas. Size: 39⅜ by 25¾ inches. New York, Museum of Modern Art; acquired through the Lillie P. Bliss Bequest.)

what the artist had in mind. In some cases, as in the Brancusi's *Bird in Space,* Honegger's *Pacific 231,* or Ravel's *The Fountain,* the name offers a real explanation of the artist's purpose and idea. In others, as in Picasso's *Ma Jolie* or Moussorgsky's *Pictures at an Exhibition,* the title gives the source for the original inspiration.

The Symbol

Another way of presenting a subject is through symbols. A *symbol* is a sign which by common agreement stands for something else. It is a kind of shorthand whereby long or complicated facts may be expressed in a short time or space. The bands on his sleeve indicate how long a railway conductor has been in the service of the company. Stars, bars, and eagles indicate rank in the army. Certain tunes on the radio tell what programs are to follow.

Often a person is recognized by his symbol. Mercury (Figure 21), the messenger of the gods, may usually be identified by his winged sandals, his staff entwined with snakes (caduceus), and his flat hat (petasos). The caduceus had magical powers over sleeping, waking, and dreaming, and as such became identified with healing. It is now the symbol of the medical profession and of the Army Medical Corps. Bacchus, the god of wine, is usually portrayed with grapes or grape leaves. In the vase painting by Execias, *Dionysus Sailing the Sea* (Figure 22), we recognize Bacchus (Dionysus) by the grapes and grape leaves which fill the upper part of the picture. The story is that one day while he was asleep, Bacchus was taken aboard a ship by some sailors who wished to sell him into slavery. Waking, the god asked them to take him to Naxos. When they refused, vines laden with grapes grew up around the mast, and the mariners were changed into dolphins.

FIG. 21. Giovanni da Bologna (ca. 1524–1608), Flemish-Florentine sculptor. *Mercury* (ca. 1574). (Bronze. Height: 5 feet 9 inches. Washington, D.C., National Gallery of Art; Mellon Collection.)

There are many symbols of the Christian Church: Peter is represented with a key because of Christ's saying that he gave Peter the keys
of the kingdom of heaven (Matt. 16:19). Paul is often represented
as a bald old man carrying a sword. The symbols of the four Evangelists Matthew, Mark, Luke, and John were commonly used in the
Middle Ages and are frequently found today. Matthew is symbolized as
a winged man, Mark a winged lion, Luke a winged ox, and John an
eagle. We see these in a characteristic setting in the tympanum, or
curved space above the door, of the cathedral at Chartres (Figure 23)..
Christ is in the center with his hand raised in symbol of blessing, and
around him are the four Evangelists.

A parable is based on symbols.

FIG. 22. Execias, Greek vase painter. *Dionysus Sailing the Sea* (550–525 B.C.).
(Black on red pottery. Diameter: 14½ inches. Munich, Antikensammlungen.)

FIG. 23. *Glorification of the Savior* (middle of twelfth century). (Stone. Height: ca. 29 feet. Middle portal of West Façade, Chartres Cathedral. Photograph by Clarence Ward.)

Behold a sower went forth to sow. And when he sowed, some seeds fell by the wayside, and the fowls came and devoured them up: Some fell upon stony places, where they had not much earth: and forthwith they sprung up, because they had no deepness of earth: And when the sun was up, they were scorched; and because they had no root, they withered away. And some fell among thorns; and the thorns sprung up, and choked them. But other fell into good ground, and brought forth fruit, some an hundredfold, some sixtyfold, some thirtyfold.

—MATT. 13:3–8

In the New Testament stories, the disciples often had to ask Jesus to explain his symbols, as they did in this case. Sometimes in literature one is not quite certain that a symbol is intended, as in the little poem by Frost:

> Whose woods these are I think I know.
> His house is in the village though;

He will not see me stopping here
To watch his woods fill up with snow.

My little horse must think it queer
To stop without a farmhouse near
Between the woods and frozen lake
The darkest evening of the year.

He gives his harness bells a shake
To ask if there is some mistake.
The only other sound's the sweep
Of easy wind and downy flake.

The woods are lovely, dark and deep,
But I have promises to keep,
And miles to go before I sleep,
And miles to go before I sleep.
                —ROBERT FROST (1875——, American poet),
                    Stopping by Woods on a Snowy Evening (1923) [2]

This poem offers no obvious difficulties; the images are clear-cut,
and the sense is clear. The poet stops to admire the scene in the snow,
but he does not pause very long because he has made promises he must
keep, and he has a long way still to go. But is this all? As one reads
he wonders if that is all the poem has to say, if there is not a further
meaning hidden in the seemingly simple lines. When Frost says:

But I have promises to keep,
And miles to go before I sleep,

does he have in mind just the trip home? Or does that seemingly simple
statement stand for something else? When he says "before I sleep,"
does he really mean "before I die"? In the "promises to keep," is he
thinking of work that he has set out to do? Does he refer to responsi-
bilities that he must meet before he dies? There is nothing in the poem
that says Frost has such a hidden meaning, but most of us think that
he has. And if we do, we decide that the poem is symbolic.

In Sandburg's *Grass*, the grass that covers all is clearly a symbol.
The poem means more than that grass grows on battlefields.

[2] From *Complete Poems of Robert Frost*, 1949. Copyright 1923, 1949, by
Henry Holt and Company, Inc.

Pile the bodies high at Austerlitz and Waterloo.
Shovel them under and let me work—
I am the grass; I cover all.

And pile them high at Gettysburg
And pile them high at Ypres and Verdun.
Shovel them under and let me work.
Two years, ten years, and passengers ask the conductor:
What place is this?
Where are we now?

I am the grass,
Let me work.
                    —CARL SANDBURG (1878——, American poet),
                        Grass (1918) [3]

Dreams and the Subconscious

Among the interesting recent ways of presenting the subject are those that have to do with dreams and the subconscious. Under the influence of Freudian psychology, the subconscious has come to be recognized as important in human conduct, and naturally it has found expression in art.

Subjects of this class attempt to show the inside of man's mind as well as the appearance of his outside world. They try to show thoughts and dreams that are not controlled by reason or any conscious order. The work which results is like its subject; it may be clear and vivid but it is not necessarily logical. Events and people are put together in unrelated and therefore irrational combinations. The reality of such scenes can best be understood if one remembers his own thoughts and dreams; he finds himself taking part in actions under circumstances which probably have to do with his ordinary life, but which are combined in forms that are strange and irrational.

Chagall's *I and My Village* (Figure 24) presents a rural scene. The two important characters are the man and the cow. Their faces are bound together in a circle and they look at each other with sympathy. The man holds a spray for the cow to eat. The cow is thinking of being milked, as we can tell from the small figures painted on her jaw. In the background are the other objects of the village—a workman

[3] Reprinted from *Cornhuskers* by Carl Sandburg, Henry Holt and Company, Inc.

FIG. 24. Marc Chagall (1887——), Russian painter. *I and My Village* (1911).
(Oil on canvas. Size: 85⅝ by 59⅝ inches. New York, Collection of the Museum
of Modern Art; Mrs. Simon Guggenheim Fund.)

with a scythe, a woman, and a row of the village houses—some of
them being right side up and some upside down.

The scene in Miró's *Composition* (Figure 25) is one of quiet and
peace. Individual details are hardly recognizable, but we can distinguish a seated dog in the upper left, and across the background a sug-
gestion of horned cattle. The whole is a spontaneous and intuitive

expression of the subconscious. Paintings of this type belong to the type called surrealism. It gets its name from its attempt to find the real *behind* the real, and to bring together the inner and the outer reality. Other painters of this school are Klee, Chirico, and Dali.

The attempt to locate and hold the subconscious is found in literature in the stream-of-consciousness novel, in which the author attempts to trap every thought or feeling that passes through the mind of a character; Joyce's *Ulysses* is an example. Time, naturally, becomes confused in the process.

In Arthur Miller's play, *Death of a Salesman,* the scene is sometimes the present and sometimes the past. When the salesman begins thinking about the past, it is acted out before him; then, just as in thought, it shifts back to the present. His two sons are sometimes men of thirty and sometimes boys playing football in high school. The man thinks of his

Fig. 25. Joan Miró (1893——), Spanish painter and print maker. *Composition* (1933). (Oil on canvas. Size 68½ by 77¼ inches. New York, Museum of Modern Art; gift of the Advisory Committee, by exchange.)

wife as a strong healthy woman bringing in the clothes from the yard, and so when she appears in those flashbacks of the past she appears about thirty-five and she carries a large hamper of freshly washed clothes. The scenes are not irrational in the sense that they are not reasonable, but they are irrational from the point of view of logical stage action in the passage of time.

There have also been examples of the fantastic and unreal in music. Saint-Saëns has written a tone poem on the dance of death, *Danse Macabre,* and Moussorgsky's *Night on Bald Mountain* describes a gathering of witches as they perform their mysterious rites.

BEAUTIFUL AND UGLY SUBJECTS OF ART

The last consideration in this chapter on subject has to do with the artist's choice of subject. What are fit subjects for art? Are there certain subjects that are not allowed in art? Almost instinctively one answers these questions by saying that the noble, the lovely, the beautiful, the distinguished, and the unusual are the proper subjects for art. Subjects such as we found in *The Fountain* or the caryatids of the Erechtheum seem appropriate subjects for art, and usually one has something of this kind in mind when he calls a subject "artistic." By the same impulse subjects that are ugly, undignified, and commonplace do not seem proper subjects for art.

But when one turns from theory to practice, this idea is not borne out. Most of us would turn away in disgust if we met in life the old man with the diseased nose, painted by Ghirlandajo in *Old Man and Boy* (Figure 26). But the old man's concern for the boy and the boy's adoration of the man are so great that we forget the man is old and ugly.

Shakespeare has painted a very clear picture of winter in a short lyric in *Love's Labour's Lost,* but muddy roads, a greasy, sweaty cook, a nose "red and raw" are not beautiful or lovely details.

> When icicles hang by the wall
>   And Dick the shepherd blows his nail
> And Tom bears logs into the hall
>   And milk comes frozen home in pail,
> When blood is nipp'd and ways be foul,
> Then nightly sings the staring owl,
>   "Tu-whit; tu-who!"

FIG. 26. Domenico Ghirlandajo (1449–1494), Italian painter. *Old Man and Boy* (undated). (Oil on wood. Height: 2 feet ⅜ inches. Paris, Louvre. Photograph by Alinari.)

A merry note,
While greasy Joan doth keel the pot.

When all aloud the wind doth blow
    And coughing drowns the parson's saw
And birds sit brooding in the snow
    And Marian's nose looks red and raw,
When roasted crabs hiss in the bowl,
Then nightly sings the staring owl,
            "Tu-whit; tu-who!"
        A merry note,
While greasy Joan doth keel the pot.
        —WILLIAM SHAKESPEARE (1564–1616, English poet
                                            and dramatist),
        Love's Labour's Lost, V, ii, 922–938 (ca. 1590)

Most emphatically, art is not limited to subjects that in themselves are beautiful, agreeable, lovely. The beautiful, the agreeable, the lovely, are subjects of art but they are not the only ones. Any subject may be a subject of art. We like in art what we do not like in nature, because we see the subject as it has been interpreted for us by the artist.

This last sentence answers the question of the relation of subject to *value* in a work of art. Does the choice of subject help to determine the final judgment as to whether a work may be counted good or bad, great or mediocre? Can we say that a work of art is good if it has a certain subject, and poor if it has another? A "beautiful" subject does not necessarily produce a good work of art, nor an "ugly" subject a poor one; a noble subject does not mean a noble work of art, nor an ignoble subject an ignoble work. The value of art does not lie in the subject but in what the artist does with his subject. The greatness of art comes not from the subject but from the artist.

FOR FURTHER EXPLORATION

1. Study the illustrations of visual arts in this text for examples of art with and without subject.

2. Do the same for the illustrations in a magazine. Study illustrations in advertisements as well as in the text.

3. Make a similar study of the illustrations of music in this text, in a magazine, in the program for a concert.

4. Experiment with program music. Play records without noting the titles, and see how often you can identify the subject.

5. Make a list of subjects found in dress goods, wallpaper, and silverware. Note the exactness (or lack of it) of the imitation.

6. Note the symbols used in the radio programs you listen to. Can you trace any connection between the symbol and the program?

7. Note the symbols used in the army and the navy, in college gowns and hoods, in the insignia employed by a railroad or a streetcar system.

8. Collect symbols used in everyday life. What per cent were auditory, what per cent were visual?

9. Compare the subjects used by two artists.

10. Make a list of examples from each of the arts that illustrate the use of the ugly in art. Do not forget *Oedipus Rex, King Lear,* and Grünewald's *Crucifixion.*

11. What is the symbolism in Blake's *The Sick Rose?*

12. In Ibsen's *A Doll's House* make a list of symbols used: card with cross on it, party dress, macaroons, etc.

13. Compare the music, literature, and painting of the past twenty years with earlier music, literature, and painting for the importance of:

    a. Nonimitative subjects

    b. Distortion

    c. Abstraction

    d. Use of ugly subjects

14. Compare, for the distortions, a figure from a fashion magazine with a figure from one of El Greco's paintings.

15. It has been claimed with reason that many of the irrational creatures in modern art derive from the fantastic drawings of Hieronymous Bosch (1450–1516). Study his painting of the temptation of St. Anthony. Can you give a reason for each of the strange malformations?

16. Professor Loran has excellent analyses of Cézanne's paintings in his volume *Cézanne's Composition.* The student should look there for further study of Cézanne's distortions.

CHAPTER 3

SOURCES OF ART SUBJECTS

> When I consider how my light is spent
> Ere half my days in this dark world and wide,
> And that one Talent which is death to hide
> Lodged with me useless, though my soul more bent
> To serve therewith my Maker, and present
> My true account, lest He returning chide,
> "Doth God exact day-labour, light denied?"
> I fondly ask. But Patience, to prevent
> That murmur, soon replies, "God doth not need
> Either man's work or his own gifts. Who best
> Bear his mild yoke, they serve him best. His state
> Is kingly: thousands at his bidding speed,
> And post o'er land and ocean without rest;
> They also serve who only stand and wait."
> —JOHN MILTON (1608–1674, English poet and essayist),
> *On His Blindness* (ca. 1655)

The subjects used in art are usually clear and obvious. They need no explanation other than the work itself. Rimsky-Korsakov's bumblebee and Emily Dickinson's railroad train are self-explanatory. Cézanne gives the name of the forest in which he found the well and grinding wheel that attracted his attention, but it is of no real importance in our understanding of the picture. On the other hand, there are many works of art which depend for their understanding upon some knowledge of the subject. When Tchaikovsky calls his suite *Romeo and Juliet,* he takes it for granted that we know the story of Shakespeare's young lovers.

Milton's sonnet, *On His Blind-ness*, tells the essential facts for the understanding of the poem: that the poet lost his eyesight when he felt his greatest work lay before him, and that through this experience he learned patience and submission to the will of God. However, one understands the poem better and enjoys it more if he knows, even vaguely, the story of Milton's life. Milton lost his sight in the service of his country before he had written the great poem he had always wanted to write and which he knew he could write, the poem he did write later in spite of his blindness, *Paradise Lost*. Moreover, one's pleasure is increased if he understands the reference to the parable of the talents in the twenty-fifth chapter of Matthew. Milton speaks of himself as having one talent which it is "death to hide," and of his Maker's chiding him on his return.

Similarly, anyone can tell, with no cause for confusion, that Michelangelo's *David* (Figure 27) is a statue of a young man, a very beautiful young man with a serious, determined expression on his face.

Fig. 27. Michelangelo (1475–1564), Italian painter, sculptor, architect, and poet. *David* (1501–1503). (Marble. Height: 18 feet. Florence, Academy. Photograph by Anderson.)

He is standing with his left arm raised and his right arm by his side. Anyone can identify the subject to this extent, and he can get a great deal of pleasure from the statue with no other information. But the sculptor has named the young man David, and we understand the statue better if we know the story of David and Goliath which Michelangelo had in mind. (It is told in I Samuel, chapter 17.)

The examples given so far can all be enjoyed without any knowledge of the subject. Botticelli's *Birth of Venus* (Figure 28) is very nearly nonsense if one accepts it at its face value. The young woman is very beautiful, but why should she be standing naked on the edge of a shell? Why does not the shell topple over? And what are the people doing on either side of her? Botticelli assumed that those who looked at his picture would know that Venus, the goddess of love and beauty, was born from the foam of the sea. In the picture, she is being blown to the shore by the winds, while one of the Horae (seasons) is waiting on the bank to receive her.

When we talk about the sources of art subjects, we are thinking primarily of subjects like those just mentioned which demand some knowledge on the part of the critic, if he is to get the idea the artist had in mind.

FIG. 28. Sandro Botticelli (1444–1510), Italian painter. *Birth of Venus* (ca. 1485). (Tempera on canvas. Height: 5 feet 3¼ inches. Florence, Uffizi. Photograph by Alinari.)

The number of subjects used in this way is limitless. Any artist may use any subject from any source, and it is impossible ever to know all the subjects of art. Even the scholar who has devoted his life to their study never expects to know all of them. There are, however, a few sources which are part of the background of every cultivated person. For convenience, they are grouped under these headings:

1. History and Legend
2. Greek and Roman Mythology
3. Christianity
4. Derived Works

HISTORY AND LEGEND

In one sense, all art is conditioned by the historical period and place in which it is created. The dress, the houses, the manner of life, the thoughts of a period are necessarily reflected in the work of the artist. Such general references, however, may be taken for granted, and we do not call a subject historical unless it refers to specific places, persons, or events.

Historical subjects are numerous. One reason is that rulers desire to see themselves and their deeds, the great events of their time, perpetuated. Another and more important reason is that artists are interested in and sensitive to the events in the world around them. Daumier was protesting against social injustice in *Rue Transnonain* (Figure 44). When a shot from one of the windows of No. 12, Rue Transnonain wounded an officer, the soldiers rushed into the building and killed the inhabitants. Daumier's lithograph depicts a scene when they had left. A similar protest is found in Picasso's *Guernica* (Figure 29), the unarmed Basque city that was bombed by the Fascists in the Spanish Civil War of 1936 to 1939. A different and more usual type of historical painting is found in portraits. Goya's portrait of *Maria Luisa of Parma* (Figure 30) is probably an excellent likeness of the lady, and at the same time it is a telling commentary on her character and disposition.

Legend and Folklore

Historical subjects as such can usually be identified and recognized with little trouble; records are kept, histories are written, and references are usually clear and easy to find. In quite a different class is legend,

FIG. 29. Pablo Picasso (1881——), Spanish painter. *Guernica* (1937). (Oil on canvas. Mural 11 feet 6 inches by 25 feet 3 inches. Collection of the artist on extended loan to the Museum of Modern Art, New York. Photograph, courtesy of the Museum of Modern Art.)

the elder sister of history. Legend may be defined as history that is not
or cannot be authenticated. It may be believed and in its earlier stages
is usually given credence, but the facts are not verifiable. Arthur and
Lear for example are legendary kings of Britain. Charlemagne is a

FIG. 30. Francisco Goya (1746–1828), Spanish painter, etcher, and lithographer.
Maria Luisa of Parma (painted between 1790 and 1792). (Oil on canvas. Size:
43⅝ by 33⅝ inches. New York, courtesy of the Metropolitan Museum of Art;
bequest of Mrs. H. O. Havemeyer, 1929. The H. O. Havemeyer Collection.)

historical king of France, but the exploits of his nephew Roland are
legendary. Till Eulenspiegel, the hero of Richard Strauss's tone poem,
Till Eulenspiegel's Merry Pranks, is the legendary bad boy of medieval
Germany.

Wagner used legend for the subject of his great tetralogy *The Ring
of the Nibelung.* In it he tells the saga of the Nibelung gold from the
time it was stolen until it was restored to the Rhine maidens after
causing the downfall of the gods themselves.

GREEK AND ROMAN MYTHOLOGY

Greek and Roman mythology has been a very important source for subjects in art. The stream of its influence on Western civilization may be traced primarily to two sources. First are the works of Greece and Rome during the period of Greek and Roman civilization, from the sixth century before Christ to the fifth century after. Those arts are so well known that they count as a definite part of our inheritance: architecture, drama, poetry, sculpture, and painting. Second are the arts of Europe during the Renaissance, the period of revived interest in things Greek and Latin between the twelfth and the fifteenth centuries. During this period, poets, painters, and sculptors drew very largely from Greek and Roman sources for their subjects.

Of the examples already mentioned, the poems of Homer and Sappho, the Erechtheum, and the vase showing *Dionysus Sailing the Sea* belong to the first period; Botticelli's *Birth of Venus* belongs to the second.

Stories from Greek and Roman mythology center around the gods and the heroes. Each of the gods had his own province and was known by some symbol. Jupiter for example was the king of the gods and was known by his thunderbolt. Bacchus, we have seen, was god of wine and was shown with grapes and grape leaves.

About each of the gods there clustered many stories. We have already noted a story about the birth of Venus. Proserpine, the daughter of Ceres (Demeter) was carried off by Pluto to be queen of the under-world. Ceres implored Jupiter for the restoration of her daughter, and at last a compromise was made whereby Proserpine will forever spend half her time with her mother, and half with her husband. The six months Ceres has her daughter with her it is summer.

In addition to the stories of the gods, there are many tales of the heroes, who were mortal men in close touch with the gods, and in whose exploits the gods themselves assisted. Each of these heroes became the nucleus for a series of stories to which any auther might add additional tales as the fancy struck him. Among the heroes are Perseus, who killed the Gorgon, Medusa, and saved the life of Andromeda; Oedipus, who was doomed to kill his father and marry his mother; and Theseus, who killed the Minotaur with the aid of Ariadne and then, tiring of her, deserted her on the island of Naxos, where she was met and loved by

Bacchus. Titian's painting *Bacchus and Ariadne* (Figure 31) shows Bacchus leaping from his chariot to greet Ariadne; she has gathered up her skirts, preparing to flee, when she looks back at the god.

The greatest of all Greek stories, however, center about the War of Troy, which was fought over Helen, whose face ". . . launched a thousand ships, and burnt the topless towers of Ilium." We find many references in art to one or another story connected with Troy, such as the judgment of Paris when the shepherd lad had to choose which of the three goddesses was the most beautiful, and the use of a wooden horse by the Greeks to obtain entrance to Troy. The *Laocoön* (Figure 32) represents the punishment inflicted on the priest when he urged the Trojans not to take the horse into the city.

The three great classical epics are concerned with the war of Troy.

Homer's *Iliad* tells of the war itself, beginning with the anger of Achilles and narrating the events through the death of Hector. Homer's *Odyssey* describes the wanderings of Ulysses, and Vergil's *Aeneid* describes the adventures of Aeneas and the founding of Rome.

Fɪɢ. 32. School of Rhodes. *Laocoön* (ca. 40 B.C.). (White marble. Height to right hand of Laocoön: 8 feet. Rome, Vatican Museum. Photograph by Alinari.)

CHRISTIANITY

Christianity has exerted a greater influence on the art of the western world than any other single source. When we say Christianity, we mean not only the Bible, but all Jewish and Christian history, legend, and ritual. They may be classified under four headings:

The Bible

The Apocrypha

Legends and lives of the saints

The ritual of the church

The Bible

The Bible, as is commonly recognized, is not a single book but a library. The books of the Bible may be grouped as follows:

Old Testament (39 books)

1. History (Genesis through Esther). The historical books give the story of the Jews from the creation to the Babylonian exile.

2. Poetry (Job through the Song of Songs). Job is a poetic drama; Proverbs is a collection of wise sayings and epigrams. Song of Songs and Ecclesiastes are, respectively, a group of marriage songs and a statement of gently cynical philosophy.

3. Prophecy (Isaiah through Malachi). The Prophets were not soothsayers, but practical men who judged and interpreted the affairs of their own times. They were patriots, reformers, preachers, and teachers.

New Testament (27 books)

1. History. The four Gospels: Matthew, Mark, Luke, and John; The Acts of the Apostles.

2. Letters. The Epistles written by Paul and others to the Christian churches that were just starting in the various parts of the world.

3. Apocalypse. The Revelation of St. John.

Any consideration of the Bible in relation to art must take into account the fact that the Bible itself is great art. For the English-speaking people, the Bible has the additional advantage of being available in the King James version, probably the greatest translation ever made. So the Bible not only is a source of art, but is itself art.

The most frequently used subjects are taken from the life of Jesus. And in the life of Jesus, the accounts of his birth and death are most often chosen. Artists of each generation have tried to picture the

Madonna, the Annunciation, the Magi, the shepherds, the scourging, the crucifixion, the deposition, and the entombment. Beckman's *Deposition,* T. S. Eliot's *Journey of the Magi,* and Rouault's *Head of Christ* (Figure 33) are modern uses of New Testament subjects. In the Old Testament, the stories of the creation are probably more important than any others, though reference is frequent to the heroes of the Old Testament: Abraham, Jacob, Moses, Samson, David, Elijah, and the others.

Narratives can be used as subjects for art more easily than songs or lyrics; and for that reason, the historical books have exerted a greater influence on art than the poetic or prophetic books. Their influence has been felt, however, especially in music. The oratorio *The Messiah* takes its text in part from the Prophets. The opening tenor recitative uses the words of Isaiah, chapter 40, "Comfort ye, comfort ye, my people."

Fig. 33. Georges Rouault (1871–1958), French painter. *Head of Christ* (*Christ flagellé*) (1905). (Oil on paper. Size: 45 by 31 inches. From the Collection of Walter P. Chrysler, Jr.)

Fig. 34. William Blake (1757–1827), English poet, painter, and engraver. *When the Morning Stars Sang Together* (ca. 1825). (Engraving. Size: 6 by 7½ inches. Photograph, Don Woolley.)

Blake's engraving *When the Morning Stars Sang Together* (Figure 34) is taken from the book of Job. When the Lord answers Job out of the whirlwind, he asks:

> Where wast thou when I laid the foundations of the earth?
> Declare, if thou hast understanding.
> Who hath laid the measures thereof, if thou knowest?

55

> Or who hath stretched the line upon it?
> Whereupon are the foundations thereof fastened?
> Or who laid the corner stone thereof;
> When the morning stars sang together,
> And all the sons of God shouted for joy?

—JOB 38:4–7

Honegger has written an oratorio on King David. Haydn's great oratorio is, as the title indicates, on the subject of the creation.

The Sistine Ceiling. It has been a practice not uncommon to tell stories from the Bible in a series of pictures. One of the greatest of these was made by Michelangelo to decorate the ceiling of the Sistine Chapel; it is therefore called the Sistine Ceiling (Figure 35). The chapel is a long narrow room, about 155 by 45 feet. In painting this space, Michelangelo chose to divide it into a number of small areas.

Down the center of the ceiling is a series of nine rectangles telling the story of the creation through the time of Noah (Figures 36, 37).

1. *Separation of Light and Darkness*
2. *Creation of Sun and Moon*
3. *Creation of Land and Water*
4. *Creation of Adam*
5. *Creation of Eve*
6. *Temptation and Expulsion*
7. *Sacrifice of Noah*
8. *The Deluge*
9. *The Drunkenness of Noah*

The pictures given odd numbers in this list are smaller than those with even numbers, and at each corner of these small sections is a figure of a nude man (Figure 38). These figures are primarily decorative. Around the central panels is a row of figures representing the Prophets of the Old Testament and the sibyls of classic mythology. Beginning with the one at the left of the first panel, they are identified as follows (Figure 39):

1. Jeremiah
2. Persian sibyl
3. Ezekiel
4. Erythraean sibyl
5. Joel
6. Zachariah
7. Delphian sibyl
8. Isaiah
9. Cumaean sibyl

Fig. 35. Michelangelo (1475–1564), Italian painter, sculptor, architect, and poet. Ceiling of the Sistine Chapel (1508–1512). (Fresco. Length: 132 feet, width: 45 feet. Rome, Vatican. Photograph by Anderson.)

FIG. 36. Michelangelo. *Creation of Adam*, detail of Sistine Chapel ceiling. (Length of Adam: 10 feet. Photograph by Anderson.)

FIG. 37. Michelangelo. *Temptation and Expulsion,* detail of Sistine Chapel ceiling. (Photograph by Anderson.)

Fig. 38. Michelangelo.
Decorative Nude, detail of
Sistine Chapel ceiling.
(Photograph by Anderson.)

Fig. 39. Michelangelo.
Libyan Sibyl, detail of
Sistine Chapel ceiling.
(Photograph by Alinari.)

10. Daniel
11. Libyan sibyl
12. Jonah

In the triangles that separate the Prophets and sibyls are the ancestors of Christ, and in the corners are other scenes from the Old Testament and the Old Testament Apocrypha.

The Apocrypha

The Apocrypha are those books of the Bible which were not accepted in the canons of the Old and the New Testaments. The Apocrypha of the Old Testament include some books found in the Greek Old Testament (the Septuagint) and the Latin version prepared by Jerome (the Vulgate). They are not in the Jewish canon or in the Protestant Bible. In them are found narratives (*Judith, Susanna,*

Fig. 40. Giotto (1266–1336), Italian painter. *Joachim Returning to the Sheepfolds* (ca. 1305). (Fresco. Height of figures: 3½ feet. Padua, Arena Chapel. Photograph by Alinari.)

Tobit), books of wisdom (*Ecclesiasticus*), history (*Maccabees*), and prophecy (*Baruch*).

The New Testament Apocrypha comprise all the early stories of the lives of Jesus and Mary. The stories that have had the greatest influence on art are those that have to do with the birth and death of the Virgin.

The story is that Joachim and Anna were prosperous and devout, but their childlessness was a source of great affliction to them. On the day when the children of Israel offered their gifts to the Lord, Joachim's offering was refused because he was without child. Joachim was sorely grieved and went off to the country alone. Later in answer to their fasting and prayer, an angel appeared to each of them, foretelling the birth of Mary, declaring her greatness, and bidding them dedicate her in the temple to the service of God. In time Mary was born, and when she was three years old her parents presented her in the temple, where she lived in the greatest piety until she was twelve years old.

In the Arena Chapel at Padua, Giotto has painted a cycle of frescoes depicting the Life of the Virgin. The picture of *Joachim Returning to the Sheepfolds* (Figure 40) shows the dejection of Joachim after his offering has been refused. In his sadness he does not even realize that he has reached the sheepfolds. The shepherds hold back in doubt and in fear of intruding, but the little dog recognizes his master and runs to meet him.

Legends and Lives of the Saints

The saints are those people formally recognized by the Christian church because of the exceptional holiness and piety of their lives. About them many stories have been told, and these have found their way into the arts. There is, for instance, the story that one day when St. Jerome was teaching, a lion walked into the room and lifted up its paw. All the students fled, but St. Jerome, noticing that the lion was wounded, pulled a thorn from its paw. After that the lion was Jerome's constant companion. In Dürer's engraving of St. Jerome (Figure 41), the saint is pictured working in his study; the scene is one of scholarly quiet and order, and right in front is a large lion, sleeping peacefully.

The legends and lives of saints present a difficult problem because they are so numerous. Many collections of these stories have been made, one of the most popular being the one made in the Middle Ages by Jacobus de Varagine, called the *Golden Legend*; but no account

FIG. 41. Albrecht Dürer (1471–1528), German painter, engraver, and wood carver. *St. Jerome in His Cell* (1514). (Engraving. Size: about 9¾ by 7½ inches. New York, courtesy of the Metropolitan Museum of Art; Fletcher Fund, 1919.)

of the lives of the saints can ever be complete, because saints are still being canonized, and new miracles are still being recorded.

Ritual

The ritual of the church has been of great importance in art. The prayers and the words of the responses are beautiful. Through constant repetition they have become familiar to everyone and they have had great influence on language and speech patterns. Just as important has been the influence on music; the various rituals were early set to music, and the composers of each generation wrote new music for the services. The most important of all the rituals of the church is the Mass, which is the celebration of the Holy Communion. It is regularly in five parts (only the opening words are given):

Kyrie: "Lord, have mercy upon us."
Gloria: "Glory be to God on high."
Credo (Creed): "I believe in one God."
Sanctus: "Holy, holy, holy."
Agnus Dei: "O Lamb of God, that takest away the sins of the world."

DERIVED WORKS OF ART

A last category of subjects may be found in those works that take their subject from other works of art. Brueghel has used the subject of Icarus for one of his paintings, and Auden was inspired by the painting to write a poem. The Greek myth tells that Icarus, the son of Daedalus the great artisan, was given wings by his father. Since the wings were fastened on by wax, Daedalus warned the boy not to fly too near the sun. But the boy, exulting in his new strength and power, could not restrain himself; soon the wax melted, he fell into the sea, and was drowned.

In Brueghel's painting *The Fall of Icarus* (Figure 42) the boy is almost submerged; only one leg is seen as it disappears into the water. Nearby is a luxurious ship, and on a slight rise a farmer is plowing with a horse; below is a shepherd who is looking up at the sky, his sheep all around him. Auden gives his poem the name of the museum in which the painting is found.

Musée des Beaux Arts

About suffering they were never wrong,
The Old Masters: how well they understood
Its human position; how it takes place
While someone else is eating or opening a window or just walking dully
     along;
How, when the aged are reverently, passionately waiting
For the miraculous birth, there always must be
Children who did not specially want it to happen, skating
On a pond at the edge of the wood:
They never forgot

Fig. 42. Pieter Brueghel, the Elder (ca. 1525–1569), Dutch painter. *The Fall of Icarus* (ca. 1554–1555). (Tempera on canvas. Height: ca. 2 feet 4 inches. Copyright A. C. L. Bruxelles.)

That even the dreadful martyrdom must run its course
Anyhow in a corner, some untidy spot
Where the dogs go on with their doggy life and the torturer's horse
Scratches its innocent behind on a tree.

In Brueghel's *Icarus,* for instance: how everything turns away
Quite leisurely from the disaster; the ploughman may
Have heard the splash, the forsaken cry,
But for him it was not an important failure; the sun shone
As it had to on the white legs disappearing into the green
Water; and the expensive delicate ship that must have seen
Something amazing, a boy falling out of the sky,
Had somewhere to get to and sailed calmly on.
        —W. H. Auden (1907——, English poet now living in the United
        States),
        Musée des Beaux Arts [1]

We have already spoken of Tchaikovsky's suite based on Shakespeare's play *Romeo and Juliet.* Debussy's *Afternoon of a Faun* is

[1] From *The Collected Poetry of W. H. Auden.* Copyright 1940 by W. H. Auden, reprinted by permission of **Random House, Inc.**

based on the poem by Mallarmé, and the ballet is based on both. Rimsky-Korsakov's *Scheherazade* finds its source in the Arabian Nights. Browning's poem *Fra Lippo Lippi* was inspired by the painting *The Coronation of the Virgin* by Fra Filippo Lippi. Strauss takes his subject *Don Quixote* from the novel by Cervantes. Maeterlinck's play *Pelléas et Mélisande* was used by Debussy for his opera of the same name.

Dramas are often based on novels, and operas on plays; it is almost a rule that cinema plots be taken from dramas or novels. Works that derive from other works of art are always individual and can never be classified or grouped together. Therefore, it is sufficient for our purpose merely to note that works of art often are so derived.

CONCLUSION

These classifications of the sources of art are by no means exhaustive, but they cover the more important ones! Yet it should never be forgotten that no matter how many classifications are made, no matter how many examples are given, these are never enough. The task, as stated at the beginning, is endless. Artists take their subjects when and where they please, and often they lead us a merry chase before we know and understand what they have referred to. But no matter how difficult the reference, a work of art can never be fully understood until its subject is known.

APPENDIX

Sources of Art Subjects—Outline

1. Norse mythology
   a. Name survivals
      Tuesday, Day of Tyr (Tiu), god of battles
      Wednesday, Day of Woden, king of gods
      Thursday, Day of Thor, god of thunder
      Friday, Day of Freya (Freja), goddess of music, love, and spring
   b. Wagner, *The Ring of the Nibelung*
      i. The operas
         The Rhinegold
         The Valkyrie (Die Walküre)
         Siegfried
         The Twilight of the Gods (Götterdämmerung)
      ii. Main characters
         The Gods

Wotan, king of the gods
Fricka, wife of Wotan
Freya, spring
Loki, fire
The Valkyrie Brunhild
The Rhine Maidens
The Giants
The Nibelungs
  Alberich
  Mime, the artificer who forged Tarnhelm (helmet), Notung (sword),
    and the ring
The Volsungs
  Sieglinde (wife of Hunding)
  Siegmund
  Siegfried
The Gibichungs
  Gunther
  Gutrune
  Hagen (son of Alberich)

2. Greek mythology and legend
  a. Important gods and goddesses (The Roman name is given first, then the
    Greek. After the names are the province and the attributes by which the
    god is recognized.)
      Jupiter, Zeus. Supreme ruler of the gods. Frequently seen with a thunder-
        bolt in his hands
      Juno, Hera. Wife of Jupiter. Shown with a peacock
      Minerva, Athene or Athena. Goddess of wisdom. On her breast is the
        aegis on which is the head of Medusa who turns men to stone
      Mars, Ares. God of war
      Vulcan, Hephaestus. God of fire
      Apollo. Sun, music, poetry
      Diana, Artemis. Moon. Usually carries a bow, often with crescent moon
        in hair
      Venus, Aphrodite. Love and beauty. Seen with swan, sparrow, and dove
      Mercury, Hermes. Messenger of gods. Represented with caduceus (staff),
        petasos (hat), and wings on ankles
      Cupid, Eros. Son of Venus. Blind. Carries bow and arrows
      Ceres, Demeter. Agriculture. Represented with sheaves of corn and
        poppies
      Bacchus, Dionysus. Wine. Shown with tiger, grape leaves, and grapes
      Pluto, Hades. King of the underworld
      Proserpina, Persephone. Wife of Pluto, daughter of Ceres
      Neptune, Poseidon. God of sea. Shown with trident
  b. Myths of the gods.
      i. Jupiter—Danaë
        Europa
        Io

    ii. Apollo—Daphne
        Phaethon
   iii. Diana—Actaeon
   iv. Venus—Adonis
        Cupid and Psyche
        Atalanta's Race
c. Myths of the heroes
    i. Perseus—Medusa
       Andromeda
   ii. Theseus—The Minotaur
      Ariadne
  iii. Oedipus—The Sphinx
     The King—Jocasta
  iv. Jason—Golden Fleece
     Medea
d. The Trojan War
    i. The origin of the war
      (*a*) Wedding feast of Peleus and Thetis
      (*b*) Judgment of Paris
      (*c*) Iphigenia in Aulis
   ii. The war—Homer's *Iliad*
      (*a*) The wrath of Achilles
      (*b*) Death of Hector
  iii. The fall of Troy
      (*a*) The Palladium
      (*b*) The Wooden Horse
      (*c*) Laocoön
  iv. The wanderings of Ulysses—Homer's *Odyssey*
      (*a*) The lotus-eaters
      (*b*) The island of Circe
      (*c*) The meeting of Nausicaä
      (*d*) The return to Penelope. The fate of the suitors
   v. The adventures of Aeneas. Vergil's *Aeneid*
      (*a*) Dido
      (*b*) Visit to hell
3. Christianity
  a. The Bible
    i. The best known stories from the Old Testament
      (*a*) The beginnings
          Creation and Fall
          The first murder, Cain and Abel
          The flood, Noah
          The tower of Babel
          The story of Abraham
            Sacrifice of Isaac
            Isaac and Rebecca
          Jacob

(*b*) Stories of heroes
      Joseph and his brethren
      Moses
      Joshua
      Jephthah
      Samson
      David
      Elijah and Elisha
ii. Most important stories from the New Testament
   (*a*) The birth of Jesus
      Birth of John the Baptist
      Annunciation, Magnificat
      Birth in Bethlehem, shepherds, Magi, flight into Egypt
      Presentation in temple, Song of Simeon
   (*b*) Events in life of Christ
      Baptism
      Temptation
      Woman of Samaria
      Calling of Disciples
      Rich young ruler
      Mary and Martha
      Mary Magdalene
      Peter walking on sea
      Keys given to St. Peter
   (*c*) Parables and sermons
      Prodigal Son
      Sermon on Mount
      Sower
      "Can the blind lead the blind?"
      Tribute to Caesar
   (*d*) Trial, death, and resurrection
      Last Supper
      Garden of Gethsemane
      Trial
        Peter's denial
        Scourging
        Barabbas
      Crucifixion
      Burial
        Pietà (pictorial representation of Mary mourning over dead
          body of Christ)
        Entombment
      Resurrection
b. Legends and lives of the saints (a few names and symbols):
   St. Barbara. Patron of buildings. Represented with a building
   St. Cecilia. Patron saint of music and musicians. Usually represented
  with a musical instrument

St. Christopher. Ferryman who carried Christ across the water

St. Francis. Founder of the Franciscan order. Represented in monastic habit with hempen cord. Usually represented with the stigmata in reference to the legend that he was transfixed with the wounds of Christ

St. George. Patron saint of England. Usually represented in full armor conquering the dragon

St. Jerome. A father of the Western church in the fourth century. The translator of the Vulgate. Usually represented as an old man studying or writing, often with a lion

St. Patrick. Patron saint of Ireland. Often shown with snakes because of the legend that he drove the snakes from Ireland

St. Sebastian. A young Roman officer who was killed for being a Christian. Usually represented as tied to a stake and shot full of arrows

FOR FURTHER EXPLORATION

1. Study all the pictures in this book for their use of subjects from Christianity, mythology, history, etc.

2. Do the same for the illustrations in any magazine.

3. Find modern uses of Greek and Christian stories.

4. Explain the references to mythology in these words:

titanic	martial	Dionysiac
chaotic	vulcanize	panic
saturnine	volcano	Plutonian
saturnalian	venereal	protean
Promethean	mercurial	Atlantean
jovial	cereal	erotic
Junoesque	Bacchic	Neptunian

5. Make yourself familiar with the great stories of the Bible.

6. Study any painter's work for his use of different kinds of subjects.

7. Do the same for a sculptor.

8. Do the same for a musician.

9. Do the same for a poet.

10. Compare the text of Haydn's *Creation* with its biblical sources.

11. Do the same for Handel's *Messiah*.

12. Three modern composers have made settings for Psalms that are well worth studying:

Stravinsky, *Symphony of Psalms*

Honegger, "Psalm of Penitence" from *King David* (Psalm 51)

Dello Joio, *A Psalm of David* (Psalm 51)

CHAPTER 4

FUNCTION

DEFINITION

Benvenuto Cellini, the famous goldsmith, made an elaborate little bowl for Francis I, King of France (Figure 43). It is of gold on a black ebony base; on it are two figures: a woman representing the land and a man representing the sea. We identify the man by the trident, which is the symbol of Neptune, the god of the sea. As we look at the bowl and marvel at its exquisite workmanship, we ask, "What is it for?"

The answer to the question "What is it for?" gives the *function* of an article. Cellini made his bowl as a container for salt, and from its function it is called a saltcellar. As used in this book, the word *function* will be reserved for such definite, practical, and usually utilitarian meanings.

FUNCTIONAL AND NONFUNCTIONAL ARTS

Obviously, function plays a larger part in some arts than in others. Architecture is entirely functional: buildings are always built for some special purpose. The applied arts are almost entirely functional. In fact, they are called *applied* arts because they have function. Rugs, blankets, clothes, jewelry, cups and saucers, plates, teapots, sugar bowls, baskets—one need only name examples to realize that each is made for some definite and specific use. Moreover, in the applied arts, as in architecture, function is so important that it has usurped the name of the art in the identification of individual works; examples of those arts are ordinarily known by their function alone. We speak of a painting, a poem, or a statue, but we do not usually speak of a building or a piece of ceramics; we say instead a school, a church, a plate, a saucer.

Compared with architecture and the applied arts no other art is so highly functional, though every art can show works that are functional. Religion, as we have seen, is the greatest single subject in all art, and most religious art was created either for worship or for instruction. Primitive peoples frequently combine the arts in their religious ceremonies as they dance and sing, and pronounce incantations before the statues or other representations of their gods.

Aside from their use in religion, painting and literature probably have least to do with purely practical values. When we think of a painting or a poem as a work of art, we think of the value it has in itself and not of some work it can do. There are, however, functional writings and paintings. *Uncle Tom's Cabin* was written for the definite purpose of fighting slavery, and it did much to arouse antislavery sentiment before the Civil War. Oliver Wendell Holmes's short poem *Old Ironsides* was written in protest against a naval order that the frigate

Fig. 43. Benvenuto Cellini (1500–1572), Italian sculptor and goldsmith. *Saltcellar of Francis I* (ca. 1545). (Gold and enamel. Height: about 8 inches. Vienna, Kunsthistorisches Museum.)

Constitution be destroyed. This ship, known as "Old Ironsides," was famous for its exploits during the War of 1812. Holmes's poem, which begins with the familiar line: "Aye, tear her tattered ensign down!" aroused so much resentment that the order to scrap the old ship was countermanded; her "tattered ensign" was not torn down.

Expository and argumentative writings are functional in so far as they are designed to accomplish some definite end. Newspaper stories and pictures are primarily functional; they want to make clear the news. All advertisements, whether in words or in lines and color, are functional in that they are designed to influence people to buy the products advertised.

Many works are cherished for themselves after their functions have ceased, and only these have the right to be considered as art. *Uncle Tom's Cabin* and *Old Ironsides* are cases in point. The war speeches of Churchill are now being printed and read. The lithographs by Daumier which appeared for forty years in the periodical *Charivari* as cartoons of the day are collected and reproduced. *Rue Transnonain* (Figure 44), as we know, shows the aftermath of an insurrection, but we like it as a drawing, not as a record of fact or a protest against abuses of the times.

FIG. 44. Honoré Daumier (1808–1879), French lithographer and caricaturist. *Rue Transnonain* (1834). (Lithograph. Size: about 11½ by 17½ inches. New York, courtesy of the Metropolitan Museum of Art; Rogers Fund, 1920.)

FUNCTION IN MUSIC

Music, in its origins, was primarily functional, its two sources being the dance and religion. The earliest peoples invoked their gods by beating the drum and singing, and from that time to the present music has been of primary importance in worship.

Dance music includes the ballet as well as tunes for social and folk dances, such as jigs, waltzes, minuets, fox trots, polonaises, mazurkas, and *rumbas*. In the dance, music is essential to mark the rhythm and so to keep the dancers together. It also sets the mood of the dance as war-like, gay, elegiac, or religious.

Closely akin to dance music are marches, work songs, and game songs. A march serves the same purpose as a dance in that it marks the time for people walking in a procession, whether it be a military occasion, a wedding, or a funeral. Work songs mark the rhythm of work. Chanteys are sung by sailors when lifting anchor or loading cargo. The popular Russian folk song, *The Volga Boatman,* helped the sailors in their struggle against the current of the river. Game songs are about halfway between dance and work songs. In *The Farmer in the Dell* or *London Bridge Is Falling Down,* the song is sung as the game is played, and the song is an essential part of the game.

Certain compositions become identified with certain specific occasions. One march is used for the President of the United States. Another, Handel's "Dead March" from *Saul,* is used for the funerals of the royal family in England. The Wagner and the Mendelssohn marches are so universally used in America for weddings that the wags have wondered if that wedding is legal which does not employ one of them.

With the development of musical instruments, music outgrew its narrow dependence on these two main functions, and we now have much music that has no connection whatever with either the dance or religion: symphonies, sonatas, and operas. On the other hand, many musical compositions retain a connection with their functional origin though they are no longer functional. Few of the polonaises and mazurkas of Chopin, for example, could be used as accompaniment for a dance. Bach's great work, the Mass in B minor, is too long to be used for church services, but it retains the form of the Mass designed for church ritual. Lullabies and serenades also are dissociated from their original use and are treated merely as musical forms, yet they retain certain connotations: the lullaby, of suave melody and swaying rhythms; the serenade, of night and love.

FUNCTION IN SCULPTURE

Sculpture is much more functional than painting or literature. One of the greatest single uses of sculpture is in religion. From the earliest times people have erected statues for religious purposes. Examples in this text are the *Hermes* (Figure 58), the *Pietà* (Figure 186), and the *Entombment* (Figure 187). Another important function of sculpture is the commemoration of individuals as in the Lincoln Memorial in Washington (Figure 96). Often a statue records an event of importance; the *Charioteer* (Figure 60) probably commemorates a victory.

Another of the important uses of sculpture, both religious and secular, is the decoration of architecture. From the days of the Greeks right down to our own times, sculpture has been used to decorate architecture. Doors and doorways are filled with figures and flowers. The bronze doors which Ghiberti made for the Baptistery at Florence (Figure 45) are so faultless that when Michelangelo saw them he exclaimed, "They are so beautiful that they might fittingly stand at the gates of paradise." And they have been called the "Gates of Paradise" ever since.

In the medieval church, sculpture was frequently used for instructional purposes. The panels of the "Gates of Paradise," for example, record scenes from the Old Testament. In the first panel the subject is the creation (Figure 46). Several different scenes are presented; in the lower left-hand corner God is bringing Adam to life while the angels rejoice; in the center of the panel is the creation of Eve, with a circle of angels surrounding the figures. On the left, behind the creation of Adam, is the temptation: Adam and Eve stand under a tree with the serpent coiled around it. On the right is shown the expulsion: Adam and Eve have been driven from the gates of Paradise by an angel, while God is seen far back in the heavens.

On the wall of the cathedral at Amiens is a calendar showing the signs of the Zodiac. Each of the signs is represented by its symbol, and under it is a relief, of the same size and shape, showing a typical occupation for that sign or month. The first of the three signs in our photo-

Fig. 45. Lorenzo Ghiberti (1378–1455), Italian goldsmith, sculptor and painter. East Door, "Gates of Paradise" (1425–1452). (Bronze. Height of door: 16½ feet. Florence, Baptistery. Photograph by Anderson.)

Fig. 46. Lorenzo Ghiberti. *Creation and Fall,* detail of "Gates of Paradise." (Height of detail: 3 feet 10 inches. Photograph by Alinari.)

graph (Figure 47) pictures a goat, the sign of Capricorn, which corresponds roughly to the month of December. Shown under it is a man putting up meat for the winter. The middle relief shows a man pouring water, Aquarius, or January. Under him is a table at which is seated a man with two heads who, as January (following the Latin Janus) looks both to the new and the old years. February, the last of the three signs, is represented by two fish, the sign being Pisces, or fish. Under them is a monk trying to keep warm. He has taken off his shoes and is warming his hands before the blazing fire.

In sculpture that is not connected with architecture, fountains take an important place. The fountain is frequently used as a medium for telling a mythological or allegorical story; for example, the fountain by

Carl Milles, opposite the Union Station in St. Louis, represents the union of the Missouri and the Mississippi Rivers.

The tombstone is one of the opportunities for sculpture that is too frequently disregarded. But tombstones can and should be beautiful. In Figures 169 and 170 we have two examples from different ages: one is Greek of the fifth century; the other is recent American, the work of Augustus Saint-Gaudens. The *Tomb of Giuliano de' Medici* is one of Michelangelo's most magnificent works (Figure 119).

Another functional use of sculpture is the coin. Every coin shows a relief: the Lincoln penny, the Jefferson nickel, the Franklin Roosevelt dime, and the Washington quarter. In the United States we are now paying more attention to the designs on coins than we did fifty years ago. And in a foreign country it is interesting to note how the spirit of the country is reflected in the designs on its coins.

FUNCTION IN ARCHITECTURE

Architecture is the only one of the great arts that is primarily functional. It is also the art in which the proper performance of function is

Fig. 47. *Signs of the Zodiac,* with corresponding occupations. Details of basement of West Façade (first half of thirteenth century). (Stone. Height of each quatrefoil: 2½ feet. Amiens, Cathedral. Photograph, Clarence Ward.)

most important. Buildings are large and expensive and they cannot easily be replaced. If a chair is not comfortable, we can buy another and use this only when we have company. But we cannot treat architecture in any such fashion; we do not keep several buildings on hand. If a building does not function we have to put up with an inconvenient and inefficient structure. Therefore it is in architecture that we see most clearly the influence of functional demands. These can be traced to demands that arise from climate and those that come from social conditions.

Climate is a factor of which everyone is acutely conscious. Is the climate wet or dry, hot or cold, sunny or dark, even or variable, windy or calm? In countries where there is strong wind, the house is planned with windbreaks and the living rooms are put in protected areas away from the wind, whereas in warm climates with temperate winds, the house is planned to take advantage of the prevailing breeze. In a cold climate, emphasis is placed on building for warmth, in a warm climate on the attempt to keep cool. When the climate is mild, the primary functions of the walls are to ensure privacy and to keep out the sun and rain; hence, they may be of very light material. In China and Japan, for instance, the walls are merely sliding screens.

The size and number of the doors and windows are likewise determined largely by climate. In hot southern countries, where the sun is blinding, the object is to shut out the light; accordingly, in Spain and in Egypt the windows are small and few in number. In the northern countries, where there is much rain and the winters are long and dark, the demand is for more light, and the windows are large and numerous. The shape of the roof depends primarily on the amount of rain and snow. A flat roof is found in warm, dry countries, as in Egypt or Greece, where the roof can be used as an extra sitting room or as a bedroom on warm nights. But a flat roof is practicable only in a dry climate. Where there is rain it is usually found best to tilt the roof to make it easier for the water to run off. The degree of slope is determined partly by the amount of rain. In countries where there is much rain the roofs are more steeply pitched than in countries that have only a little rain. The amount of snow is an important factor, also. Snow is very heavy; a large quantity will break through a roof; hence, in mountains where there is a great deal of snow, the roofs are very steeply pitched and are left unbroken by windows so that the snow will slide off. The steeply pitched, broken roofs that are found on the châteaux are useful in France, where there is much rain and little snow, but they would not be practical in the Alps. In China there are very heavy rains during the monsoons. Accordingly the roofs are steeply pitched and project over the house; at the eaves they are turned up to admit light.

Here in the United States both the Northern and the Southern states have beautiful examples of the colonial type of architecture. But there are interesting differences due primarily to differences in climate. In the South there are many more verandas than in the North. And in the South the columns of the porch often extend to the roof in order to shade the windows of the second story. There is a difference, too, in the arrangement of the buildings. In New England, because of the cold and the snow, the barns and the other outbuildings were often attached to the main residence so that the men of the house could do the chores without going out in the cold. In the South, with its mild winters, the outbuildings were scattered all around the yard as separate structures. A very moderate home would have a smoke house (for meat), a hen house, a carriage house, and probably an ice house (for storing ice) and a cellar (for keeping food cool), as well as the barns.

The term *social conditions* is used here to mean all those factors in architecture that are determined by man, in contrast to those that are governed by nature. A first consideration in any building is the use to which it is to be put, its function in the narrower sense of the term. A building is designed for a special purpose: it may be an office building, a church, a residence, a garage, and so on. These primary functions are influenced by the physical conditions of the land, as we have just seen, but they are even more dependent on social forces. Again the walls of a building may be used as an example. Heat and rain are always determining factors, but in olden times there was also the need for protection. Castles and fortifications were made with very thick, strong walls, as defense against the enemy. Palaces had to be strong enough to ward off possible attack. The palace which Michelozzo built for Cosimo de' Medici served both as palace and fortress (Figure 48).

Another example of social influences on architecture can be found in buildings for worship (Figure 49). To Christians a church or a cathedral is primarily a place where large numbers of people can assemble, because corporate worship is an integral part of the Christian faith. Hence the cathedral at Amiens is large, the construction is open, and

FIG. 48. Michelozzo (1396–
1472), Italian architect.
Medici-Riccardi Palace
(1444–1452). (Stone.
Length: 300 feet; height:
90 feet. Florence. Photograph
by Alinari.)

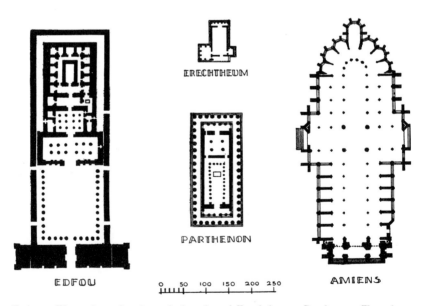

FIG. 49. Floor plans showing relative size of Erechtheum, Parthenon, Temple at
Edfu, and Cathedral of Amiens.

it will hold many people. The Greeks, on the other hand, had no service in the same sense; their gatherings for religious purposes were infrequent and were held out of doors. For them the temple was primarily a shrine for the statue of the god, and in consequence their temples were small, accommodating only a few people at a time. The Parthenon, though large for a temple, is only about one-fourth the size of the cathedral at Amiens. And small as is the Parthenon, it was divided into two rooms: a large room in which the statute of Athena was kept, and a smaller one for the treasures. The Erechtheum, another Greek temple, is even smaller. The Egyptian temple had a different arrangement because the ritual was different. In Egypt the temple was primarily a sanctuary which could be visited only by the Pharaoh and the priest. In front of the sanctuary was a series of rooms to which other people were admitted according to their rank. Accordingly an Egyptian temple such as that at Edfu consisted of four parts: first, the pylon, a huge gateway covering the entire front of the building; second, a large open court accessible to everyone; third, a hall or hypostyle made up of columns. This hall, which was dimly lighted because the columns covered the entire floor, was reserved for dignitaries who occupied a position midway between the people and Pharaoh. And finally, there was a small inner sanctuary for the priest and the king.

Sometimes the government steps in with laws which affect architecture, though not directly concerned with building as such. A tax on the number of windows, for instance, will result in houses with fewer windows. It is supposed that a tax on the number of stories of a house had much to do with the development of the mansard roof, which gave all the space of an extra story while technically it was only an attic.

One of the interesting examples of this type is to be found in the zoning law of New York City. This law was made necessary by the skyscrapers, for if very tall buildings are placed on each side, the street between is left dark, like a very narrow canyon. The purpose of the law is to ensure that a street should always have the proper amount of air and sunshine, and it accomplishes this end by regulating the height of a building in proportion to the width of the street and the size of the lot. An imaginary triangle is drawn with the lot as its base, and the law requires that the building should not project beyond that triangle, except for a tower, not to exceed one-fourth the area of the plot. In order to utilize their plots to the best advantage, builders designed structures in which the upper floors were set *back* of the lower floors.

In the McGraw-Hill Building (Figure 50) there are three such set-backs before we reach the central tower, the height of which is not restricted by law.

FORM FOLLOWS FUNCTION

Whenever art has function, the function influences and often determines the form. This is just another way of stating the obvious fact that if an object is made for a certain function it should be made in such a way that it can perform that function. As the function changes, the form changes, and if there are many functions there will be many forms. Take an object of everyday use such as a spoon. There are spoons for babies and spoons for adults, spoons for cooking, spoons for eating, spoons for serving, spoons for coffee if it is served with the meal, and spoons for coffee if it is served in the drawing room after dinner, deep spoons and shallow spoons, spoons with long handles and spoons

FIG. 50. Raymond Hood (1881–1934), American architect. McGraw-Hill Building (completed 1931). (Steel frame construction, 33 stories and basement. New York.)

with short handles. Even a rather small household will probably have a variety of spoons because there is a variety of functions to be served by them.

Door keys offer another interesting example. Keys are now carried by many individuals, and one person often has to carry more than one; accordingly keys are small. But when gates and doors were in the charge of special porters who were always in attendance, keys were large and massive; they were in fact a visible symbol of the power and importance of the place to be locked.

These examples have all been taken from the industrial arts, but instances may be cited from any art that is functional. A lullaby must not be so loud as to wake the baby. A march or a jig must keep the time exactly so that one may march or dance in time to it. A coin must be small and flat, and any decoration on it must also be flat. Advertisements, whether in words or in pictures, should make clear the desirable qualities of the object advertised.

FUNCTION AND BEAUTY

Some arts are functional and some are not. Is there any relation between function and value as art? Can we say that functional arts are greater or less great than arts that are not functional? The value of any work of art depends on the work itself, not on its being functional or nonfunctional. Architecture, which is always functional, is not superior or inferior to painting, which is usually nonfunctional. In the evaluation of two works of art, the presence or absence of function, just as the presence or absence of subject, is a matter of no consequence. If one were asked to name the world's greatest works of art he would certainly include the plays of Aeschylus and Shakespeare, the cathedrals at Chartres and Amiens, and the symphonies of Beethoven and Brahms. The plays have subject but no function; the cathedrals have function but no subject; the symphonies have neither subject nor function.

However, in the evaluation of functional art, the problem is different. Obviously the function should be known if the work is to be understood; if it is a birdbath or a saltcellar, it should be known as a bath for birds or as a container for salt when it is judged. It cannot be adequately judged just as shape.

But when the function is understood is there any relation between the function of a work and its value as art? Yes, in a general way, there is. There has been a great deal of discussion on this point, and any statement may be contradicted by excellent examples to the contrary, but it will usually be granted that a functional object is not beautiful unless it can perform its function adequately and acceptably. If it is desirable for people to see and hear in church, a church should be constructed so that they can see and hear in it. A chair that is uncomfortable is not as good as one that is comfortable. A residence should be so planned that the business of housekeeping may be carried on in it with the maximum of ease and efficiency. A beautiful teapot that is useless is like a beautiful bridge that one cannot cross or a beautiful car that will not run.

In this respect we must admit that the saltcellar of Cellini fails if considered as a saltcellar. The figures are well conceived and executed, but the affair is too elaborate for its function. On the other hand it was a custom at this time to have on the table a large and elaborate saltcellar known as "the salt." The salt was placed before the master of the house, between him and the guest of honor, thus serving to indicate rank. For this function the Cellini saltcellar was admirably adapted.

In fact, adequate performance of function usually tends to make for beauty of design. Why this should be true we do not know, but it is true. The shapes in nature that are the most beautiful are also the most efficient, as for instance the wings of a bird. Practical design offers many examples; everything is eliminated except what is essential and the result is beautiful. Examples of such shapes are found in the canoe, the canoe paddle, the handle of an ax or a scythe, and the blades of an electric fan.

Nevertheless, it is true that, although efficiency does make for beauty, efficiency and beauty are not the same. An article that adequately performs its function is not necessarily beautiful. Art demands something beyond function, something in addition to efficiency and proper performance of function. The shape of a spoon may be the best possible for its particular function, but the spoon is not a work of art for that reason. In the economy of nature the best shape for an object's use *tends* to be the most beautiful, but it is our pleasure in the shape and not its usefulness that makes it art.

FOR FURTHER EXPLORATION

1. Check any ten advertisements for their functional quality; i.e., do they accomplish what they attempt to do?

2. Choose one advertisement which you think good and check it for these points:

    a. How does it attract attention?

    b. Does this primary attraction reinforce the message of the advertisement?

    c. What are the logical implications?

3. Find other examples of painting and literature that have function.

4. Look through the contents of (*a*) a literary magazine and (*b*) a trade magazine for the number of articles with definite and obvious function.

5. What examples of architectural sculpture do you find in your home town?

6. Study as many different coins as you can find. Which do you like best?

7. Could the paper money of the U.S.A. be improved from the point of view of design? Compare with English and French money.

8. Study some article of furniture for its functional value.

9. Do the same for some article of dress.

10. Make a list of twenty different knives, noting in each case how the function determines the form.

11. Study ten articles in the kitchen from the point of view of:

    a. Function

    b. Beauty

12. Make a list of ten examples to prove or disprove the statement that much more attention is being paid to beauty in industrial design than was usual ten years ago. Notice everything from egg beaters to refrigerators, from house plans to table decorations, from automobiles to fountain pens.

13. Study the climate of your home town. How has it influenced the town's architecture?

14. What problems arising from the climate have not been met? Can you suggest ways to meet them?

15. Study a typical farm setup in your state.

16. What are the particular demands for worship in your church which are not found in the churches of other faiths? Are there arrangements for baptism? Note the position of the choir.

17. Visit any home that was built over a hundred years ago. Note ways that servants were considered in its plan.

18. Cite examples of government regulation of building in your town.

19. Study for its functional value the plan of the church in which you worship. Make a list of objectives for which a church is built, and see how this church meets them. Do you find that the function of the building has been hampered by the desire for beauty?

20. Answer Question 19 for the house or apartment in which you live. Do not forget to notice:

    a. The amount of light and sunlight

    b. Accessibility. Can you get from one part of the house to another?

    c. Adaptation to the number and character of the people living in it

21. In Cellini's autobiography read the story of the making of the saltcellar (Everyman edition, p. 340).

PART TWO

MEDIUM

CHAPTER 5

MEDIUM—GENERAL CONSIDERATIONS

DEFINITION

Many widely diverse objects go under the name of art. A song, a sonata, a symphony, a statue, a skyscraper, a tapestry, a tragedy, a teapot, a poem, a painting, a palace, an oratorio, a cathedral, a chest, an etching, an engraving, an epic, a dance, a novel, a lyric—all these and more may be classed as art. A single reading of this list, however, is sufficient for certain obvious classifications. The song, the symphony, the sonata, and the oratorio belong to the art of music; the cathedral, the palace, and the skyscraper are examples of architecture; the poem, the tragedy, the epic, the lyric, and the novel are literature. The basis for these classifications is primarily the way the artist has communicated his idea to us, his medium. The word *medium,* which comes from the Latin word *medium* signifying "means," denotes the means by which an artist communicates his idea; it is the stuff out of which he creates a work of art. Architecture makes use of wood, stone, brick, concrete; sculpture makes use of marble, bronze, wood; painting makes use of colored pigments on wood or canvas.

Medium is essential to art. Subject and function, as we have seen, are not essential. There is art without subject and there is art without function, but there is no art without medium. A work of art could not be known if it did not exist in some medium. And both the art and the artist get their names from the medium. Emily Dickinson and Arthur Honegger were both inspired by the railway train. Because she used words to express her idea she is called a poet, and because he used tones he is called a musician.

On the basis of medium the arts are classified as *visual* and *auditory*. Painting, sculpture, architecture, tapestry, glassware, etc., are visual arts; they are seen. Music and literature are auditory arts; they are heard. Even when one reads silently a musical score or a page of poetry, he hears the sound in his mind. On the basis of medium also the arts are classified as *time arts* and *space arts*. The visual arts are space arts. The auditory arts are time arts. The theater, the opera, and the cinema are known as *combined arts,* being both visual and auditory, existing in both space and time. Though it is largely visual, the dance is classed with the combined arts because it employs both time and space.

By a third classification on the basis of medium the arts are divided into *major* and *minor arts*. The five major arts are music, literature, painting, sculpture, and architecture. The minor arts are the applied arts: metalwork, weaving, ceramics, glass, furniture, photography, lettering, bookmaking, etc. The terms major and minor, however, are of no importance in determining the value of any single work of art. A good piece of glass or porcelain is better than a poor painting; a beautiful Oriental rug is finer than a poor statue, a good saltcellar than a poor building. Any work of art is good or not in itself and should be judged as such regardless of its medium.

THE ARTIST AND HIS MEDIUM

When an artist uses a medium, he employs the one which can best express what he wants to say. Often an artist uses more than one medium. William Blake used three different mediums: color for his paintings, lines for his engravings, and rhythmic words for his poetry. He chose each medium because it could express the exact idea he wanted to make clear at that time. And what he said in painting he could not say in engraving or in poetry.

In the determination of medium, however, the words *choice* and *selection* give a false impression, for they imply that the artist makes a deliberate choice. The artist does not make a conscious, reasoned choice of his medium; the selection of medium is a part of the artistic inspiration. The idea which Blake put into a poem came to him as an idea for a poem. He did not have an idea out of which he might make a poem or an engraving. When the unknown Greek sculptor of the fifth century before Christ made the little bronze horse now at the

Metropolitan Museum (Figure 51), he chose sculpture because what he wanted to say demanded volume. The poet is a poet rather than a painter because he thinks in terms of words. As one poet said, "When I enjoy a scene, I find myself hunting for words that will exactly express the impression it has made on me."

FIG. 51. Greek sculpture. *Horse* (ca. 480 B.C.). (Bronze. Height: ca. 14 inches. New York, courtesy of the Metropolitan Museum of Art.)

Moreover, the artist thinks in terms of a specific medium. Two of Dürer's great prints are of horsemen; for one the artist has used engraving, for the other woodcut. He chose each medium to express the exact idea he wanted to make clear in that print. The engraving is called *The Knight, Death, and the Devil* (Figure 52). The knight probably represents the Christian who is not led astray by temptations. A very solid and praiseworthy person, he rides across the picture apparently bound for the ideal city shown against the sky. He pays no attention to his companions: Death, who holds an hourglass before him, and the Devil, half pig and half wolf.

The woodcut is called *The Four Horsemen of the Apocalypse* (Figure 53). According to the passage in the New Testament (Revelation, chapter 6) the first horse is white, and its rider who carries a bow "went forth conquering and to conquer." Some think Christ is this conquering rider. The second horse is red, symbolizing war; its rider carrying a sword takes peace from the earth. The third horse, which is black, represents famine; the scales in the hands of its rider show that food is scarce and must be weighed. Last is a pale horse, "and his name that sat on him was Death."

FIG. 52. Albrecht Dürer (1471–1528), German painter, engraver, and wood carver. *The Knight, Death, and the Devil* (ca. 1513). (Engraving. Size: 9¾ by 7¼ inches. New York, courtesy of the Metropolitan Museum of Art.)

A sculptor plans his statue not for wood in general but for oak or mahogany. The architect does not plan a house and then decide whether it shall be of brick, wood, or stone; the demands of brick, wood, and stone are different, and he must design his house according to his material. The jeweler does not imagine a design and then say,

FIG. 53. Albrecht Dürer. *Four Horsemen of the Apocalypse* (ca. 1498). (Woodcut. Size: 15 13/16 by 11 1/2 inches. Boston, courtesy of Museum of Fine Arts.)

"Shall I make it in copper or gold?" It is a design for gold or for copper. The artist thinks and feels in terms of his medium.

Moreover the artist loves and respects his medium for itself; he uses it because it has certain qualities and he tries to bring out and emphasize those qualities. The sculptor gives life to his statue not by denying that it is wood or stone, but by incorporating the qualities of wood or stone into the meaning of the sculptured piece. In the statues of Henry Moore, we are always conscious of the texture of wood as wood, or bronze as bronze. To the poet the words are the poem. They are not one of many ways he has found to express his idea, they *are* the idea. His poem cannot be separated from the words of the poem.

In studying any work of art, therefore, it is always worth while to ask why the artist chose the particular medium in question. Why did Wagner give the sword theme to the trumpet? Why did the unknown artist of the *Horse* want it in bronze? Why did Dürer use engraving for *The Knight, Death, and the Devil,* and woodcut for *The Four Horsemen of the Apocalypse?* How do these works suit the inherent qualities of the medium chosen?

THE DISTINCTIVE CHARACTER OF MEDIUM

If what is said in one medium cannot be said in another, it follows that no work can ever be translated from one medium to another. There is no argument about this point if it is a question of two different arts. A description of a scene and a painting of the same scene do not tell the same story; inevitably what they say is different. And the same is true, though to a lesser degree, when it is a question of two mediums within a single art. If the artist's intuition demands a statue of marble, it follows that a copy of the statue in bronze will miss something essential to the original.

It is in music and literature that the problem of translation arises most often. Music that was written for the orchestra is arranged for piano, and music written for piano is arranged for orchestra. Works in foreign languages are translated into English, and English works are translated into foreign languages. In this kind of translation, however, something of the original is always lost or changed. Every time Stokowski transcribes the music of Bach, the result is Stokowski as well as Bach. Gilbert Murray's translations of Euripides show us Euripides plus

Gilbert Murray. The orchestral score of *The Afternoon of a Faun* transcribed for piano has lost something that was essential to the music. Even when a great artist like Casals plays a Chopin piano prelude on the cello we have lost something of Chopin's music.

On this point, however, a caution is necessary. It is better to know a Greek play in a translation than not to know the play. It is better to hear Bach arranged by Stokowski than not to hear Bach. It is better to know the famous masterpieces of painting and sculpture in reproductions than not to know them at all. One should strive not to be too learned on the one hand, or too easily pleased on the other; one should not refuse to know Bach's music as played by the orchestra, but one should hear it on the harpsichord if he has the opportunity. It is well to study the works of Botticelli in reproductions until one has a chance to see the originals. One should read translations from the Greek but remember that one will know Sophocles and Euripides best when he reads their plays in Greek.

INFLUENCE OF MEDIUM ON CHOICE OF SUBJECT

Sculpture

The nature of the medium inevitably influences the type of subject it can portray. Traditionally sculpture in the round has tended to emphasize mass and weight, and its subjects are objects of definite form and solidity. Michelangelo said that sculpture should look as though it could be rolled downhill without injury, and we have learned to expect a certain compactness in sculptured form. Trees and clouds are not common in sculpture. Moreover, the sculpture of the past has been limited almost entirely to the bodies of animals and, especially, the bodies of men. It has emphasized not only the human body but in large measure the nude human body. We do not really suppose that David was naked when he fought Goliath, but the body of David is more nearly ideal when it is naked, and therefore better suited to the meaning and purpose of the statue. When clothes are used we want them to be simple and straightforward, as in the figures of the caryatids of the Erechtheum.

Sculpture in relief, because the figures are attached to a background, has shown more subjects and more varied treatment of subject than

sculpture in the round. On the background may be carved many
subjects not so appropriate to sculpture in the round: trees, clouds,
birds, fish, anything. In the famous "Gates of Paradise" Ghiberti seems
almost as free as a painter in his choice of subject. In the so-called
Ludovisi Throne (Figure 54), which is supposed to portray the birth
of Venus, the goddess is being lifted from the water by two attendants.
The representation of cloth, especially the delineation of the form seen
through the cloth, is exceptionally fine.

With the interest in abstract art there have developed new styles,
as we have seen in Moore's *Two Forms*. This new sculpture differs
from older forms in treatment of medium as well as in subject. Whereas
older sculpture is solid, the new sculpture is often hollow, playing up
concave as well as convex surfaces. Thin strips of metal are combined
with plastic or glass, even with wood and wires, to make interesting
arrangements. Often they are suspended where they can move, and
one gets various lights and shadows from them. Such sculptures, called
mobiles, are associated primarily with the name of Alexander Calder.
An example is *Lobster Trap and Fish Tail* (Figure 55), which hangs in
the stair well of the Museum of Modern Art in New York City. Of his
mobiles Calder said in 1951: ". . . the idea of detached bodies floating in space, of different sizes and densities, perhaps of different colors

FIG. 54. *Ludovisi Throne,* ca. 460 B.C. (Marble. Height at center: 3 feet 4½
inches. Rome, Terme Museum. Photograph by Alinari.)

Fig. 55. Alexander Calder
(1898——), American sculptor.
Lobster Trap and Fish Tail
(1939). (Mobile. Steel wire and
sheet aluminum. Size: 8½ feet
high, 9½ feet in diameter. New
York, Collection of the Museum
of Modern Art; gift of the
Advisory Committee.)

and temperatures . . . some at rest, while others move in peculiar manners, seems to me the ideal source of form." [1]

Painting

Painting has a much wider field than sculpture; it may concern itself with anything in space. Whatever can be seen can be painted: lakes, trees, clouds, houses, mountains, fields, anything that has form to the eye either in reality or in the artist's mind.

Painting and sculpture are both limited in time. Each can represent its object only at a single moment of time. In life the running horse or the smiling girl does not stay the same for ten consecutive seconds; the sculptor or the painter chooses one of those seconds and preserves the object at that instant. He may create a feeling or an illusion of movement so that we are conscious of the action that is taking place or is about to take place. In El Greco's *Resurrection,* Christ seems to be really rising out of a mass of bodies. In Botticelli's *Birth of Venus,* the goddess is being blown to the shore. Even in Ghirlandajo's *Old Man and Boy,* we feel that it is just for a moment that they will be in this position, that one or both will move very soon. In each case the artist is showing the characteristic motion or gesture of the person about to move; we feel that the next second there will be movement, but the scene as presented is still, the action does not change.

Several years ago there was a great deal of talk about a painting by

[1] Barr, *Masters of Modern Art,* p. 146.

97

Duchamp called *Nude Descending a Stair* (Figure 56). The artist was trying to picture just what the title indicates, the appearance of forms in motion. He did this by presenting a succession of pictures of the same thing from slightly different points of view. Some modern artists, notably Picasso, have given a sense of movement to a painting by presenting at one time different aspects of a head or figure. Here as in everything connected with art we must admit that all standards are empirical; that is, they are derived from experience. The artist may do anything he can do. In other words, if Duchamp and Picasso can persuade us that we can see action in a painting and that we like to see action portrayed in that way, then painting becomes a medium for the portrayal of action.

Literature

Painting allows a wider range of subjects than sculpture, and literature allows a wider range than painting. If painting can present anything that might be seen, literature can present anything than can be put into words. Moreover, it is not limited to a second of time as are the visual arts. Literature can describe a situation at any given moment and can tell what happened before and after that time. Literature differs from the other arts in another respect. Since the language of literature is the same as the language of abstract thought, it can express abstract thought as the other arts cannot. Shakespeare can have Hamlet say,

> There's a divinity that shapes our ends,
> Rough-hew them how we will,—
> —*Hamlet,* V, ii, 10–11

The sculptor or the painter may portray a thoughtful face. The musician may make one think of immortality, but no one of the three can express the idea as clearly as the poet can.

On the other hand, imitation through literature is less exact than imitation through either painting or sculpture. The statue of a dog may conceivably be mistaken for the living dog, but a poem about a dog may never be. And yet the poem may call to mind the characteristics of a dog better than the statue.

Music

As we have seen, music can never portray any subject clearly. And since music can only suggest the subject, it can suggest any subject.

FIG. 56. Marcel Duchamp (1887——), French painter. *Nude Descending a Stair* (1912). (Oil on canvas. Size: 58⅜ by 35⅜ inches. Philadelphia, Museum of Art; Collection of Louise and Walter Arensberg.)

Subjects that cannot even be put into words can be expressed in music. Vague ideas, half-formed opinions and emotions, feelings that can never be given tangible form, all these are found in music.

Thus each art is limited in the subjects it can portray, and it is a general rule that the more subjects an art can portray, the less lifelike it is. A statue of an animal is more like the original than the work in any other art, but sculpture can depict fewer subjects. As the medium gets less like the original, the number of subjects it can portray increases until, as in music, any subject is allowed, though the imitation is so little exact that we cannot even be sure what the subject is.

ORPHEUS AND EURYDICE

The limitations and possibilities of medium can be illustrated clearly if we compare the use of a single subject in several mediums. Take, for instance, the myth of Orpheus, the great musician who went to the other world to demand back his wife Eurydice. His request was granted on condition that he should not look back until he had reached the upper world. But just before he arrived he looked back and his wife was lost.

This legend is the subject of a Greek relief of about the third century before Christ (Figure 57), though the work is known only in a Roman copy. The sculptor had to choose one second and only one from the entire story. He chose the moment just after Orpheus had looked around, when both Orpheus and Eurydice realized that she must return to Hades. In that one instant he has had to show all the love and longing of the lovers. The legend says that when Orpheus turned Eurydice disappeared. Sculpture could not show a person in the act of disappearing, and hence Hermes, the messenger of the gods, is shown waiting to take Eurydice back to the realm of Pluto.

In this change, however, what seems a limitation of the medium becomes an opportunity, for the sculptor shows the contrast between the mortals and the gods, not in physique but in attitude. The mortals, Orpheus and Eurydice, are pathetic in their fruitless yearning and powerlessness; the god is patient, conscious of the inevitability of the gods' decree, but quite detached from the sufferings of men.

The story is told again by Ovid, a Latin poet who lived about the time of Christ, in his *Metamorphoses*. Since he was using words, Ovid could give minute details of all kinds. He told, for instance, how the wild beasts and even the trees and rocks responded to the playing of Orpheus. He described the bad omen at the wedding when Hymen's torch smoked, and how Eurydice, while running away from the unwelcome advances of a shepherd, was bitten by a snake and died. Orpheus, inconsolable, at last made the desperate resolve to seek her in Hades. Playing on his lyre, he passed all the people being tortured there. Finally, he reached the throne of Pluto and Proserpine, where he declared boldly that if they would not give him back his wife, they would have a new inhabitant of Hades, for he would not leave without Eurydice. They agreed that she might go on condition that he should not look behind to see if she were following. When he had almost reached the entrance, he looked back and she disappeared. The Thracian maidens tried to captivate him, but when he refused to have anything to do with them, they tore him to bits and threw the pieces into the river.

Gluck, an eighteenth century German composer, used this story as the subject of his opera *Orpheus and Eurydice*. The change in medium necessarily involved changes in presentation. In the first place, an opera is limited in time, and singing is much slower than speaking.

FIG. 57. *Orpheus and Eurydice*. Roman copy in Pentelic marble. Original marble of ca. 430 B.C. (Height: 3 feet 10½ inches. Naples, National Museum. Photograph by Alinari.)

Therefore, the story had to be shortened; the opera begins after the death of Eurydice and ends with the departure from Hades. Moreover, it would be impossible on the stage to show the various punishments of Hades, Ixion rolling a stone, the daughters of Danaüs carrying water in a sieve, or Tantalus immersed in water up to his lips. Instead, Gluck introduced bands of Furies who assail Orpheus and challenge his approach.

The most interesting change comes in the return of Orpheus and Eurydice. Ovid says simply that Eurydice followed Orpheus until they were almost out in the world, when he looked around. Orpheus was, of course, playing on his lyre, but there is no other indication as to what was happening on the journey. Such a scene would be foolish if enacted on the stage, a man singing and a woman following in silence. Hence, Eurydice is made to talk; she asks where they are going. Why does Orpheus not look at her? Has he ceased to love her? At last, she says in desperation she would rather be back in Hades if her husband does not love her any more; at this Orpheus can stand it no longer, he turns, and she dies.

It is not important for our study to notice that in this version the god Amor (love) brings her to life again with the statement that they have suffered enough, and the lovers leave Hades happily. This ending, however, changes the entire tone of the play, taking away its tragedy and making it all rather sprightly and sophisticated.

PRESERVATION OF ART

Since it can be known only as it is expressed in some medium, art is lost if the medium is lost. We cannot study the architecture of Mesopotamia as we can that of Greece, for the houses were made of sun-dried brick and almost all of them have been washed away. The Angles and Saxons, when they settled in England, must have known many stories about the heroes of their native home; but only one of these stories was written down, *Beowulf;* the others have been forgotten.

About some of these lost works of art a great deal is known. The great statue of Athena called the *Athena Parthenos,* for which the Parthenon was a shrine, was described by the historians. It was about forty feet in height, and it was made of gold and ivory. Standing as it did in the Parthenon, lighted by the beams of the early morning sun, it must have been an object of rare beauty. But the statue itself has not been preserved, the two known copies are inadequate, and while we may learn various facts about the statue, we cannot experience its beauty. Other examples might be cited almost indefinitely, but the point is clear. If the medium of a work of art is gone, the art is gone. It is therefore extremely important that the medium be preserved.

In this matter of preservation we find a sharp difference between the visual and the auditory arts. The visual arts are material realities and as such can be preserved. A painting, a statue, building, even a bit of embroidery or lace may be kept; and when we want to study it we can see the original work. It may not be in as good condition as when it was made, but we can see the thing itself. In a painting by Rembrandt we see the actual paint which was put on by the artist; the colors may be darkened by time, but the picture we see is the work of the artist himself. The statues of Michelangelo are the figures made by Michelangelo. In the visual arts, therefore, the problems of preservation are all problems of keeping the medium safe and in good condition: of finding paints that will not fade, of seeing that houses and statues are made of materials that will endure and that they are not destroyed.

PRESERVATION OF THE AUDITORY ARTS

In the auditory arts the situation is entirely different. Music and literature exist in time, and time once passed is gone forever. The only way we can keep the time arts is to reproduce them. We cannot hear the song as it was sung a half hour ago; we must sing it over again. We cannot listen today to the poem as we heard it yesterday, but we can repeat the poem. The problem of preserving the auditory arts, therefore, is the problem of finding some means of keeping them so that they can be reproduced.

Originally music and literature were kept by memory and by oral transmission. One man taught another; the grandfather told tales to his grandson; the mother sang songs to her child. In most countries, songs and stories were handed down in this way for a long time, often for centuries, before they were put into permanent form. Even today some of our literature and music comes to us by word of mouth. The stories we tell of Santa Claus, the verses and songs we sing in games, and the simple steps to which we dance them are learned from others, not from books. Children in Idaho or Mississippi sing of London Bridge and the farmer in the dell, not because the words have any significance for them, but because they have learned the songs from their parents and friends.

The difficulties with this kind of transmission, however, are very great. The song or the story may be forgotten. Moreover, it does not remain the same. When a new singer tells a story or sings a melody, he often changes it, sometimes unconsciously, sometimes consciously. The poet who does not understand one word will substitute another he does know. In the Kentucky mountains songs have been preserved since the time of Shakespeare, but they are not exactly the same: words and music have changed.

A better way to preserve a time art is to convert it into symbols that can be kept. Hence, from the very earliest times, there have been attempts to find such symbols. The symbols for words came first; they are old. In fact, we can almost say that they are as old as history, for we know comparatively little history earlier than the symbols of written language. Moreover, these symbols are accurate and can be accurately interpreted. We know the writings of the Egyptians, the Greeks, and the Hebrews, and we know that we are reading those writings in the main correctly.

The symbols for music were invented much later, and hence we do not know music of as early a date as we do literature. We know that the early peoples had music and musical instruments; the Hebrews talk of the cymbals and the psaltery, and the Egyptians and the Greeks drew pictures of people with musical instruments. We know also that the Greeks had a very elaborate musical system; they have written its laws and principles; much of our present theory derives directly from the Greeks. But none of these people had a precise way of writing the music itself, and very little has been preserved. The earliest music that can be read with any degree of accuracy is that of the Middle Ages. Before that time there were various attempts at musical notation, but either these early examples were not exact or we have not learned how to interpret them accurately. Hence, for us, the history of music is vague until about the year 1000.

More recent devices for preserving the auditory arts are the phonograph record and the tape recorder. These can preserve the exact tone, the exact speed, the intonation, and many other characteristics that are lost in the written symbol. They have not, however, superseded writing;

music and literature are still known primarily through written symbols.

For the combined arts there are even yet no good methods of preservation. In the drama and the opera we have, of course, symbols for words and for music; and we can take photographs of stage sets and actors, of singers and dancers. But for the combination of various effects that make up the theater, the opera, or the dance, we have no adequate means of preservation. The cinema with its sound track would seem to be a perfect means for preserving the combined arts; and it is probably the best we have today. The conditions for the making of a motion picture, however, are so different from the conditions of a stage performance that it is difficult, not to say impossible, to get the same effects. Furthermore, as the cinema is developing now, it is becoming more and more a new art rather than a means for reproducing or preserving a stage performance.

It is too soon to know how good television will be for the preservation of the combined arts. It seems to have great possibilities, but if we can judge by present indications it is apt to develop like the cinema into an independent art.

For the preservation of all the arts there will undoubtedly be improvements in the future. Within the past fifty years we have seen so many changes effected by the cinema, the phonograph, and television that we cannot say what the future will hold. Several hundred years from now a library may consist almost entirely of phonograph records and sound films, and it may be that we shall listen to a record of a book or magazine as naturally as we now read it. Future generations may look on our failure to preserve the dance with as great wonderment and lack of comprehension as we have in viewing the period before writing was invented or adequate music notation devised. But whatever may happen in the future, for the present dancing, opera, and theater are almost entirely lost, and music and literature are preserved primarily through written symbols.

ADVANTAGES AND DISADVANTAGES OF SYMBOLS

The symbols of music and literature have the disadvantages of all symbols: they are arbitrary, and they must be known to be interpreted correctly. A child or an entirely unlettered person can recognize a picture, but he must know how to read notes or written words before he can get the meaning of written music or literature. Moreover, the symbols themselves are not too exact. The printed page gives only the word; one cannot tell how long a word is to be held, in what tone it should be uttered, or how much stress it is to be given, and, unless one knows the language, the symbol does not even tell the sound. Printed music is in this respect much more exact, for it can give duration and pitch and can indicate accent. Even so, however, it is far from accurate and, besides, it is so cumbersome that comparatively few can read it and even fewer can write it, whereas the simpler symbols for language can now be read and written almost universally.

The disadvantages of the symbol have, however, a corresponding advantage. In the auditory arts, especially in music, there is often a third person coming between the artist and his audience helping to explain to the audience what the artist is trying to say. We hear the music of the composer and the drama of the author as interpreted by the performer. Under the best circumstances the performer is himself an artist. Reading the lines or playing the music is not to him merely a mechanical performance; it is a new interpretation, a re-creation.

This element of re-creation in the auditory arts is so important that we do not even admit the artist's right to decide on a fixed interpretation. Robert Frost may read one of his poems with a certain emphasis, but anyone has the right to change that emphasis if he desires. A pianist will remember how the music was played by the composer if he was fortunate enough to hear him, but he will not hesitate to change the emphasis as he thinks best. In both these respects the auditory arts are in marked contrast to the visual. When a painter draws a line or puts on a color, no one has the right to change it, and there is usually no artist-interpreter to make the meaning clear. Hence it may be said that the visual arts, as we know them, are exact and definite; they tend to be finished, complete, and static; and the auditory arts tend to be vague and indefinite; they are always subject to various interpretations, but they are dynamic and creative.

TECHNIQUE

Technique is the ability to do *what* you want to do, *when* you want to do it, *in the way* you want to do it. Technique is the artist's control of his medium. Technique, in short, has to do with the way the artist uses his medium in expressing an idea, not with the value of the idea itself.

A musician's technique is his ability to make the music sound as he wants it to sound; a sculptor's technique is his way of handling chisel and hammer to produce the effect he wants from them. In the same way there is a technique of blowing glass, casting bronze, making etchings, laying bricks. And that technique is perfect which enables the artist to do just what he desires with his medium. Browning states this ideal when he makes Andrea del Sarto say,

> I can do with my pencil what I know,
> What I see, what at bottom of my heart
> I wish for. . . .

Obviously techniques differ not only in the different arts but in various mediums of a single art; a person's technique in one medium will be quite different from his technique in another. A painter may be a good technician in oil but a poor one in water color. A musician may have fine technique with the bassoon but a poor one with the flute.

Technique is the actual doing of something; it is the handling of material; it does not usually apply to mental labor. We speak of the technique of Botticelli in painting the picture but not of his technique in planning the composition. We notice that Michelangelo has used different techniques in *David* (Figure 27), and in the *Entombment* (Figure 187); in the one the surface is smooth, in the other rough. But it was not a matter of technique that made him decide the smooth surface was right in the one case and the rough in the other.

On the basis of technique the distinction is made between an art and a craft. For the artist, the technique is not the end but the means; it is the language of which he is master; through his technique he is able to say what he wants to say. For the craftsman, technique is the end. He is concerned only with techniques, he does not go beyond techniques. He may make an excellent copy of a picture; he may make an engraving or an etching from it. But he will follow the design of the artist; the artist must make the design.

At various times, however, technique has been considered of great, if not primary, importance, especially in music. It is as though the best singer were the one who could do the most difficult cadenzas and the most amazing trills, as though it were a virtue that the song is hard to sing, not that it is beautiful music. It is fun, of course, to observe a difficult feat well done, whether it be a player hitting a tennis ball or an acrobat hanging by his teeth. So, likewise, it is fun to hear a soprano reach a high note or to see a dancer poise on one toe for an inordinately long time. Nevertheless, the real point is not whether the performer is master of a difficult bit of technique but whether that passage helps the music or the dancing. Is the dancer merely giving an exhibition of her ability to stand on her toe, or is it the climax of the dance? Is the high note appropriate or is it merely difficult? Probably the best commentary on technique is the story told of Kant. After a singer's performance, an admirer said, "Was that not difficult?" and Kant replied, "Would to God it had been impossible!" Technique should always be the means, not the end.

Technique impinges on the question of value in art in yet another way, in the problem of whether an artist's work may be hampered by poor technique. We hear much talk of this kind: "A good artist but poor technique!" "He has good ideas for a landscape, but he cannot paint them!" "He is Milton, but mute and therefore inglorious!" To this problem, as to all other problems in art, no immediate or summary solution may be given that will fit all cases. In the re-creative phases of art, technique is of great importance. A man who speaks with a monotonous voice cannot make as forceful an actor as one who has learned to control his voice. A pianist must know how to play; a singer must be able to sing. In these situations an artist is truly hampered by poor technique.

When, however, it is a matter of creative as against re-creative work, the disparity between technique and artistic ability is much less real. A poet or a musician can write down any words or melodies he can think. Or if he is illiterate, he can dictate to his friends. The architect is not expected to execute his own designs. Painting and sculpture are more difficult, but in them the artist who knows exactly what effects he wants can usually get them. In general the artist's creative ability and his technique go hand in hand.

This point is of importance in the criticism of art. In judging any work of art it is wise to take it for granted that the artist has done what he wanted to do, in other words that he has not been hampered by lack of technique. It is easy to look at the distortions and abstractions of Rouault and Picasso and say, "If only he would learn how to draw," or to hear the discords of Hindemith and say, "If only he had had a few lessons in harmony!" But such criticisms are almost always false. The artist who distorts does so not because he cannot make a life-like figure but because he wants the effect gained through distortion, and the composer who makes discords in his music knows how to make harmonies but he wants the effect of the discord.

FOR FURTHER EXPLORATION

1. List some of the stories and songs that, so far as you know, have been preserved only by oral transmission.

2. Plan a number of works on the same subject in different mediums. What changes in the treatment of the subject does the change in medium necessitate?

3. Compare an orchestral version of a piece by Bach with the organ or harpsichord version.

4. Compare Michelangelo's statue of Moses with the account in the Bible. Note the strength and weakness of each.

5. Compare for mediums the versions of the story of Camille:

    a. Novel: Dumas, *La Dame aux camélias* (translated as *Camille*)

    b. Play: Dumas's dramatization of his novel *Camille*

    c. Opera: Verdi, *La Traviata*

    d. Cinema: *Camille*

6. Compare the opera *Carmen,* by Bizet, with the short story by Mérimée from which it was taken, or Donizetti's *Lucia di Lammermoor* with Scott's *The Bride of Lammermoor.*

7. Listen carefully to the next concert you attend to see if there are any numbers that are designed primarily for display of technique.

8. Find examples of sculpture that emphasize mass and solidity and some that emphasize space.

9. Study the work of some one sculptor for his subjects.

10. Do the same for his choice of mediums.

11. Study Picasso's paintings that show two views of a face at the same time. Do they give you the illusion of seeing the face in the round?

12. Find poems that could not be made into paintings because they deal with abstract subjects.

13. Answer the criticism that the "Gates of Paradise" is not good art because Ghiberti has followed the methods of a painter rather than a sculptor.

14. Study any ten reliefs for the subjects used.

15. Compare the work of Michelangelo in painting, sculpture, architecture, and poetry.

CHAPTER 6

MEDIUMS OF THE VISUAL ARTS

ARCHITECTURE

Traditionally the material of which a building is made is determined by the materials at hand when the building is erected. In Greece marble was easily available and many of the buildings were made of marble. In Rome concrete was used because there were great quantities of an earth called *pozzuolana* which, when mixed with lime, made a hard and enduring cement. Throughout Europe limestone was easily available and the cathedrals were built of limestone. In most sections of the United States there were heavily wooded forests, and the first houses were built by chopping down trees and putting up log cabins. In some parts of the country clay was to be had for the digging, and settlers dug the clay and fired the brick where the house was to be put. In the Southwest the Indians had no stone and no way of firing brick, and so they built their houses of brick dried in the sun, *adobe*. The Eskimos build with blocks of hard snow. In most circumstances buildings have been constructed of the materials at hand.

This condition is changing because new building materials are being made in factories, and the architect is less dependent on local materials than he used to be. The most important of the new materials are structural steel and reinforced concrete. But many other new materials have gained wide acceptance. Plate glass makes possible huge expanses of uninterrupted glass. Glass bricks have the advantage of letting in light, i.e., of being translucent, while not being transparent. There are fabricated woods made of thin sheets of wood glued together with grain running in opposite directions in order to obviate the possibility of warping or bending, as in ordinary wood. Under these conditions, wood can take its place with steel and reinforced concrete as a scientific material that lends itself to exact calculation. Aluminum and enameled surfaces are being tried. Linoleum, rubber, and concrete tiles are used for floors. Plastics are being used increasingly; their development has been such that we can count on other new materials of plastic in the future.

The choice of medium determines or is determined by the type of construction used in the building. For buildings in wood, the post-and-lintel type is generally used. For stone, post-and-lintel is used if the slabs are large; if the stones are small, the arch is usually employed. The arch is the typical method for stone construction, as post-and-lintel is for wood. Steel and reinforced concrete, which are very strong and very light, can be used in any type of construction. The type that is characteristic of them is known as skeleton construction. (See Chapter 12.)

SCULPTURE

Stone and Bronze. The two mediums most commonly used for sculpture are stone and metal. Of the stones marble is one of the glories of the *Hermes* of Praxiteles (Figure 58). The stone is so smooth that one wants to feel it, to run his hand over the surface. So well has the sculptor followed the contours of the body, one almost believes that if he could touch the skin, he would find it soft and pliable.

In medieval cathedrals the figures were carved of the material of which the church was made, usually limestone. Limestone is soft and for that reason it does not polish well. Even in photographs one can tell the difference between the surface of a marble statue, like the *Hermes* of Praxiteles, and that of softer stones, such as we find in the *King of Judah* (Figure 59) from Chartres. Granite is coarse but hard and is suited for bold effects. In the *Adams Memorial* (Figure 170), Saint-Gaudens has used granite for the background, its hard uncompromising texture and speckled color being used to contrast with the soft clothing of the bronze figure.

Of the metals, the one most commonly used is bronze. The processes used in making stone and bronze statues are exactly opposite. Stone statues are made by cutting away the stone until only the figures are

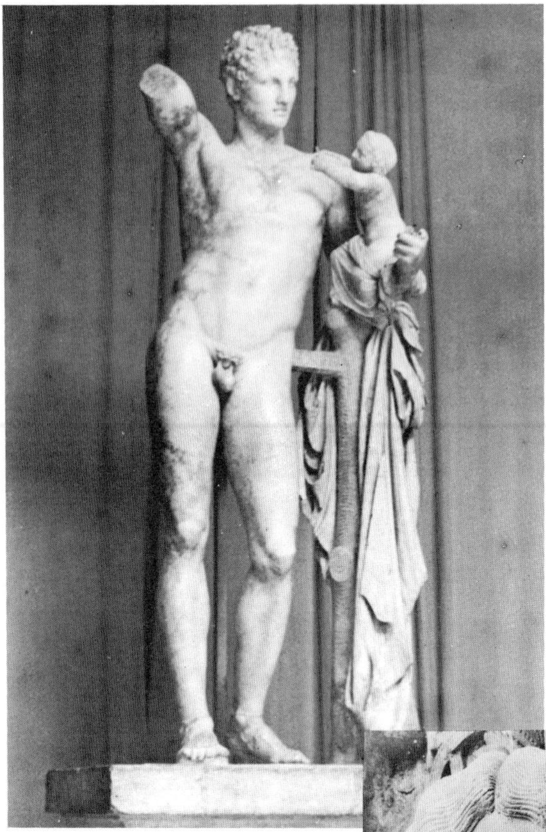

FIG. 58. Praxiteles (fourth century
B.C.), Greek sculptor. *Hermes and
Dionysus* (ca. 350 B.C.). (Parian
marble. Height: 6 feet 11 inches.
Olympia, Museum. Photograph,
Saul Weinburg.)

FIG. 59. *King of Judah* (twelfth
century). (Stone. Above life-size.
Chartres, Cathedral of Notre
Dame. Photograph by Houvet.)

left. Metal statues are first mod-
eled in clay; the sculptor builds
up the figure he wants, and then
has it cast in bronze.

In small statues the bronze is
solid, but in large ones the solid
metal is too heavy and expensive;
besides it has a tendency to crack
when it is cooled. Most bronze
statues therefore are hollow. The
process of casting bronze is a very
difficult and intricate one, so difficult that it constitutes one of
the disadvantages of the medium.
Another disadvantage is that it
is easily melted down for other
uses; many a bronze statue has
been poured into bullets. Its rich
color, however, and the smooth
texture, reflecting lights as they
can be reflected only in metal,
make it one of the most beautiful
of all the mediums for sculpture.
Moreover, it is relatively light,
and the figure can support itself
in many positions that would be
impossible in stone. In the *Charioteer* (Figure 60) and the
Hermes of Praxiteles (Figure 58),
we have two original Greek statues, the *Charioteer* in bronze, the
Hermes in marble. The *Charioteer* stands on his own feet, and
though the figure is large, it

FIG. 60. *The Charioteer* (ca. 475 B.C.).
(Bronze with enamel and silver inlay.
Height: 5 feet 11 inches. Delphi,
Museum. Photograph, Saul Weinburg.)

needs no other support. In the *Hermes,* however, extra support is given by a tree trunk partially covered with a cloak on which the god is leaning his left elbow. The marble would break if the entire weight of the statue were concentrated on the legs.

A large number of Greek statues in bronze were destroyed, but copies in stone were made by the Romans, and the stone copies are now all that are left. Since the stone would not support the figure in the position used in the bronze, stone supports, often poorly disguised, were added. This is the reason that one often sees a trunk of a tree in a Greek statue where it is not expected.

Because of the differences in method and medium the effects to be gained in stone and metal are very different. Stone tends to be hard, strong, solid, but brittle, whereas metal tends to be light, tensile, and graceful.

Wood. Besides stone and metal, wood, terra cotta, and ivory are important mediums for sculpture. Wood has an initial advantage in that it is cheap, easily available, and easy to cut. More important is the fact that it polishes well, has a smooth shining surface and a beautiful color. Furthermore it is relatively light and can be made into varied shapes. It is, of course, limited in size. Often the grain of the wood can be seen, and if used well, it adds greatly to the effect of the whole, as in Henry Moore's *Reclining Figure* (Figure 14) and *Two Forms* (Figure 11).

Ivory. Ivory and terra cotta may almost be counted lost mediums for they are used very little today, though they have been important. As we have said, the great statue of Athena in the Parthenon was of gold and ivory. In the Boston Museum is the small statuette of ivory called the *Snake Goddess* (Figure 61); it dates from the little-known Aegean, or Minoan, civilization, which preceded the Greek. When excavations were being made in Crete, a woman interested in the Boston Museum of Fine Arts bought a mass of earth just as it came from the spade because it contained fragments of gold and ivory.[1] When the pieces were put together this little figure emerged, and it is now counted one of the treasures of the Museum. The snakes and the bands of her skirt are of gold. There are holes in her tiara which would indicate that gold was wound through it also. The lady looks very modern with her small waist and full skirts. Probably she was a priestess,

[1] Pijoan. *An Outline History of Art,* Vol. I, p. 203.

for she carries two snakes in her hands. Certainly she was an aristocrat; her face and bearing both give witness to a noble lineage.

From the Middle Ages on, ivory has been much used for small pieces in which very delicate carving is needed, for example, crosses, chessmen, and the backs of books. Usually carvings in ivory are of small size, the reasons being the great expense of ivory and the difficulty of securing it in large pieces. The color of ivory is a rich, creamy yellow. Like wood, ivory cracks.

Terra Cotta. The word *terra cotta* means "baked earth." Terra cotta is made by firing clay, as in pottery. It is usually painted and covered with a heavy glaze. The great advantages of terra cotta are its cheapness in comparison with stone or bronze, and the brilliant colors made possible by glazing. Like all pottery, terra cotta is easily broken and chipped. As a medium for sculpture, terra cotta has been used at all times. Excellent examples are to be found in the work of many early peoples, notably the Greeks, the Chinese, and the Etruscans.

Fig. 61. *Snake Goddess* (ca. 1500 B.C.). (Gold and ivory. Height: 6½ inches. Boston, courtesy of Museum of Fine Arts.)

A frequent subject in Chinese art is the lohan, a disciple of the Buddha. Usually, as in the example shown (Figure 62) we find the emphasis on meditation characteristic of Buddhism. In the Renaissance, terra cotta was the favorite medium of the della Robbias.

Artists in all arts at all times have experimented in new mediums, and sculptors of the present day are no exception. Henry Moore's little figure *The Bride* is of cast lead and copper wire. Zorach's *Head of Christ* is of black porphyry. Cast stone, wrought iron, aluminum, glass, and steel are other mediums used today.

FIG. 62. *Lohan*. Chinese, T'ang Dynasty (A.D. 618–906). (Pottery, hard reddish-buff clay, green and yellow glazes. Height, 42 inches; base, 7 inches; depth, 35 inches; width, 38 inches. Toronto, Royal Ontario Museum.)

PAINTING

Painting may be defined as the application of colored pigments to a flat surface, usually canvas, paper, wood, or plaster.

Pigments

Pigments used in making colors come from many different sources: clay, coal tar, vegetable matter, etc. Some are manufactured; some are found in nature almost as they are used. Most of the pigments used today are obtained from natural sources and have been known for a very long time. The reds and browns now obtained from clay are the same reds and browns used by the cave men when they painted on the walls in prehistoric times. Vegetables are the source for many pigments; indigo produces blue and madder red. Ultramarine, which is the *blue* blue, the most expensive of all blues, is made by grinding the stone lapis lazuli. Purple, one of the most famous colors, is extracted from a shellfish, the murex. Blacks are usually made by burning some substance such as wood, ivory, or oil.

Vehicles

Though the sources of color have been pretty much the same throughout the generations, the way the color is applied to the surface has changed. Since the colors as procured either from nature or from artificial sources are dry, they must be mixed with something to be spread on a surface. This substance, usually a fluid, is called the *vehicle*. In oil paintings the colors are mixed with oil; in other words oil is the vehicle. In water color, water is the vehicle. The surface on which the paint is spread depends chiefly on the vehicle used. Canvas is not a good surface for water color, nor is paper a good surface for oil. Since the pigments are essentially the same no matter what surface or vehicle is used, a medium is commonly distinguished by the surface and vehicle used. We do not speak of painting in earth colors but of painting in oil on canvas. Each medium also determines its own brush stroke and produces an effect not to be obtained in another.

Oil. Probably the most widely used medium for painting at the present time is oil. The vehicle is oil and the surface is usually canvas though various other surfaces are used. The special advantage of oil is that it stays moist for a long time. The artist can work over what he is doing, and if he wishes he may change today what he painted yesterday. The paint may be applied in any way that suits the artist, so thinly that the canvas shows through or so thickly as to produce a rough surface. The rough surface of van Gogh's *Self-Portrait in a Straw Hat* may be seen in the photograph (Figure 63); the paint is so thick that each stroke shows clearly. In contrast, the paint in Gauguin's *Sulking Woman* (Figure 64) is applied smoothly, and individual brush strokes do not show at all.

There are two methods of painting in oil, the direct and the indirect. In the direct method the paints are opaque and are applied to the surface just as they are desired in the finished picture. In the indirect method the paint is put on in many thin layers of transparent color; the effect produced in this way is very rich and luminous. Unfortunately it cannot be distinguished in a photograph. The direct method is the more flexible medium of expression; the artist can use his pigment very freely and express in it any fleeting change in his thought. And, if it has not the richness of the transparent colors, it can obtain great vitality through the use of colors in high intensity. What may be called a third method of using oil is called *pointillism*, because small dots, or

Fig. 63. Vincent van Gogh (1853–1890), Dutch painter, etcher, and lithographer. *Self-Portrait in a Straw Hat* (1888–1889). (Oil on canvas, on wood. Size: 13¾ by 10½ inches. Detroit, courtesy of Detroit Institute of Arts.)

strokes, of opaque paint are placed close together so that the eye looking at them mixes them. One can see the little dots of paint in Seurat's *Sunday on the Island of La Grande Jatte* (Figure 65).

The disadvantages of oil have to do with the preservation of the picture. Because the paint takes a long time to dry, the oil has a

Fig. 64. Paul Gauguin (1848–1903), French painter. *The Sulking Woman* (1891). (Oil on canvas. Size: 36 by 27 inches. Worcester, Mass., Art Museum. Photograph by Worcester Art Museum.)

tendency to rise to the surface and form a film over the picture, making the colors dull. Moreover, it tends to become yellow, and in time the paint cracks.

Water Color. In water color the pigments are mixed with water and applied to a fine, white paper. The paper shines through the paint and makes the color brilliant. It is difficult to produce warm, rich tones in water color. Once the paint has been applied, changes may be made, but usually a change tends to make the color less brilliant. In Marin's painting (Figure 66), the characteristic "watery" look of water color can be clearly seen. Water color is best for spontaneous, evanescent expression.

Opaque water color is called *gouache*. Enough white is added to keep the paper from shining through. As a result the color is lacking in brilliance. Picasso's *Blue Boy* is done in *gouache* (Figure 17).

Fresco. In fresco the pigment is mixed with water and applied to wet plaster. The color dries into the plaster, and the picture thus becomes a part of the wall.

Since fresco must be done quickly it is a very exacting medium; there is no rubbing out and no changing once the design is begun. It is accordingly a medium of broad, bold, direct work, usually with great simplification of form and freedom in the treatment of the subject. Moreover, because of the chemical action of the plaster on the paint, only earth pigments may be used, and the colors lack intensity; there

Fig. 65. Georges Pierre Seurat (1859–1891), French painter. *Sunday on the Island of La Grande Jatte* (1886). (Oil on canvas. Size: 81 by 120⅜ inches. Chicago, courtesy of Art Institute of Chicago; Helen Birch Bartlett Memorial Collection.)

FIG. 66. John Marin (1870–
1953), American painter.
Maine Islands (1922).
(Water color. Size: 16¾ by
20 inches. Washington,
Phillips Gallery; courtesy,
Phillips Collection.)

FIG. 67. Michelangelo.
Decorative Nude. Detail of
Sistine Chapel ceiling.
(Fresco. Photograph by
Anderson.)

is, however, uniformity of tone with no glaring contrasts. The disadvantages of fresco are two: first, it is almost impossible to move a fresco; second, the painting, being permanently fixed to the wall, is subject to any of the disasters that may happen to the wall. If the plaster cracks or has a hole punched in it, the picture is hurt to that extent. The Sistine Chapel ceiling is in fresco (Figure 67).

Egg Tempera. Tempera and fresco were favorite mediums throughout the Middle Ages and early Renaissance before oil was generally adopted. Tempera painting is usually done on a wooden panel that has been made very smooth with a coating of plaster called *gesso*. The colors are mixed with egg. The paint dries almost immediately; therefore there is in tempera painting little blending or fusing of colors; the colors are laid on side by side or are superimposed. Hence the painting is composed of a large number of successive small strokes, and the effect

Fig. 68. Simone Martini (ca. 1284–1344), Italian painter. (The saints on either side are probably the work of Lippo Memmi.) *Annunciation* (1333). (Tempera on wood. Height: 5 feet 11¼ inches. Florence, Uffizi Gallery. Photograph by Anderson.)

is largely linear. It is hard to obtain rich, deep tones or dark shadows. Because tempera paint dries quickly, the artist must be precise and exact in his work. It is a medium well designed for careful detail. The advantage of tempera is its great luminosity of tone, the colors being clear and beautiful. On the other hand, the precision needed tends to produce a certain hardness of outline. Botticelli's *Birth of Venus* (Figure 28), and Simone Martini's *Annunciation* (Figure 68) show most of the characteristics of tempera.

Encaustic. Wax was used by the Egyptians for portrait paintings on mummy cases. There were several different ways of preparing the wax, but in general the color was mixed with the warm wax and burned in. This method was also used by the Greeks and the Romans, and it was employed to some extent during the Middle Ages. Paintings with wax have a definite body and a pleasing sheen which seem to show at their best in portraits. The *Portrait of a Boy* (Figure 69) dating from the second century is an example. In recent

FIG. 69. *Portrait of a Boy* (second century A.D.). (Encaustic on wood panel. Size: about 10 by 16 inches. New York, courtesy of Metropolitan Museum of Art. Gift of Edward S. Harkness, 1917–1918.)

years painting in wax has been revived by some modern painters, notably Diego Rivera.

Pastel. Pastel is a kind of colored chalk. Its colors are brilliant, and it is a very flexible medium, one in which very rich and varied effects may be produced. As a medium, however, it has never won a high place because no one has yet discovered a way to preserve it in its original freshness. Even if it is covered almost at once with a fixing medium or with a protecting surface such as glass, the chalk rubs, and the picture loses some of its brilliance.

Illumination. In the Middle Ages, when books were lettered by hand, the pages were often decorated with gold, silver, and bright colors. Capital letters, especially, were made large and important. Decorative borders were common, and frequently the artist added miniature paintings of people or scenes. In the page from the *Tickhill Psalter* (Figure 70), all the capitals are emphasized, but special attention is given the initial letter B with which the first Psalm begins, "Beatus qui non abiit in consilio impiorum" (Blessed is the man that walketh not in the counsel of the ungodly). Each half of the letter is filled with a miniature, and there are further miniatures at the foot of the page. These miniatures tell the story of the anointing of David, the supposed author of the Psalms. The illuminations were made with opaque water colors, much like present-day *gouache*.

Mosaic. Mosaic, stained glass, and tapestry are usually classed with painting, though the medium is not pigment. A picture in mosaic is made by putting together small pieces of colored glass or stone, called *tesserae*. These tesserae are usually square in shape. They are set in cement to hold them in place, the underside of the tesserae being roughened to make them fast in the cement. The use of stones makes simplification of design necessary. Moreover, the stones can never be set very smoothly in the cement, and hence the surface is always rough, with the light reflected from it in many ways. This creates a lively, vibrant effect. The greatest mosaics were made in the Middle Ages before painting became usual in churches. Some of the most famous are found in the church of San Vitale at Ravenna (Figure 71). The enlargement shows the tesserae clearly (Figure 72).

Stained Glass. Like the mosaic, the stained-glass window is a kind of patchwork. It is made by combining many small pieces of colored glass which are held together by bands of lead. In a large window, the lead is reinforced by heavy iron bars that make very heavy black lines in the picture. The windows at Chartres are considered among the greatest of a great period. Our illustration shows one section of the window of *St. Eustace* (Figure 73). The saint is shown riding to the hunt, his horn to his lips. At his feet are the dogs, and just before him, the stags; behind him is an attendant urging on the chase.

Tapestry. Tapestries are large fabrics in which a design is woven by hand. In the Middle Ages they were hung on the walls of palaces and in the cathedrals on festive occasions, both as decoration and for warmth. Being of very firm texture, they shut out the cold and helped

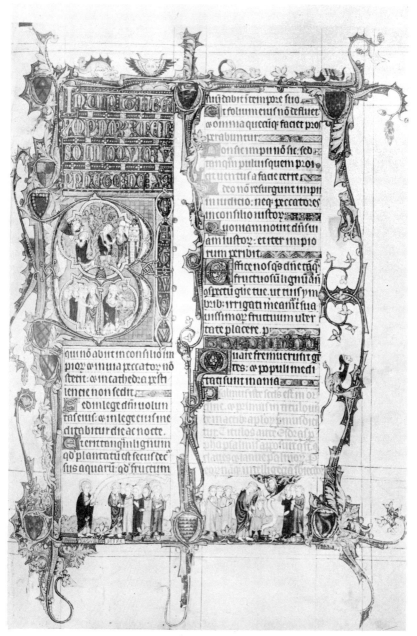

FIG. 70. First page of the Psalms from the *Tickhill Psalter* (ca. 1310). (Illuminated manuscript. Size: 12⅞ by 8⅝ inches. New York, Spencer Collection of the New York Public Library.)

Fig. 71. *Theodora and Her Attendants* (ca. A.D. 525). (Mosaic. Figures slightly above life-size. Detail from copy of original mosaic in church of San Vitale, Ravenna. New York, Metropolitan Museum of Art; courtesy of the Metropolitan Museum of Art.)

Fig. 72. "Portrait of Theodora," detail of *Theodora and Her Attendants*. (Photograph by Alinari.)

to preserve the heat from the fireplace. In the *Unicorn in Captivity* (Figure 74) we have the famous *mille fleur* or "thousand flower" background.

DRAWINGS

Drawings and prints are of special interest to the student, both for their intrinsic value and because they are comparatively inexpensive. In them the person of small means can afford original works of artists.

Fig. 73. *St. Eustace Hunting* (twelfth century), window, Bay 13. (Stained glass. Height of diamond about 3 feet. Chartres, Cathedral of Notre Dame. Photograph by Houvet.)

Fig. 74. *The Hunt of the Unicorn:* VI. *The Unicorn in Captivity* (late 15th or early 16th century). (French or Flemish Tapestry, from Chateau of Verteuil. Silk and wool with silver and silver gilt threads. Size: about 12 by 8 feet. New York, courtesy of the Metropolitan Museum of Art. The Cloisters Collection.)

A drawing may be a finished work as in Ingres's *Lady and Boy* (Figure 75). Or it may be made as a study for a painting to be completed, as Michelangelo's studies for the *Libyan Sibyl* (Figure 76). Notice in the latter Michelangelo's sketches of the big toe, and his change from the masculine face in the center to the feminine face at the left.

Drawings are known chiefly by the mediums used, such as pencil, pen, and silverpoint. *Pencil* is one of the most common because of its general utility, especially for the making of rapid notes. The French

Fig. 75. Jean Auguste Dominique Ingres (1780–1867), French painter and maker of pencil portraits. *Lady and Boy* (1808). (Pencil drawing. Size: 9¾ by 7¼ inches. New York, courtesy of the Metropolitan Museum of Art; bequest of Mrs. H. O. Havemeyer, 1929. The H. O. Havemeyer Collection.)

FIG. 76. Michelangelo (1475–1564). Studies for *Libyan Sibyl*. (Red chalk. New York, courtesy of the Metropolitan Museum of Art; Joseph Pultizer Bequest, 1924.)

FIG. 77. Leonardo da Vinci (Attributed) (1452–1519), Italian painter. *Head of a Woman*. (Silverpoint with white on bluish paper. New York, courtesy of the Metropolitan Museum of Art; Hewitt Fund, 1917.)

artist Ingres made many pencil portraits as one means of support while
he was living in Rome. A typical example is the *Lady and Boy. Silverpoint,* a drawing with a gold or silver wire on a specially prepared
paper, is very pale in tone and has little vitality but is very delicate.

Fɪɢ. 78. Georges Pierre Seurat (1859–1891), French painter. *The Artist's Mother*
(ca. 1883). (Conte crayon on paper. Size: 12⅞ by 9½ inches. New York,
courtesy of the Metropolitan Museum of Art; Joseph Pulitzer Bequest, 1951,
from the Museum of Modern Art, Lillie P. Bliss Collection.)

The difference between the line of the pencil and that of silverpoint can be seen by comparing the Ingres portrait with the *Head of a Woman* attributed to Leonardo (Figure 77). *Charcoal* and *Conte crayon* give rich shadows, great brilliancy of light, and strength of tones, but the lines are often vague (Figure 78).

Ink makes a clear crisp line; often ink is combined with a wash as in the Rembrandt drawing (Figure 79). Drawing with a *brush* is char-

FIG. 79. Rembrandt Harmensz Van Rijn (1606–1669), Dutch painter. *St. Peter and St. Paul at the Beautiful Gate of the Temple.* (Pen and bister, washed. New York, courtesy of the Metropolitan Museum of Art; Rogers Fund, 1911.)

FIG. 80. Kyosai (1831–1889), Japanese painter. *Animals, Children, and Men.* (Brush drawing. Height: 10⅞ inches. New York, courtesy of the Metropolitan Museum of Art; Fletcher Fund, 1937.)

acteristic of the Chinese and Japanese, who, it will be remembered, *write* with a brush instead of a pen. The brush gives very quick results and allows great freedom in handling. See Kyosai's *Animals, Children, and Men* (Figure 80).

PRINTS

A print is something printed; that is, it is the impression left on paper or some other surface from an inked plate. Usually the printing is in black ink on white paper. The plate is made by the artist and he does the printing. For these reasons a print is counted the authentic work of an artist and is signed by him.

The number of copies that are made from any plate depends on the type of print, the qualities of the particular plate, and the wishes of the artist. Often an artist decides on a certain number—thirty, fifty, one hundred—and destroys the plate once that number has been reached. There are four major types of prints: woodcut, engraving, etching, and lithograph. Each print can be distinguished by the type of line found in it, and the line in turn is determined by the way the plate is made. Therefore it is convenient to know both the kind of line characteristic of a print and the way the plate is made.

Woodcut. The woodcut, as the name implies, is made from a plate of wood. The design stands out in relief, the remaining surface of the block being cut away. A wood block prints just like the letters of a typewriter. The lines of the design being of wood, they can never be very fine, and woodcuts can be identified by their firm, clear, black lines, as we see in Dürer's *Christ on the Cross* (Figure 81), and his *Four Horsemen* (Figure 53).

The design is left standing in relief, and any part of the plate that is not cut away will print a solid black. Older makers of the woodcut such as Dürer used solid blacks very sparingly. In more modern prints, as in

FIG. 81. Albrecht Dürer (1471–1528), German painter, engraver, and wood carver. *Christ on the Cross,* from the Small Passion (1511). (Woodcut. Size: 4 by 5 inches. Photograph, Don Woolley.)

The Miraculous Draught of Fishes by Schmidt-Rottluff (Figure 82), large areas of black are used in the design.

The woodcut is made from a plate of softwood like peach, apple, pear, or sycamore, sawed parallel with the grain of the wood. The print often shows the grain. In recent years prints have been cut from linoleum as well as from wood. Sometimes these prints are called linoleum cuts, but there is so little difference in the two that ordinarily no distinction is made, and both are called woodcuts.

Colored woodcuts are made by preparing a separate block for each color to be used; only the parts to be printed in one color appear on the block of that color. The finished print, however, will show more shades than there are blocks, because one' color is printed on top of another and so the colors are mixed. The Japanese, especially, have excelled in this type of woodcut, though the technique has been used widely (Figure 92).

Fig. 82. Karl Schmidt-Rottluff (1884———), German painter and print maker. *The Miraculous Draught of Fishes* (1918). (Woodcut. Size: 15½ by 19⅝ inches. From *Kristus,* a portfolio of 9 woodcuts, published by Kurt Wolff, Leipzig, 1919. Collection Mrs. Gertrud A. Mellon, New York. Photograph, The Museum of Modern Art.)

Engraving. The engraving is in many ways the opposite of the woodcut. In the woodcut, the parts that are to be black are left standing, and the remainder of the block is cut away; in engraving, the lines of the design are cut into a metal plate. These lines are then filled

Fig. 83. Martin Schongauer (1440–1491), German painter and engraver. *The Annunciation* (undated). (Engraving. Size: 6½ by 4¾ inches. Boston, courtesy Museum of Fine Arts.)

with ink and transferred from the plate to the paper. The lines of an engraving are cut by hand with an instrument called a *burin,* and since the copper plate is hard to cut, they are very fine, much finer than the lines of a woodcut. For the same reason they are hard and stiff, precise and formal. Shadows are made by lines either very close together or crossing at regular angles. Blake's engraving *When the Morning Stars Sang Together* shows the typical quality of the line (Figure 34). Other engravings are Dürer's *The Knight, Death, and the Devil* (Figure 52) and Schongauer's *The Annunciation* (Figure 83).

FIG. 84. Paul Klee (1879–1940), Swiss painter and print maker. *Why Does He Run?* (ca. 1932). Etching. Size: 9⅜ by 11¹³⁄₁₆ inches. New York, The Museum of Modern Art.)

Etching. Etching differs from engraving in the way the lines are made. In engraving, as we noted, the lines are cut directly in the plate by hand. In etching the plate is covered with a coating of a thin wax-like material called a ground. Through it the etcher draws his design. He does not attempt to cut the plate itself; he merely scratches through the wax, leaving the metal uncovered. The plate is then put in an acid bath, and the design is *etched* or eaten into the plate. The lines on an etched plate therefore are made much more easily than on an engraved plate, and we see the difference in the finished print. The etched lines

Fig. 85. Francisco Goya (1746–1828), Spanish painter, etcher, and lithographer. *No Grites Tanta* from *Los Caprichos* (*Caprices*) (1793–1798). (Etching and aquatint. Size: 5 by 7⅜ inches. Photograph, Don Woolley.)

have the freedom of a penciled line, go in any direction, and cross at any angle. In *Why Does He Run?* (Figure 84), Klee uses his etching needle almost like a pencil or a pen.

Obviously neither etching nor engraving can show solid blacks as can the woodcut, and in both prints grays must be made by putting lines close together or by crisscrossing. The etched lines are very clear in Goya's *No Grites Tanta* (Figure 85), and in Rembrandt's *Three Trees* (Figure 88).

Lithography. The lithograph is the most recent of the four common types of print. It was discovered just before 1800, whereas woodcuts, engravings, and etchings go back to the fifteenth and sixteenth centuries. In a lithograph the design is drawn with a heavy greasy chalk on a specially prepared stone, and ink impressions are made from it. Every line or shadow made on the stone is transferred to the paper; in fact a lithograph looks very much like a charcoal or chalk drawing. And it is the only print that can show values shading one into the other as in a drawing or a painting. Daumier's *Strangers in Paris* (Figure 130) and Bellows's *Dempsey and Firpo* (Figure 86) both show the characteristic shading of the lithograph.

Dry Point, Mezzotint, Aquatint, Serigraph. *Dry point* stands halfway between engraving and etching. It is like engraving in that the lines are cut directly in the metal. It is like etching in that the needle is held as a pencil and is used very freely. It merely scratches the metal. As it scratches, it leaves a little ridge at one side like the ridge left by a pin run across a cake of soap. This ridge, called the *burr,* takes the ink and makes a very rich, velvety line. A similar ridge is thrown up in engraving, but it is cleared away before any prints are taken. Dry point can rarely be distinguished from etching in a photograph, but in the original the rough line of the dry point is clear.

Mezzotint and aquatint are two means of giving a solid tone to a print. *Mezzotint* is made on a copper plate which is artificially roughened by an instrument known as a "rocker" or "cradle." The engraver then scrapes away more or less of the roughness in the parts he wants light. The parts not scraped, or only partially scraped, make a rich, velvety black like the burr of the dry point. Mezzotint is frequently combined with some other type of print, such as etching or dry point.

In *aquatint,* powdered resin is sprinkled on the plate and heated so that it adheres to the plate. When the plate is immersed in the acid, the

FIG. 86. George Bellows (1882–1925), American painter and print maker. *Dempsey and Firpo* (1924). (Lithograph. Size: 18½ by 22⅜ inches. New York, The Museum of Modern Art; Mrs. John D. Rockefeller, Jr. Purchase Fund. Photograph, Museum of Modern Art.)

FIG. 87. Francisco Goya (1746–1828), Spanish painter, etcher, and lithographer. *Los Caprichos*, Plate 39, *Back to His Grandfather* (Aquatint. New York, courtesy Metropolitan Museum of Art; gift of M. Knoedler and Co., 1918.)

parts not protected by the resin are bitten, and a very fine shadowy gray is produced (Figure 87).

The *serigraph,* or silk screen, is a color print made by squeezing color through a silk screen. For it a stencil method is employed. The artist has a series of silk screens, one for each color. He leaves open all areas using a certain color, but paints over or "stops" the remaining sections of the silk, thus allowing the paint to penetrate only the parts designed for it. The serigraph can show broad flat areas and vivid coloring.

FOR FURTHER EXPLORATION

1. What are the most common building materials used in your home town? Are they found in the neighborhood?

2. Study the houses around you for their construction. Look especially for skeleton construction. Do you find any arches, domes, or buttresses?

3. Buy dry pigment from an art store, and experiment with different vehicles: water, oil, egg, and wax. Note the effect of the vehicle on the stroke.

4. If possible, visit an exhibit of paintings and one of prints to study the characteristics of the different mediums.

5. Make note of any new materials for architecture or sculpture you may see.

6. Study in detail three statues in different mediums. Put into words the influence of the medium on the statue.

7. Do the same for three buildings.

8. Do the same for three paintings.

9. Use a cake of soap and a bit of clay to try out the two methods of making sculpture. What effect does the method have on the finished work?

CHAPTER 7

MEDIUMS OF MUSIC, LITERATURE, AND THE COMBINED ARTS

MUSIC

Music and literature are the arts of sound. A word is a sound and it is also a meaning. In music, however, a sound is only a sound; it may be a high sound or a low sound, a long sound or a short sound, a sweet sound or a harsh sound, but it is only a sound. A tone is only a tone; it has no other significance. The symbol for a tone is only a symbol for a tone. Moreover, that symbol is the same throughout the civilized world. We do not have one set of symbols for Russian music and another for French or German music.

Music and literature differ also in the way the sounds are made. In literature all the sounds are made by the human voice. In music the human voice is but one of a number of instruments used. The sound and hence the music are quite different when produced by one instrument or another.

KINDS OF MUSICAL INSTRUMENTS

Musical instruments may be classified roughly according to the way the sound is produced, by beating, blowing, or bowing. Those in which the sound is made by beating are called the instruments of percussion: drum, xylophore, cymbals. Those in which the sound is made by blowing are wind instruments: horn, trumpet, flute. Those in which the sound is made by bowing are stringed instruments: violin, viola, cello. The name of the last group is not satisfactory, however, because certain of the stringed instruments, the harp, for example, are not bowed. Therefore, they are called stringed instruments, not bowed instruments. This is the usual classification of instruments: percussion, wind, strings. It is believed that instruments of percussion came first, then wind instruments, and last, strings. A child follows this order in his natural development; at first he likes rattles and other toys that make noise by beating. Later he learns to whistle, and he likes to pipe on wind instruments of all kinds. Still later he begins to play on the strings such as violin, cello, or harp.

Wind instruments are further subdivided into (1) wood winds: piccolo, flute, oboe, clarinet, English horn, and bassoon; and (2) brasses: trumpet, horn, trombone, and tuba. The names originally corresponded to the materials of which the instruments were made; most of the instruments of the brass family are still made of brass, but the name wood winds has stuck though the flute and piccolo now are made of metal.

Thus we have four families or choirs of instruments:

1. Strings
2. Wood winds
3. Brasses
4. Percussion

For obvious reasons the human voice, the organ, and the piano are not usually classed in one of these groups but are put in a separate section by themselves.

The Strings

The string section is the most important group in an orchestra. It carries the main burden, though it is helped and relieved by the other choirs. There are four instruments in this section:

1. Violin   Soprano
2. Viola   Contralto
3. Cello (violoncello)   Tenor
4. Double bass   Bass

Each instrument has four strings which are normally set in vibration by a bow moving across them, though they can be plucked by the fingers (called *pizzicato*). When the strings are played at their full length, an instrument can make only four tones. Other tones are made by *stopping,* that is, by putting a finger on a string. In this way the performer shortens the amount of string that vibrates and so raises the pitch; by this means the performer can thus produce a large number of tones on a single string. The Second Movement of Bach's Suite No. 3 in D major has been arranged for solo violin to be played on one string. It is commonly known as the "Air for the G String."

The Violin. The most important member of the string section, the violin, is so well known as to need no description. Of all the strings, it is the most versatile and expressive. It has a wide range of tone, its tone can be indefinitely sustained, and it is capable of expressing almost any emotion. César Franck's Sonata in A major for Violin and Piano (page 217) shows the instrument clearly.

In an orchestra the violins are usually divided into two groups, the first and second violins.

The Viola. The second member of the violin family is the viola, which is similar to a violin but larger, with thicker strings and a heavier bow. It plays at a lower pitch and might be called an alto violin. It is tuned a fifth lower. Like the violin, it is held under the chin.

The Cello. A still larger violin is the cello. Its strings are thicker and heavier, and its bow heavier and shorter than those of the viola. The cello is too large to be held under the chin; it rests on the floor and is held between the knees of the seated performer. The cello is an octave lower than the viola and has a wider range. The tone of the cello is rich and romantic, deep and full, and unlike the viola it is often used as a solo instrument. A classic example of writing for cello is Haydn's Cello Concerto in D.

The Double Bass. Also known as the contrabass or bass viol, the double bass is the largest member of the violin family. It rests on the floor and the player must stand to play it. Because of its size and the depth of its tone, it has a limited range of expression. It usually does no more than supply the bass notes of an ensemble, though at times it is given a solo part. In the Scherzo of Beethoven's Fifth Symphony, it plays a lumbering, almost grotesque role. Berlioz compared this famous passage to "the happy gambols of an elephant." In recent years, the bass has been used in jazz bands, being plucked or played in a "slapping" fashion to emphasize the beat, almost like a percussion instrument.

The Wood Winds

In all the members of the wood-wind family, tone is produced by air vibrating in a tube. Differences in tone are caused by the way the air in the tube is set vibrating. There are two kinds of wood-wind instruments: air and reed. In the first class, which includes the flute and piccolo, the air of the human breath is blown across a hole in the tube. The principle is the same as that involved when one blows across the top of a bottle or jug. In the second class of wood wind, a reed, which is a very elastic tongue of wood or metal, is placed in or upon an opening through which the air passes. By blowing, the player causes the reed to vibrate and so produces sound. The principle is the same as that of blowing upon a piece of grass held between the hands. Reeds may be single or double. In the single-reed instruments (clarinet and saxophone), a single reed flutters back and forth between the air in the player's mouth and the air in the instrument. In the double-reed instruments (oboe, English horn, and bassoon), the air passes between the two reeds, causing vibration.

The members of the wood-wind choir are:

High soprano	Piccolo
Soprano	Flute
	Clarinet
	Oboe
	Saxophone
Contralto	English horn
Tenor	Bassoon
Bass	Contrabassoon

The Flute. The coloratura soprano of the wood-wind family is the flute. The tone is very pure and "silvery," cool and liquid. The classic illustration of the flute is the "Dance of the Blessed Spirits" in Gluck's *Orpheus and Eurydice*.

The Piccolo. The little flute, or piccolo, is shrill and piercing. When played with the flute it adds brilliance and bite.

The Oboe. The lyric soprano of the wood-wind family is the oboe. The tone is soft and tender, yet penetrating and especially beautiful for pastoral effects. It is slightly nasal. The Second Movement of Tchaikovsky's Fourth Symphony begins with a short theme on the oboe.

The English Horn. Although called a horn, this instrument is really a large oboe, with a lower tone. It has a melancholy sound. It is heard in Sibelius's *Swan of Tuonela*. It also has the famous melody of the slow movement of Dvořák's *New World Symphony* (page 211).

The Bassoon, and the Contrabassoon. These instruments are respectively the tenor and bass of the oboe family. The tube is so long (bassoon, eight feet, and contrabassoon, sixteen feet) that it must be doubled back on itself. The contrabassoon produces the lowest tones in the orchestra. The bassoon is often used to represent clumsy, awkward movement, as when it is used for the hopping of the broom in Dukas's *Sorcerer's Apprentice*. In Ravel's "Beauty and the Beast" from the *Mother Goose Suite* the contrabassoon is used to depict the Beast.

The Clarinet. The dramatic soprano of the wood-wind family is the clarinet. It is less nasal than the oboe. It has a wide range and wide variety of tones. The minor melody with which Tchaikovsky's Fifth Symphony begins is played first on the clarinet.

The Bass Clarinet. The other principal member of the wood-wind family, the bass clarinet, has similar tones but of course is lower in pitch than the ordinary clarinet.

The Saxophone. Because it has a single reed, the saxophone is frequently classed with the wood winds.

The Brasses

The instruments of the brass choir are:

Trumpet	Soprano
French horn	Contralto
Trombone	Tenor
Tuba	Bass

The brass instruments have no reeds. Instead the air in the tube is set vibrating by the lips of the player against a cup-shaped metal mouthpiece. In all but the trombone, the tones are raised or lowered by valves which shorten or lengthen the tube. In the trombone the tube slides back and forth and so is shortened or lengthened to make the correct tone.

The Trumpet. The highest of the brasses is the trumpet. It has a rich but piercing tone, and it can be one of the most beautiful. It connotes war, fury, vengeance, triumph. No one who has heard Beethoven's *Leonore Overture* No. 3 will soon forget the trumpet call heard off stage.

The Horn. The French horn, as it is usually called, because it was so widely used by the French kings in their hunts, is one of the most beautiful of the voices of the orchestra—noble, poetic, expressive, sonorous, pure, soft. If played softly, it can be romantic and mysterious. If very loudly, it can be threatening and ominous. Probably the best-known French horn solo is the Andante Cantabile of Tchaikovsky's Fifth Symphony.

The Trombone. While similar to the trumpet, the trombone is more mellow in sound. The tone is solemn and majestic; it has beauty and dignity. It is heard in characteristic form in the "Pilgrim's Chorus" of Wagner's *Tannhäuser* Overture.

The Tuba. The deep bass foundation for the brasses is provided by the tuba. The tone is dignified and rich, powerful and brilliant. Like most of the bass instruments, it is rarely used alone, and then it represents some awkward, clumsy person or action. It depicts the bear in Stravinsky's *Petrouchka*, and the dragon in Wagner's *Siegfried*.

In all the wind instruments, both wood wind and brass, the mechanism is far from perfect and the difficulties of playing in tune are extremely great. In order to keep the instrument in tune with the rest of the orchestra, it is constantly necessary to correct the pitch by means of the breath and the lips of the player.

Percussion Family

The instruments of the percussion family are very varied, but they have one thing in common: the instrument is made to sound by being struck. Most of the instruments of this family contribute to effects of rhythm, dynamics, and tone color, rather than melody or harmony. Since each instrument is played only at times and in a rather conspicuous way, by watching the performers the beginner can easily learn the special qualities of each instrument and the way it is played.

The Drums. The *timpani*, or *kettledrums*, the most important members of the percussion group, are huge copper "kettles" across which skin has been stretched. They can be tuned to definite pitch. Change in pitch is produced by tightening or loosening the skin of the head. There are usually three or four kettledrums in an orchestra. The man who is playing them must have perfect pitch, for often he needs to tune his drums in the middle of a selection; specifically, he must get ready for a change in key while the orchestra is playing in the original key. The timpani are used for getting volume of sound, for dramatic suspense, and for big climaxes. A muffled roll on the timpani is always ominous, presaging doom and arousing terror.

The snare drum and the bass drum are the other drums. The *snare,* or *side drum,* is a small military instrument. Parchment is stretched on both sides, and on one side there are strings or "snares" which give the rattling sound characteristic of this drum. The tone is sharp and incisive and the drum is usually associated with the fife or piccolo.

The *"big bass drum"* is commonly used to accentuate rhythm. It is the largest of the drums, and is usually used in military compositions. Muffled, it plays a big part in funeral marches. It has a deep, booming sound. It is played with a single stick which has a large padded head.

Instruments of Indefinite Pitch. Besides the snare drum and the bass drum, there is a wide variety of instruments without definite pitch. *Cymbals* are large, slightly cupped plates of brass with leather hand straps on the back. They may be clashed together, rattled, or struck with a drumstick. They are dramatic and add to the excitement of a climax. The *gong* is a heavy metal disk hit with a padded stick. Its tone, which is a hollow sound, can be ominous or mysterious.

The *triangle* is a steel rod bent in the shape of a triangle and suspended by a string. It is hit with a metal rod. The sound is light and tinkling. The *tambourine* is a small wooden hoop with skin stretched over it. In the wooden hoop are small metal disks which jingle or tinkle when the tambourine is shaken or hit. *Castanets* are hard wooden pieces which are clicked together by the player.

Instruments of Definite Pitch. The percussion family includes several types of instruments of definite pitch. The *celesta* has a set of steel plates attached to wooden resonators. It is played from a keyboard, and the sound is sweet and cloying. It is appropriately used by Tchaikovsky for the "Dance of the Sugarplum Fairy" in the *Nutcracker Suite.* The *xylophone* is made of a set of small wooden bars and is played with two hammers. The tone is hollow and clanking. It is used by Saint-Saëns in *Danse Macabre* (*Dance of Death*) to imitate the rattling of bones. The *marimba* is a xylophone with resonators. The *glockenspiel,* or orchestral bells, is a set of steel bars played with hammers. *Chimes* (tubular bells) are pipes of various sizes, hung from a frame and struck with a hammer.

The Harp

Although it is a stringed instrument, the timbre of the harp is so different from that of the violin family that it is not counted with the strings but occupies a position all by itself. It is a large triangular-shaped instrument with forty-six strings which correspond to the white keys of the piano. When the performer wishes to play on the black keys, he must lengthen or shorten the strings by means of pedals operated by the feet. The strings are plucked by hand. The tone is silvery and dreamlike. Sparingly used the effect is beautiful. Unfortunately the harp has been used so much to suggest angels that it is hard to escape heavenly connotations when the harp is played. On the harp, chords are frequently "broken," that is, one tone is played after the other. Thus we get the name of a broken chord, *arpeggio,* from *arpa,* a "harp."

Piano, Harpsichord, Organ

In the piano, the harpsichord, and the organ, the tones are produced from a keyboard, and the performer has no responsibility for pitch. Each instrument is capable of producing complete harmonies.

The Piano. The piano is so well known as to need no discussion. Small hammers played from a keyboard strike the strings and produce the tone. There is a separate string or group of strings for each tone.

The Harpsichord. The harpsichord is like the piano, but the strings are plucked by quills or pieces of leather which are attached to small wooden bars. The harpsichord was one of the earlier forms of the piano; today it is used chiefly for the music of Bach and his predecessors.

The Organ. The organ is often called the "King of Instruments." It enjoys the distinction of being the only instrument on which a single performer can cause many different timbres to sound. The organist is like the conductor of an orchestra who plays all the instruments at the same time. The pipes of an organ are arranged in sets, each set with one pipe for each note of the keyboard. Each set has its own timbre, and all the sets are connected mechanically with the keyboard (or keyboards). From his seat on the organ bench the organist can control all the sets, and it is his business to combine these tones to secure the ensemble he desires. Most of the pipes of an organ are like the flute in that a column of air is played against an opening to make the sound. However, there are *reed stops* in which a single reed is used as in a clarinet. In the *electric organ* tones are produced by radio tubes or by other electromagnetic devices.

The organ is one of the oldest and greatest of instruments, and some of the greatest musicians like Bach have composed for it. Of recent years, however, the organ has fallen more or less into disfavor; we do not know the brilliant organist as we know the brilliant pianist or the brilliant violinist. There are probably a number of reasons; we will name only two. The organ is often poorly played. In the popular mind it is associated primarily with church services where the standard may be low. A more valid reason springs from the nature of the instrument itself. A pianist or a violinist may take his instrument with him, and therefore he may count on having an adequate instrument no matter where he is. The organist cannot carry his organ with him. He can play only in halls where there are organs, and he is dependent on the instrument he finds. In recent years there has been a renewed interest in organs, and we may hope for better opportunities for hearing organ music in the future.

The String Quartet

There are certain combinations of instruments that have proved to be good, and are often used by composers, such as the *piano trio* for violin, cello, and piano, and the *string orchestra,* which comprises the whole violin family. Of the small groups, however, the most important by far is the string quartet.

As its name indicates, the string quartet is composed of four stringed instruments, first violin, second violin, viola, and cello. The violins play the parts of both soprano and contralto, the viola plays the tenor part, and the cello the bass.

Since the sound is not large, music for the quartet falls into the classification called *chamber music.* Some of the greatest music has been written for this medium. The slow movement from Tchaikovsky's Quartet, Op. 11, Andante Cantabile is justly popular.

The Orchestra

By far the most important combination of instruments is the orchestra, which is composed of the four families: strings, wood winds, brasses, and percussion. Each of the first three has the four voices: soprano, contralto, tenor, and bass.

The strings are largest in number and constitute the most important group. They are divided into first and second violins, violas, and cellos. The double basses are used primarily to emphasize the low notes of the cellos. The strings form the backbone of the orchestra, and are largest in number. The leader of the first violins, called the *concertmeister,* is, next to the conductor, the first man of the orchestra. He always sits on the left of the conductor. In the string family, there is a strong family likeness and great unity of effect.

In the wood winds, on the other hand, we have seen that there are three different ways of producing the tone, whether by a column of air, or a single or a double reed. This means there is great variety of tone, and we can easily distinguish between the different instruments. Therefore we pick them out individually for specific parts played, and the tones are so piercing that we do not need many wood winds.

The brasses are strident; they can be heard very easily and very few are needed.

The number of instruments in any orchestra varies. In the score of his Ninth Symphony, Beethoven called for these instruments:

Wood wind: 2 flutes, 1 piccolo, 2 oboes, 2 clarinets, 2 bassoons, 1 double bassoon.

Brass: 4 horns, 2 trumpets, 3 trombones.

Percussion: 2 timpani, triangle, cymbals, bass drum.

Strings: First and second violins, violas, violoncellos, double basses.

Wagner in *The Ring of the Nibelung* increased the orchestra greatly:

Wood wind: 3 flutes, 2 piccolos, 3 oboes, 1 English horn, 3 clarinets, 1 bass clarinet, 3 bassoons.

Brass: 8 horns, 3 trumpets, 1 bass trumpet, 4 trombones, 5 tubas.

Percussion: 4 timpani, side drum, bass drum, triangle, cymbals, glockenspiel, gong.

Strings: 16 first violins, 16 second violins, 12 violas, 12 violoncellos, 8 double basses, 6 harps.

Since the time of Wagner the orchestra has gone on increasing the number of its instruments. But the multiplication of instruments does not mean that all are playing all the time. The strings have the most work to do, the brasses the least. In Brahms's First Symphony, for instance, there are over twelve hundred bars, and the trombones play fewer than a hundred.

The Conductor. At first it may seem that the conductor stands up in front, waves his arms, and takes the bows, while the men in the orchestra do all the work. Actually he is the most important member of the group. His duties are various. First he must keep the time. It is essential that all the instruments keep together, and obviously the different players cannot hear each other. The conductor needs also to control the volume of the various instruments. The horns cannot tell how loud they are blowing, and the conductor, by his leadership, must get a correct mixture of sound so that one hears all the instruments in a proper balance. Last, the conductor must know his music so accurately that he can detect and correct any instrument that is not doing its part to produce the effect of the whole. His is the voice that determines the expression of the composition as a whole.

Chart of Instruments Giving the Approximate Range in Terms of the Human Voice

	High Soprano	Soprano	Contralto	Tenor	Bass
Strings		Violin	Viola	Cello	Double bass
Wood winds Air (no reed) One reed Two reeds	Piccolo	Flute Clarinet Oboe	English horn	Bassoon	Contra-bassoon
Brasses		Trumpet	French horn	Trombone	Tuba

A number of compositions illustrate clearly the sound of the different instruments. Some of them are:

Benjamin Britten, *The Young Person's Guide to the Orchestra*
Ravel, *Bolero*
Tchaikovsky, *Nutcracker Suite*
Saint-Saëns, *Carnival of the Animals*
Prokofiev, *Peter and the Wolf*

LITERATURE

The medium of literature is language, that is, words put together in sentences to express ideas. It is the only medium in any art which is used by everyone. Many of us do not try to draw or paint, we cannot play or sing, but we all talk. We may talk much or we may talk little, we may express our ideas easily or with difficulty, but we talk. Furthermore we use this medium creatively. We make up new sentences to express our ideas. If we sing, we usually stick to the tunes we have learned from other people, but in using language we put words together in new sentences. We are not repeating old ideas verbatim. They are our ideas we are expressing and we are expressing them in a way to suit us.

The mediums of literature are the various languages of the world: English, French, German, Italian, Russian, Chinese, Japanese, and so on. And as is true of all mediums of all arts, each has its own special characteristics, and what can be said in one cannot be said in another. It is said that the novelist Conrad wrote his novels in English rather than in French, a language he knew much better, because in French he could not say what he wanted to say. A recent writer on the subject of communication has said, "When I read French I need to become as a different person, with different thought; the language change bears with it a change of national character and temperament, a different history and literature." [1] In a small way all of us have experienced this change in assuming a dialect. The man who talks as an American Negro, a Southerner, or an Irishman assumes the character and personality of that person for that time.

A delightful account of the difficulties with a foreign language is found in Clarence Day's *Life with Father*: [2]

I got out another Bible that Mother had lent me. This one was in French, and it sometimes shocked me deeply to read it. As my belief was that when God had created the world He had said, "Let there be light," it seemed to me highly irreverent to put French words in His mouth and have Him exclaim, "Que la lumière soit!" Imagine the Lord talking French! Aside from a few odd words in Hebrew, I took it completely for granted that God had never spoken anything but the most dignified English.

Instead of the children of Israel fearing lest the Lord should be wroth, the French said "les enfants d'Israel" were afraid lest "le Seigneur" should be "irrité." This word "irrité" appeared everywhere in the French version. It wasn't only the Lord. Cain was "très irrité." Möise (which seemed to me a very jaunty way of referring to Moses) was "irrité" again and again. Everybody was "irrité." When my regular Bible, the real one, impressively described men as "wroth," their anger seemed to have something stately

[1] Colin Cherry, *On Human Communication,* p. 70.
[2] From *Life with Father* by Clarence Day. Copyright 1935, by Clarence Day. Used by permission of Alfred A. Knopf, Inc.

and solemn about it. If they were full of mere irritation all the time, they were more like the Day family.

LITERATURE IN ENGLISH

Literature is the only art whose medium is not international. A German can enjoy French painting or Russian music without knowing a word of French or Russian. Painting, sculpture, architecture, and music can be known and studied without national barriers; but we must know the language if we are to understand the literature of a foreign country.

In a text of this kind it is not safe to assume that the readers will know more than one language. Therefore, we are limiting our study of literature to the one medium, English. In doing so we are obviously restricted and are at a disadvantage. In the other arts we can study the work of all countries with equal ease. We can hear the music of Russia, see the sculpture of Greece, and enjoy the architecture of France and the paintings of Italy as clearly and as easily as we can those of England. In literature we are confined to writings in English or to translations from other languages into English.

Fortunately, the English language is a very flexible medium, and a very wide variety of effects can be obtained in it. Fortunately, also, it is a language with a very great literature. But the fact remains that, knowing only English, we are missing other and different types of effect to be obtained in other languages.

When it is necessary to use translations, the best practice is to compare several different versions. Often a different translation gives a new insight into a passage. Take, for instance, the verse from Deuteronomy with which we are famiilar in the King James version:

Love ye therefore the stranger; for ye were strangers in the land of Egypt.

—DEUT. 19:9

This takes on a new meaning when we read it in the Smith-Goodspeed translation:

So you should love the resident alien; for you were once resident aliens yourselves in the land of Egypt.

Or suppose we compare several versions of a very familiar passage such as the Lord's Prayer (Matt. 6:9–13):

Our Father which art in heaven
Hallowed be Thy name.
Thy kingdom come,
Thy will be done, in earth as it is in heaven.
Give us this day our daily bread;
And forgive us our debts, as we forgive our debtors;
And lead us not into temptation, but deliver us from evil.
—KING JAMES VERSION

Our Father in heaven,
Your name be revered!
Your Kingdom come!
Your will be done on earth as it is done in heaven!
Give us today bread for the day,
And forgive us our debts, as we have forgiven
    our debtors,
And do not subject us to temptation,
But save us from the evil one.
—SMITH AND GOODSPEED (1939)[3]

Our Father in heaven,
thy name be revered,
thy Reign begin,
thy will be done on earth as in heaven!
give us today our bread for the morrow,
and forgive us our debts as we ourselves have
    forgiven our debtors,
and lead us not into temptation
but deliver us from evil.
—JAMES MOFFATT (1934)[4]

THE COMBINED ARTS

By definition, the combined arts are those which use more than one medium. The special emphasis of a dance is on the movements of the body, but the dancer uses also costume and lighting, usually music, and sometimes stage scenery. The theater presents a story told in dialogue and acted out on the stage; usually it also employs scenery, costumes, furniture, lighting, and at times music. Ideally, the various

[3] The Bible: An American Translation. Published by the University of Chicago Press, Chicago, Ill.

[4] The Bible: A New Translation by James Moffatt, copyrighted in 1935 by Harper & Brothers, New York, used by permission.

mediums are combined with just the right emphasis on each to make clear the idea in the mind of the artist. One of the major problems of the artist is the decision as to which of his mediums he will stress at any particular time.

An example is found in *Hamlet,* in the scene in which Hamlet makes his formal renunciation of Ophelia. Hamlet is a young man just returned from the university, and he is sorely perplexed by the condition in which he has found matters at home. His father is dead, and his mother has married again so quickly that Hamlet says in contempt: "She did it to economize on the pies and meats baked for my father's funeral." Shortly afterward he learns from a ghost about his father's murder. Hamlet does not know whether to believe the ghost or not, and he needs help desperately. For a long time he has been in love with Ophelia, and naturally he turns to her now. But, looking in her face, he realizes that she cannot help him; so he shakes his head and leaves the room without saying a word.

This might seem just the scene to be enacted on the stage. But, instead, Shakespeare uses words only. Ophelia tells her father of Hamlet's coming:

> My lord, as I was sewing in my chamber,
> Lord Hamlet, with his doublet all unbrac'd,
> No hat upon his head, his stockings foul'd,
> Ungart'red, and down-gyved to his ankle,
> Pale as his shirt, his knees knocking each other,
> And with a look so piteous in purport
> As if he had been loosed out of hell
> To speak of horrors,—he comes before me.

*   *   *

> He took me by the wrist and held me hard;
> Then goes he to the length of all his arm,
> And, with his other hand thus o'er his brow,
> He falls to such perusal of my face
> As he would draw it. Long stay'd he so.
> At last, a little shaking of mine arm,
> And thrice his head thus waving up and down,
> He rais'd a sigh so piteous and profound
> That it did seem to shatter all his bulk
> And end his being. That done, he lets me go;
> And, with his head over his shoulder turn'd,

He seem'd to find his way without his eyes,
For out o' doors he went without their help.
And, to the last bended their light on me.
—SHAKESPEARE (1564–1616, English poet and dramatist),
Hamlet, II, i, 77–84, 87–100

The scene as described by Ophelia is so vivid that most people who read the play remember the event as one that took place on the stage. Why, then, did Shakespeare have Ophelia tell of it? There are many reasons; one is that in this way he kills two birds with one stone: the father is told at the same time that we learn of the action. That is a good but unimportant reason. More important is the fact that a scene of that kind would not be easy to enact. The real reason probably is that Shakespeare wants to be sure that the audience understands the scene as he meant it, and so he must interpret it for them in words.

The mediums used in the combined arts are the mediums used in the separate arts. In this short discussion we shall attempt only to show the mediums that are used in each art and to state some of the possibilities and limitations that arise from their being combined.

THE DANCE

Dance movements fall into two classes: movement within the body, such as movement of the head, arms, or torso, in a single space; and movement from one space to another, such as walking, running, or jumping. These may be the movements of a solo dancer or the movements of a group of dancers.

Dances may be divided into four general classes:

1. Folk dancing. Dances of groups of people following certain traditional patterns.

2. Social dancing. Dancing in the ballroom, usually of single couples. Traditionally social dancing follows set patterns, but recently many innovations have been introduced; now a couple on the floor may improvise.

3. Ballet. A formal type of dancing using set steps and gestures.

4. "Modern" dancing. Free movements with emphasis on expression.

The dance is one of the most direct of the various mediums of art; its emotions are communicated without delay to the spectators.

THE THEATER

The term theater, as used in this text, refers to the drama in action. The play is drama; it becomes theater when it is acted. The theater adds to the drama the speaking voice, action, costume, lighting, scenery, and properties. Voice, action, and costume are essentially individual mediums. Through them the actor makes clear the content of the play, the characterization of each person, and the interpretation of each remark. The possibilities in each type of medium are almost limitless. A slight change in costume may be used to indicate that years have passed or that the person has grown richer or poorer. The accent may betray nationality or social status, and the manner of speaking may indicate character. The actor may make use of all the movements of the dancer as well as those of the ordinary person in walking, running, or standing.

In many of the great periods of the theater the setting has been of very little importance. In the Greek theater, for instance, the setting was the same for all plays, a street before a building. In the Elizabethan theater, also, it was very simple, a set of curtains with a few pieces of furniture to indicate the type of room, as for example a bed for a bedroom. The Greeks and the Elizabethans, moreover, had no control over lighting; both performed their plays in the daytime with natural lighting. Now the producer has full control over the lights and the setting of his play, and he can change them to suit his performance. In his hands the setting and the lighting have become mediums for the artist just as truly as speech, action, or costume.

OPERA

Opera may be defined briefly as a play set to music. As a medium of art it employs all the arts of the theater, plus the fact that the characters *sing* their parts and that usually there is choral singing and dancing. Opera thus combines some of the greatest appeals of all art: music, story, action, and spectacle. It is one of the greatest and most appealing of all the arts. As a medium, however, it is probably the most difficult; certainly it is the most complex. There are the obvious demands made of the performers who are supposed to act as well as sing. Physical limitations are important. The soprano singing a long and heavy aria needs all her strength for the singing; she cannot move around the stage with the freedom of a person not so occupied.

There are difficulties in the writing as well as in the performance of opera. One of the greatest comes in finding the *libretto,* or "book of words." When a musician writes the music for a song, he takes the poem just as it is. He chooses the poem because he likes it and it appeals to his musical imagination. But the writer of an opera cannot do this. Even if the story he selects is already in the form of a play, it must be recast to meet the demands of the music. Wagner wrote the words for his operas, but this is by no means the rule. Sometimes a composer finds a librettist with whom he can work well and sometimes he does not. There have been a number of happy combinations, the best known being that of Gilbert and Sullivan.

In the working together of mediums so different as music and drama, many compromises must be made. One is in the matter of time. Speech takes only a fraction of the time necessary for singing, and the action must be greatly simplified on that account. In Verdi's opera *Otello,* based on Shakespeare's play, *Othello,* the entire first act of the play is omitted. The great speech of that act, the one in which Othello tells of his courtship of Desdemona, appears as a duet between Othello and Desdemona after they have been reunited in Cyprus. Additions are made, too. In the opera, Desdemona prays to the Virgin, singing an "Ave Maria" just before she is killed, although that scene is not found in Shakespeare's play.

CINEMA

The cinema, which was originally only a way of presenting news and minor incidents, has developed into a separate art with its own possibilities and limitations. It has absolute freedom of time and space; it can show any time and anywhere what a person is thinking as well as what he is doing and saying. The cinema is an exception to the statement about the preservation of the combined arts, since it can be reproduced at will. The pictures are usually photographs, though they may be drawings or paintings. At present, photographs seem to be preferred for serious, realistic drama; drawings and paintings are used for cartoons (e.g., *Mickey Mouse*) and for fantastic and unreal scenes (e.g., *Fantasia, Bambi, Boundary Lines*).

TELEVISION AND RADIO

Television is too young for us to know what will be its artistic development. It is, however, so closely akin to the cinema, we may expect it to develop as the cinema has done. In fact, the performance of Prokofiev's *War and Peace* has already shown that it can be a serious and satisfying medium for opera.

The radio is a way of reproducing or extending sound just as the moving picture was originally a way of reproducing sight. It has not yet been developed into an art, but it is making rapid strides.

FOR FURTHER EXPLORATION

1. The best way to learn instruments is to play in an orchestra. The next best way is to pay attention to the individual instruments at a concert: go early enough to hear the men tune up. If possible, attend rehearsals.

2. There are excellent records for the study of instruments. Both recordings and a cinema can be had of Benjamin Britten's *Young Person's Guide to the Orchestra.*

3. Study old pictures of instruments: note how they have changed.

4. Find three or four different translations of a favorite passage from the Bible. How do the differences in the translations help you to know the meaning?

5. Do the same for a passage from Dante or from one of the Greek tragedies.

6. Study one play carefully for:
   a. The scenes enacted on the stage in pantomime
   b. The scenes enacted with words
   c. The action narrated by the other characters

7. From their nature the combined arts cannot be known in the library. They can be known only in actual performances. The student should witness as many performances of each as is practicable, and notice (a) the part that each of the separate arts plays in the whole, and (b) the art that is dominant.

8. It is worth while also for the student to plan the whole when only a part is given; e.g., if he has the music to an opera or the words of a play, let him plan costume, staging, and action; if he has the steps of a dance, let him find music, staging, and costume; if he has the music for a dance, let him plan steps, staging, and costume.

PART THREE

ORGANIZATION

CHAPTER 8

ELEMENTS OF THE VISUAL ARTS

MEDIUM AND ELEMENTS

Medium and elements are together the materials the artist uses in making a work of art. The distinction between them is easy to see but hard to define. Both answer the question "What is it made of?" but from different points of view. If, for instance, we say that the building is made of brick and stone, we are talking of the medium; if we say it is made of right angles and vertical lines, we are talking of the elements. If we say that the music is played on the horn, the oboe, or the piano, we are talking of the medium; if we say it is fast or slow, that it has a good tune or a catchy rhythm, we are talking of the elements. If we say that the picture is made of oil or water color, we are talking of the medium, but if we say it is made of red and green and blue, we are talking of the elements.

An element can be known only in some medium, but as an element it is independent of medium. If we see a straight line we necessarily see it in some medium such as chalk, pencil, ink, or the corner of a house; but when we think of line we do not necessarily connect it with any medium. And so we talk of line dissociated from medium. Similarly, if we hear the song *America*, we must hear it sung by some person or played on some instrument, but we think of it as a tune without regard to any instrument. Therefore, when we study elements, we consider them with no attention to the means by which we know them. The medium is the physical means through which we can come in contact with a work of art; the elements are its qualities or properties. Mediums are concrete; elements are abstract.

The elements of the visual arts are six:

1. Line
2. Color
3. Texture
4. Value
5. Volume
6. Perspective

Line

Line is the simplest, most primitive, and most universal means for creating visual art. Ask a child to draw an apple, a man, or a house; he will make it first in lines, that is, he will try to outline it. Lines are active. They always seem to be moving, and we follow them with our fingers, our gestures, or our eyes. Color has none of this activity. We see a wall of blue or red with no idea of motion of any kind, but whenever we see a line we begin following it no matter how long or winding its path.

Straight Lines. Lines are straight or curved. Straight lines are horizontal, vertical, or diagonal. The horizontal line is primarily the line of rest and quiet, relaxation and contemplation; a long horizontal line gives a sense of infinity that is not easily obtained in any other way. Horizontal lines are found in landscapes; the quieter the landscape, the more prominent the horizontals. In Rembrandt's etching *Three Trees* (Figure 88) the sense of rest and quiet and peace derives largely from the long line of the horizon.

The vertical line is the line of a tree or of a man standing, the line of chimneys and towers. The vertical is a line of rest, but it is not the rest of relaxation we find in the horizontal. The vertical is poised, balanced, forceful, and dynamic. The vertical is ready for action though it is not acting. The early Greek bronze found at Delphi, known as *The Charioteer* (Figure 60), illustrates the vertical line. In it there is no deviation from the vertical except the arms, which are outstretched to hold the reins. Even a slight deviation from the vertical takes away from its force. In the caryatids of the Erechtheum (Figure 9), for example, each figure is perfectly straight except for one bent knee, but that break from the vertical gives a sense of relaxation. One feels that the load is not too heavy and that the maidens can easily hold up the roof for a few more centuries.

The diagonal is the line of action. A man running makes a diagonal line with his body and leg; a beating rain, trees in a hard wind, almost

Fig. 88. Rembrandt Harmensz van Rijn (1606–1669), Dutch painter and etcher. *Three Trees* (1643). (Etching. Size: about 8⅜ by 11 inches. New York, courtesy of the Metropolitan Museum of Art; bequest of Mrs. H.O. Havemeyer, 1929. The H. O. Havemeyer Collection.)

everything in action assumes a diagonal line. The degree of action is shown in the angle of the diagonal. The diagonal that approaches the vertical shares the force and self-sufficiency of that line; the one that approaches the horizontal shares its abandonment. At an angle of forty-five degrees the diagonal represents the maximum of action, being halfway between the independence of the vertical and the powerlessness of the horizontal. In Daumier's painting *The Uprising* (Figure 89), the forward movement of the mob is shown in the diagonals, especially in the upraised arm of the leader. In Duchamp-Villon's statue (Figure 90) the horse's head is turned to one side and his feet are drawn together for action. The energy and incipient action of the statue are derived primarily from its diagonals.

Diagonals meeting at sharp angles form jagged lines that are harsh and unpleasant; they connote confusion, disturbance, lightning, battle, war, and sudden death. In El Greco's *Expulsion from the Temple* (Figure 91) the main interest is centered on Christ and the unfortunate tradesmen who are being driven away. The lines made by their arms

FIG. 89. Honoré Daumier (1808–1879), French lithographer and caricaturist. *The Uprising* (1860?). (Oil on canvas. Size: 24½ by 44½ inches. Washington, D.C., courtesy of the Phillips Collection.)

FIG. 90. Raymond Duchamp-Villon (1876–1918), French sculptor. *The Horse,* 1914. (Bronze. Size: 40 inches high. New York, The Museum of Modern Art; van Gogh Purchase Fund.)

and bodies are predominantly diagonal, meeting at acute angles. In contrast, the figures to the right of the center are quiet, being formed largely of vertical and curved lines.

Curved Lines. Curved lines show action and life and energy; they are never harsh or stern. Most things to which we attach the adjective "pleasing" have curved lines: rounded hills, trees bent with fruit, curved arms and cheeks.

Curves may be single or double, slow or quick. A quick curve is an arc of a small circle, the type of curve found in a fat baby. A slow curve is an arc of a large circle, the type of curve of a long oval face. A single curve is but a single arc; a double curve turns back on itself, an S curve. The double slow curve is the famous "line of grace" or "line of beauty" of Hogarth. The quick curve is more exuberant than the slow curve; when used in great abundance it becomes coarse and gross.

A great deal of the elegance of Harunobu's *Lovers under Umbrella*

FIG. 91. El Greco (1541–1614), Spanish painter. *Expulsion from the Temple* (1595–1600). (Oil on canvas. Size: 41⅜ by 50 inches. Copyright, The Frick Collection, New York.)

in Snow (Figure 92) comes from the long single curves. In contrast, van Gogh's *La Berceuse* (Figure 93), in its round curves, is solid and substantial. All the curves are ample; the flowers and other ornaments in the background are circular.

FIG. 92. Suzuki Harunobu (1725–1770), Japanese print maker. *Lovers under Umbrella in Snow.* (Wood block. Size: 11 by 8 inches. New York, courtesy of the Metropolitan Museum of Art; Rogers Fund, 1936.)

Curved lines tend to become restless, and if emphasized too much they may get out of control. Even a dress pattern or a rug may be too full of curves. Curves need the steadying influence of adjacent straight lines. An artist will often go out of his way to introduce a hard, straight

FIG. 93. Vincent van Gogh (1853–1890), Dutch painter. *La Berceuse* (Mme. Roulin Rocking the Cradle) (1889). (Oil on canvas. Size: 36⅝ by 28⅛ inches. Chicago, courtesy of The Art Institute of Chicago; Helen Birch Bartlett Memorial Collection.)

line near his curves. Harunobu puts a straight tree along the right side of the picture, and van Gogh has straight supports for the arms of the chair.

Examples of the characteristics of lines are to be found everywhere. In advertisements, the shape of the letter and the quality of the line are frequently used to indicate the character of the thing advertised. For example, the lettering that advertises farm machinery may also try to suggest its product, in solid, heavy, square strokes that sit flatly on the paper. Articles that are supposed to appeal to the dainty or the fastidious will be advertised in thin lines with thin slow curves.

Gesture and carriage in dancing and in the theater show the same characteristics. Youth and beauty move in long, graceful curves, uprightness is square and erect. The uncompromising old maid carries herself stiffly, and the typical posture for a sycophant like Uriah Heep is that of bending, with the hands constantly making small spirals as they are rubbed together.

Color

Hue. Colors differ in hue, value, and intensity. Hue is that quality by which we distinguish one color from another. The three primary hues are red, blue, and yellow. All others can be made from them. The secondary hues are green, violet, and orange, each being halfway between two of the primary colors: orange is halfway between yellow and red, etc. This relation is easily seen on the diagram.

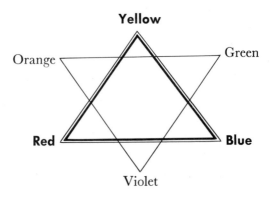

The diagram has another advantage in that each hue is just opposite its complementary hue. Two hues are said to be complementary when they comprise the three primary colors. Complementaries intensify each other if placed close together. Red and green mixed make a gray, but a red near a green makes each color seem brighter than when alone.

Colors are either "warm" or "cool." The greens and blues on the right of the palette, from yellow to violet, are cool; the reds and oranges on the left of the palette, from violet to yellow, are warm. Yellow and violet are neither warm nor cool. The cool hues probably seem cool from their association with cool subjects in nature: green grass, green trees, blue sky, and blue or green water. The warm hues are associated with warm objects: yellow sun, red coals, and orange fire. The cool colors are for the most part restful and quiet. The warm colors are more exciting, but we tire of them more quickly. The warm colors always seem closer than the cool colors; therefore, they are called *advancing colors,* and the cool colors are called *retreating colors.* If red, green, and blue circles are placed one beside the other, the red seems closest to the spectator, and the blue farthest away. For this reason warm colors are usually put in those parts of a picture which are nearest the spectator, and the cool colors are reserved for the shadows.

Value. Colors differ in value as well as in hue. There are light blues, dark blues, medium blues. Any color may be seen at any degree of darkness, from a dark that can hardly be distinguished from black to a light that is almost white. In some colors, however, a good deal of confusion is produced by the fact that certain values have been given special names, and for that reason they are not recognized as being the same. A light red, for instance, is called pink; and dark yellows and oranges are called brown.

Intensity. Colors differ also in intensity or brightness. Two colors may both be blue, one just as dark as the other, but one may be brighter than the other. Powder blue is a dulled blue; old rose is a dulled red. When a hue is found in its most vivid form it is said to be in "full intensity." The same hue dulled is said to be "partly neutralized." A hue completely neutralized loses its color and becomes a gray.

Color Combinations. There are, in general, two types of color combinations: we may combine colors that are alike or colors that are different. Colors that are alike produce paintings in values and intensities of a single hue, with little use of the adjacent hues. Unlike or contrasting colors are found in the use of complementaries. The red-green contrast is one of the most common in nature and in art. Blue-orange is also a favorite; yellow-violet is not often found.

But though each color has certain very definite properties, it is almost never seen as it is. A color is changed by the presence of other colors. It reflects and changes with all the colors around it. It looks dark beside a lighter color and light beside a darker color. A blue placed beside a violet makes the violet seem red, and a red placed beside a violet makes the violet seem blue. Delacroix was merely stating emphatically the influence of colors on each other when he said that he could paint a face of the mud from the streets if he were allowed to select the colors that were to go around it.

Painting is predominantly the art of color, but color is also important in sculpture and architecture. In terra cotta, the molded surfaces are colored, and houses made of wood are painted. In the other mediums of sculpture and architecture the color of the material is itself a factor in the appeal of any work—the rich brown of polished wood or bronze, for instance, or the creamy whiteness of ivory or marble.

Texture

Texture has to do primarily with the perception of touch. It is the element that appeals to our sense of the feel of things, whether they are rough or smooth, bumpy or slippery. It is the difference we feel between satin and velvet, between linen and silk, between the roughness of tweed and the smoothness of serge, between marble and bronze. Texture is first known by the actual touch of objects. Later it is interpreted by the eye without physical contact, although there is always the sense of contact; it is as though we had run our hands over the marble or the satin even if we have not touched it.

Texture is found in all the visual arts. In many cases, differences in textures are due primarily to differences in medium. We know the different "feel" of brick and concrete, of shingles and smoothly dressed boards, of rough and polished stone, of wood and bronze. We feel the smooth bronze of the Maillol (Figure 106), and the rough skin of the *King of Judah* (Figure 59). In painting, the term *texture* is used for the representation of skin, cloth, metal, jewels, furniture, etc. In van Eyck's *Annunciation* (Figure 94) we are very conscious of the heavy

Fig. 94. Jan van Eyck (1370?–1440?), Flemish painter. *The Annunciation* (ca. 1425–1430). (Transferred from wood to canvas. Size: 36½ by 14⅜ inches. Washington, D.C., The National Gallery of Art; Mellon Collection, 1937.)

silk and the jewels of the Virgin's dress, the gold and jewels of her crown, the wood of the footstool, the silk of the cushion on the stool, the tiles of the floor, etc.

Still Life. In the type of picture known as *still life* the representation of texture may be the primary interest. As the name suggests, still life represents inanimate objects such as flowers, fruits, and vegetables.

Fig. 95. Jean Baptiste Siméon Chardin (1699–1779), French painter. *Bowl of Plums.* (Canvas. Size: 17¾ by 22½ inches. Washington, D.C., courtesy of the Phillips Collection.)

These subjects offer abundant opportunity for the display of texture, and with them are combined other effects, the play of light on china or glass, the gleam of a knife blade, the color of wine, or even the rich glow of freshly baked bread. One of the greatest painters of still life is the Frenchman Chardin. In the *Bowl of Plums* (Figure 95) he shows us the texture of the plums and that of the pitcher. In a painting such as this there is very slight interest in subject; interest is found entirely in color and texture and in their organization in the design.

Value

Value has to do with the amount and kind of light, or we may say it is the name given to relative degrees of light and dark. In ordinary speech, only the terms *light* and *dark* are employed, but this use is rather vague. We need greater discrimination. If white is recognized as the lightest value and black as the lowest, a point halfway between them is called medium; the point halfway between white and medium is called light, and the point halfway between medium and black is called dark. This makes an exact scale:

White
Light
Medium
Dark
Black

Values that do not fit one of these points exactly may be defined in terms of the nearest value.

Values in Arts of Three Dimensions. Values have two sources. The first and obvious source is the value of the object itself, as, for instance, the color of a piece of cloth. This is called its *local color*. The second is the creation of value through shadows or reflection of light. If a cloth is hung as a curtain, its folds will show many different values. Such values are subtle because they change with every change in the light. If, for instance, a white cloth is held in a dark closet and gradually brought into the light, the hue that seemed black in the darkness appears in all values from black to white as the cloth is brought out into the light. Tooled leather, weaving, chased gold and silver all depend for their effects on differences in value produced by shadows.

The same is true of architectural design and ornament in general. A molding, whether inside or outside a building, can be seen because of the way the different surfaces reflect the light. Patterns in shingles or in the arrangement of boards or brick can hardly be seen except for the shadows they cast. A cornice casts a shadow on the wall below and makes a definite change in the design. An architect frequently makes a model of the building he is designing in order that he may learn the exact effects of the shadows. One of the beauties of the cathedral of Notre Dame in Paris is found in the varied carvings of the façade, and the play of lights and shadows over them.

If the artist has not studied the effects of shadows carefully, he may find the finished work quite different from the one he planned. French's statue of *Lincoln,* for example, was made in the studio with an overhead light. When it was placed in the Lincoln Memorial in Washington all the light came from below (Figure 96). This lighting completely changed the expression on Lincoln's face, making it little better than a caricature, as seen in the picture on the right. Fortunately the lighting could be and was easily changed, and now visitors to the Memorial see the statue as French planned it.

Relief Sculpture. In relief sculpture values are especially important, since the design can usually be seen only in the shadows cast. In *high relief* the figures project from the background; they are almost in the round. The shadows are deep and the lines bold and distinct as in the metopes of the Parthenon (Figure 97). In *low relief,* as in the *Panathenaic Procession* (Figure 98), also from the Parthenon, the figures are only slightly raised from the background. The shadows are not very deep and the lines are delicate. Therefore a low relief should be in a dimly lighted place where the light shadows make clear the outlines of all the figures. A high relief should be in bright light, because the

FIG. 96. Daniel Chester French (1850–1931), American sculptor. *Abraham Lincoln* (1920): head before (right) and after (left) change of lighting. (White marble. Size: about three times life size. Washington, D.C., Lincoln Memorial. Photograph, courtesy of Mrs. Margaret French Cresson.)

FIG. 97. *Lapith and Centaur* (ca. 447–443 B.C.) metope from the south side of the Parthenon. (Pentelic marble. Height: 3 feet 4 inches. London, British Museum.)

FIG. 98. *Panathenaic Procession* (fifth century B.C.), detail of Parthenon frieze. (Pentelic marble. Height: 40 inches. London, British Museum.)

higher the relief the deeper the shadows. In high relief, moreover, the design must be very simple; if there are too many figures the shadow of one figure tends to efface its neighbor. In low relief the design may be more complicated. In the reliefs on the Parthenon both these points were observed. The *Panathenaic Procession* is found in the frieze, which was placed on the wall of the building where it was protected from direct sunlight by a row of columns. The metopes were placed above the columns, where they receive direct sunlight.

Values in Painting. In architecture and sculpture the values change with the light; in painting the values are fixed. When a painter makes an area dark or light, puts in a shadow or leaves it out, it stays that way regardless of the time of year or the source of light.

In studying values in painting we notice first the value tone: is the painting predominantly light or dark? And since there can be no painting without contrasts in value, the second question asked is whether

Fig. 99. Rembrandt Harmensz van Rijn (1606–1669), Dutch painter. *The Night Watch* (1642). (Oil on canvas. Height: 11 feet 9 inches. Amsterdam, Rijks Museum. Photograph, courtesy of Netherlands Information Service, Netherlands Museum.)

those contrasts are great or slight. In Rembrandt's *Night Watch* (Figure 99) the values are dark and the contrasts are great. Ingres's drawing *Lady and Boy* (Figure 75) is light, and there are no great contrasts.

The next point to notice about values is the way they are separated one from the other. Do they merge one into the other or are they separate? Are the boundary lines blurred or distinct? In the *Night Watch*, boundaries are kept clear in the prominent figures of the foreground, but in the background all sense of boundary lines is lost.

A third point to consider about values in painting is the character of the dark areas. Is there a single flat area, or is it subtly varied? This is really a matter of slight variations in value within a single tone, variations so slight as to be almost imperceptible. It is the difference between a wooden box painted sky blue and the actual blue of the sky. Ruskin complained that the artists before Turner painted hard, flat skies, and it is one of the excellencies he finds in Turner that you look into and not at his skies. The shadows of Rembrandt have this same quality. In the *Night Watch* there is only a little light in the picture, and the remainder of the scene is buried in darkness. But this darkness is not hard blackness, against which one might strike his head, but a soft, penetrable shadow; one feels that he can see into the shadows. The effect is much the same as that which is produced by a small light in a large room; only a small space is clearly lighted, and the light fights against the shadows in the remainder of the space.

In emotional connotation light values are, in general, bright, gay, and happy; sometimes they are unsubstantial. Dark values are solid and substantial, sometimes gloomy and melancholy. Sharp contrasts are dramatic, and values that merge hazily one into the other, especially in the darker tones, tend to be mysterious, even mystical. The hazy dark values of Ryder's *Death on a Pale Horse* (Figure 100) are largely responsible for the mood of mystery and doom.

Volume

Volume is often called solidity. It is that quality of an object which enables us to know that it has thickness as well as length and breadth. As children we lift and punch, pinch and squeeze objects to find if they are solid, but soon we learn to interpret solidity by sight.

If we use only our eyes we perceive volume primarily in two ways. The first is by contour lines, that is, by outlines or shapes of objects.

Fig. 100. Albert Pinkham
Ryder (1847–1917), American
painter. *The Race Track* or
Death on a Pale Horse (ca.
1910). (Oil on canvas. Size:
28¼ by 35¼ inches.
Cleveland, courtesy Cleveland
Museum of Art; J. H. Wade
Collection.)

Fig. 101. Michelangelo
(1475–1564), Italian painter,
sculptor, architect, and poet.
Cumaean Sibyl, detail of
Sistine Chapel ceiling
(1508–1512). (Fresco. About
life size. Rome, Sistine Chapel.
Photograph by Alinari.)

The second is by surface lights and shadows. When we look at Michelangelo's *Cumaean Sibyl* (Figure 101) we see the figure as rounded and solid. In it both ways of judging volume are found. We see the outlines of the face, the shoulder, the headdress, and we notice the subtle shadows in face and dress.

Usually the artist uses all the means at his disposal, and usually he achieves the effect he desires. They are not all necessary however. The Japanese give the effect of solidity through the use of line alone as in the Harunobu print (Figure 92). They leave out shadows because they say that shadows are temporary and that only the permanent should be represented in painting. Their work, however, is done so skillfully that one may look at it a long time without realizing that the colors are flat and the shadows are missing. In Rembrandt's *Old Woman Cutting Her Nails* (Figure 102) volume is secured almost entirely through shadows.

Since painting is two-dimensional it can only represent volume. The shadows and contour lines are painted in and do not change. Sculpture is three-dimensional: the outlines and the shadows change with each shift in the position of the person viewing them. And we

Fig. 102. Rembrandt. *Old Woman Cutting Her Nails* (1658). (Oil on canvas. Size: 49⅝ by 40⅛ inches. New York, courtesy of the Metropolitan Museum; bequest of Benjamin Altman, 1913.)

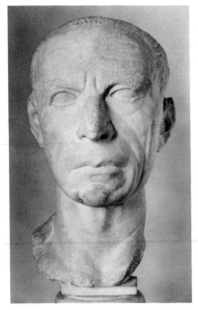

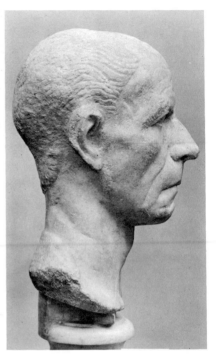

FIG. 103. *Roman Portrait* (first century B.C.). (Marble. About life size. New York, courtesy of the Metropolitan Museum of Art; Rogers Fund, 1921.)

FIG. 104. Profile view of FIG. 103.

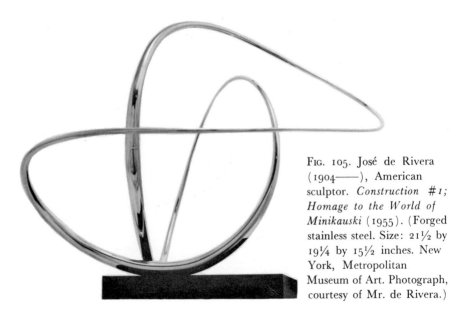

FIG. 105. José de Rivera (1904———), American sculptor. *Construction #1; Homage to the World of Minikauski* (1955). (Forged stainless steel. Size: 21½ by 19¼ by 15½ inches. New York, Metropolitan Museum of Art. Photograph, courtesy of Mr. de Rivera.)

obtain not one but many different impressions from a single work, as we see in the two views of the Roman Portrait (Figures 103 and 104). In José de Rivera's *Construction* #1 (Figure 105), or in Maillol's *Ile de France* (Figure 106), the photograph shows the work from a single point of view, but we are aware that it would present a different appearance if the camera were moved. The shadows and the contour lines would both be changed. These statues of José de Rivera and Maillol also illustrate the difference in emphasis referred to earlier. The *Construction* depends almost entirely upon linear effect, whereas the surface modeling in the body of the *Ile de France* is all-important. These two statues illustrate another point of importance in sculpture. The Maillol is not only three-dimensional but it is also solid. The José de Rivera is not. The statue seems to comprise the space within the composition as well as the material of which it is made.

Architecture like sculpture exists always in three dimensions. A great building, like a great statue, is seen from many points of view. As we walk around it or through it the appearance changes with each shift in our position, and each view should be pleasing.

Perspective

Perspective has to do with our perception of distance, our ability to see the position of objects in space.

The two arts in which space is of great importance are architecture

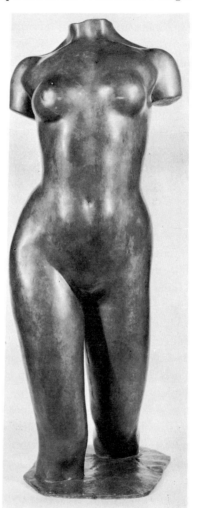

Fig. 106. Aristide Maillol (1861–1944), French sculptor. *Ile de France* (torso) (1910). (Bronze. Height: 43 inches. New York: courtesy of the Metropolitan Museum of Art; Edith Percy Chapman Fund, 1953; from the Museum of Modern Art, gift of A. Conger Goodyear.)

and painting. Architecture is primarily an art of space. The other arts exist in space; architecture uses space as one of its elements. We can see the exterior of a building only as it appears in space. And if we are within a building we see it as enclosing space. One of the great beauties of a building like Hagia Sophia (Figure 149), or the church of Sant' Apollinare in Classe (Figure 151) comes from the sense of majesty one gets when he enters the building and feels the spaciousness of the interior.

Painting does not deal with space directly as does architecture; it can only represent space on a two-dimensional surface.

Sculpture has in itself little to do with the perception of space or of space relations. Even when it shows a large number of people as in a frieze, they are usually presented in a single long line, with no other spatial relationship.

With perspective as with volume the act of judging has become instinctive, and most of us do not realize that we are making such judgments, nor do we know on what basis we make them. Briefly stated there are two major kinds of perspective; that is, there are two kinds of data on which we form opinions or make judgments about distance. These are known as linear perspective and aerial perspective.

Linear Perspective. Linear perspective has to do (1) with the direction of lines, and (2) the size of objects. Everyone has stood in the middle of a road, or on the track of a railroad, and noticed that the lines seem to rise and to meet in the distance. In the same way parallel lines above the eye seem to meet but they fall to the level of the eyes. These facts can be easily demonstrated in the photograph of the Taj Mahal (Figure 107). The lines of the pool, the paving, and the trees rise and tend to meet, whereas the tops of the minarets fall as they approach the center. If the camera is placed at one side, not between the parallel lines, the lines tend to meet just as in the examples studied, but at one side. This can be clearly seen in the picture of the aqueduct at Segovia (Figure 145). Curved lines above the level of the eye seem to drop and those below the eye to rise, as we see in the picture of the *Colosseum* (Figure 148).

In painting of course the lines do not vary with the position of the camera; therefore the artist must paint his lines of perspective, as Raphael has done in *The School of Athens* (Figure 108). Here we notice how the lines of the pavement and of the arches concentrate on the heads of Plato and Aristotle, the two principals in the scene.

FIG. 107. Taj Mahal (seventeenth century). (Marble. Size: 186 feet long by 186 feet wide by 187 feet high. Temple built by Shah Jehan in memory of his wife. Agra, courtesy Press Information Bureau, Government of India.)

FIG. 108. Raphael (Raffaello Sanzio) (1483–1520), Italian painter. *School of Athens* (1509–1511). (Fresco. Figures about life size. Rome, Vatican, Stanza della Segnatura. Photograph by Anderson.)

Size of Objects. Objects appear smaller as they recede into the distance. This is a necessary corollary of the facts we have been studying about the direction of lines, and it is illustrated in the examples already given. In the photograph of the Taj Mahal, the minarets are of equal height, but those farther away look smaller. In the *School of Athens* the arches are drawn successively smaller. And if we study the picture we find that Raphael has adapted the height of the men to the distance. Measured in inches, the figures of Plato and Aristotle are shorter than those of the men in front.

Foreshortening. This is a term of linear perspective applied primarily to the human figure. An arm held even with the eye and parallel to the plane of vision is seen in its entire length. If it is turned slowly the arm seems to grow shorter until, when it is pointing directly toward one, the arm has disappeared and little more than the end of the

Fig. 109. Mantegna (1431–1506), Italian painter. *Pietà* (1459). (Tempera on canvas. Size: about 32 by 26 inches. Milan, Brera Gallery. Photograph by Anderson.)

fingers can be seen. The name of such a shortened appearance is foreshortening. In Mantegna's *Pietà* (Figure 109) the body of Christ is foreshortened.

Obviously foreshortening is a problem only for the painter. The sculptor makes his figure of normal size. If it is seen from one point of view an arm appears full-length; if from another, it seems foreshortened. The arms of the *Charioteer* are seen in full length if the statue is viewed from the side; if the statue is seen in front the arms are foreshortened. The painter, however, is limited to one point of view and must choose one pose for each figure. Botticelli always draws the arms and legs in full length, as though he were trying to avoid the problems of foreshortening. Michelangelo on the other hand likes foreshortened poses for his paintings.

Aerial Perspective. Aerial perspective has to do with changes in appearance due to atmosphere. Objects become lighter in color and hazier in outline as they approach the horizon. In Monet's *Waterloo Bridge* (Figure 110), the buildings on the horizon are so hazy they can hardly be-seen.

Accurate painting of aerial perspective is at its best in landscape

Fig. 110. Claude Monet (1840–1926), French painter. *Waterloo Bridge* (1903). (Oil on canvas. Size: 25½ by 36 inches. Worcester, Mass., courtesy of Worcester Art Museum.)

Fig. 111. Tung Yuan (Sung epoch). Landscape scroll (late tenth century). (Brush drawing. Size: about 1 foot 3 inches by 5 feet. Boston, courtesy of the Museum of Fine Arts.)

painting, and the greatest of landscape painters are the Chinese. With a few blurred outlines they give an impression of a foreground and a background with infinite space in between. A very good example is the landscape scroll of Tung Yuan (Figure 111).

Perspective as defined in this chapter is primarily an affair of the Renaissance. Artists like Raphael, Perugino, and van Eyck were very careful to make perspective lines clear and exact. Before that time artists in general did not show what we now call realistic perspective. In the paintings of Giotto the buildings and landscapes that form the background for the figures are more nearly symbols than actual presentations. In the *Flight into Egypt* (Figure 112), the mountain and trees are intended only to give the *idea* of mountain and trees.

In more recent years there has been a turning away from exact representation of perspective. There are several reasons. One· is the impressionist movement. The impressionists wanted to give the momentary appearance of objects and the emphasis was on color. "Try to forget what you are seeing," said Monet, "merely think little squares of blue." All parts of a picture were of equal importance and interest and accordingly perspective was minimized or omitted.

Another reason lies in the importance of the camera. If a machine can reproduce lines of perspective accurately, there is not much point in doing it in a painting. The ability to draw accurate perspective has therefore become a technique, which the artist uses or not as it fits his design. Often an artist will change or falsify exact perspective to bring

Fig. 112. Giotto (1266–1336), Italian painter. *Flight into Egypt* (ca. 1305). (Fresco. Height of figures: about 3½ feet. Padua, Arena Chapel. Photograph by Alinari.)

out more clearly the idea he wants to express. In the first chapter of this book we found Cézanne changing a scene in nature to suit his design. At other times he will tilt a table or change the direction of a wall to give a greater appearance of solidity. Compare one of his still-life pictures (Figure 113) with the one by Chardin (Figure 95). In Chardin we are chiefly conscious of the texture of the objects; in Cézanne the fruit and the table are tilted toward us so that they seem solid.

In the woodcut by Schmidt-Rottluff, the two scenes of the story are juxtaposed, and difference in size is the only indication of a difference in space. In his *Melancholy and Mystery of a Street* (Figure 114), di Chirico has changed the perspective lines to give an impression of mystery and melancholy. We see a little girl playing in the street. "At first glance the scene looks solid enough, and yet we feel that the unconcerned little girl with the hoop is endangered by a world that is about to crack along invisible seams or to drift apart in incoherent pieces." [1]

Fig. 113. Paul Cézanne (1839–1906), French painter. *Still Life with Apples* (ca. 1890–1900). (Oil on canvas. Height: 27 by 36½ inches. New York, Museum of Modern Art; Lillie P. Bliss Collection.)

[1] Arnheim, *Art and Visual Perception*, p. 242.

Fig. 114. Giorgio di Chirico (1888———), Italian painter and print maker. *Melancholy and Mystery of a Street* (1914). (Oil on canvas. Size: 34⅜ by 28⅛ inches. Collection of Mr. and Mrs. Stanley R. Resor. Photograph, Museum of Modern Art.)

FOR FURTHER EXPLORATION

1. Experiment with lines of all kinds. Make a drawing to show rest by emphasis on the horizontal, or one of action by emphasis on the diagonal.

2. Draw abstractions—force, security, war, joy, etc. by the use of lines.

3. Study in detail some one painting for its use of color. Name the colors used. Has the artist chiefly used colors that are alike or unlike? How does one color influence another? For this study, an original is better than a copy.

4. Study values in the work of any two artists. What values does each prefer? What value contrasts?

5. Experiment with shadows. Try different ways of lighting your room and notice the difference in effect.

6. Choose the most important object in your room. What is the best way to light it?

7. Why does brass appear best in a room that is fairly dark?

8. What do footlights on the stage do to the shadows on the characters' faces? What do overhead lights do?

CHAPTER 9

ELEMENTS OF MUSIC

The elements of music are six: rhythm, tempo, dynamics, timbre, melody, and harmony.

RHYTHM

If we try to analyze what we hear in music, one of the first things we notice, if not the very first, is a sense of movement. Something is going forward and it is getting somewhere. It may be going fast or it may be going slowly, but it is going. In its going too it has a pattern. Trap the forward movement of a tune by clapping your hands, one clap for each tone of the composition, and you find a definite relation between the claps. If it is a tune you know, you recognize it from the pattern of claps. What you hear is the *rhythm* of that musical composition. Rhythm may be defined as the order or plan of progression in time.

Time

Ordinarily rhythm is based on regularity of accent. Listen again to the sounds when you clap the rhythm of a tune. Some of the claps are stressed or accented more than others. Moreover these stressed tones come at regular intervals and between them it is easy to make a count such as one-two, or one-two-three, using *one* as the stressed unit. For *Yankee Doodle,* the count is one-two, for *America,* one-two-three. We name these counts *beats* or *pulses,* and their regular succession makes the *time* or *meter* of the composition.

There are basically only these two kinds of time: *duple,* in which the accent falls on every other beat, and *triple,* in which it falls on every third beat. The human ear does not seem able to adjust to any time except the basic duple and triple. Four time is an expansion of duple time with a strong (or primary) accent on one and a lesser (secondary) accent on three. 1 2 *3* 4. This time is used so much that it is frequently called *common time. Praise God from Whom All Blessings Flow* is an example.

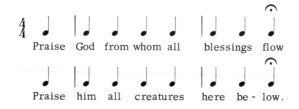

There are also multiplications of triple time called *compound time.* The most used is six time with a secondary accent on four. (1 2 3 *4* 5 6) as in *Oh! Dear, What Can the Matter Be?* Less common are nine and twelve time (1 2 3 *4* 5 6 *7* 8 9 – 1 2 3 *4* 5 6 *7* 8 9 *10* 11 12).

Oh! Dear, What Can the Matter Be?

English folk song

Even when it is marked as different, the time will be found to be some combination of the duple and triple times. A five time is a combination of two plus three or of three plus two. The famous five time in the slow movement of Tchaikovsky's Symphony No. 6 (*Pathétique*) is three plus two. And the very infrequent seven time is a combination of four and three.

Time and Rhythm

Time or meter differs from rhythm in that the beats or pulses of time are always the same, equally spaced, whereas the claps of the rhythm are not. Take *America* again; there are three beats to a unit or measure, and we count it one-two-three. In the first measure, *My country,* time and rhythm are the same, but in the second, *'tis* is slightly longer and *of* is proportionately shorter, while *thee* is exactly one beat.

This relationship, which is so awkwardly expressed in words, is clearly and simply expressed in written music.

In the last phrase of *America* we have two short tones for the beat, and in the final measure one tone is held for the time of three beats.

To summarize what we have said, there are four ways in which the time and the rhythm may be related:

1. They may be the same; the effect is usually simple and direct, clear, unaffected. A rhythm which sticks too closely to the time is stupid. The doxology tune, *Praise God from Whom All Blessings Flow,* and *Yankee Doodle* are both good tunes but their excellence is not seen in the rhythm alone. Most composers bring some variety into their rhythmic patterns.

2. The tones of the time may be amalgamated so that one tone of the rhythm will get several counts, as in *sing* and *ring* of *America*. The lengthened notes give stability and dignity; they are solid and substantial. The pause that comes from lengthened notes is practically universal at the end of a composition.

3. There may be short notes, usually two or four to a beat, as in "*Let* freedom ring." These are light, easy, and graceful. The world is not too desolate when we can sing two notes for one.

4. Dotted rhythm. A dotted note followed by a short note has the advantages of both the other variations, for it combines the lengthened with the shortened note, as in " '*tis of* thee." It often gives a touch of grace when the rhythm might be too sober without it, as in *America the Beautiful,* or in the second movement of Beethoven's Fifth Symphony.

Motives and Phrases

If one listens to rhythm as rhythm he finds that it begins very quickly to divide itself into units or *motives* that are quite small, and these motives repeat themselves. The first movement of Tchaikovsky's Symphony No. 6 (the *Pathétique*) has a characteristic rhythmic motive in four tones.

These short motives are repeated and are gathered together into longer units. The motive from the First Movement of Tchaikovsky's Sixth Symphony is repeated four times, then there is a pause. This group of four is again repeated, but now the motive is brought in for a fifth and sixth time, as an echo.

These longer groups are called *phrases*. A phrase usually consists of at least four measures, though it may easily be reduced or extended as in the example from Tchaikovsky. *America* is made up of two phrases; the first ends with "Of thee I sing," and the second with the close of the stanza "Let freedom ring." The motive which is heard in the first line, "My country 'tis of thee," is heard twice in the first phrase and

Symphony No. 6 in B minor
(Symphonie Pathétique)

Peter Ilich Tchaikovsky
Russian (1840-1893)

Adagio

etc.

The Blue Bells of Scotland

First Phrase

Popular Scottish Air

1. Oh where, and oh   where is your— High-land lad-die gone?   Oh
2. Oh where, and oh   where did your— High-land lad-die dwell?   Oh

Second Phrase

where, and oh   where is your— High - land lad - die   gone?   He's
where, and oh   where did your— High - land lad - die   dwell?   He

Third Phrase

gone to   fight the foe   for King— George up - on the throne, And it's
dwelt in   mer - ry Scot - land at the sign   of the Blue Bell, And it's

Fourth Phrase

oh,   in my heart,   I _____ wish him safe   at   home.
oh,   in my heart,   I _____ love   my lad - die well.

197

three times in the second. A phrase usually ends on a lengthened note, frequently with a rest.

In hymns and folk songs the phrases are usually definite and precise. Note the phrasing of the *Blue Bells of Scotland*. The same rhythm is used in the first, second, and fourth phrases, while that of the third is changed only slightly.

Long phrases tend to be gentle and may be romantic. Short phrases tend to be nervous and exciting.

Variety in Rhythm

We are told that savages can repeat a single short motive for a long time without getting tired, but more civilized people want variety. In a simple song such as *America* or the *Blue Bells of Scotland*, our interest is partly in the words and we are not conscious of a sameness in rhythm. But we would not like hearing the tune many times without words. Therefore the composer is always anxious to introduce some variety. Tchaikovsky begins to make changes very soon; the two first notes of his motive are doubled. This was the method found earlier in *America*.

The number of ways a composer may vary his rhythm are endless, but there are some well known means of getting variety that we may mention. One is a shift in the general temper or mood of the piece. *Dixie,* for instance, is a rather hurried affair, but it gains considerable relief by the variety afforded in lengthened tones of *away*. In another patriotic song, the *Battle Hymn of the Republic,* there is a distinct shift in emotional tension just before the chorus from the regular beats of "'His truth is marching on" to the slower tempo of the chorus, "Glory, glory, hallelujah." The entire tune is vigorous and energetic, but the refrain is more confident and relaxed than the stanza.

Another means of getting variety in rhythm is to change the time; duple measures may be inserted in triple rhythms or triple measures in duple. A notable example is the very popular Andante Cantabile from the Quartet, Op. 11, by Tchaikovsky.

A popular variant from regularity of accent is found in syncopation. Syncopation of rhythm is a kind of "robbing Peter to pay Paul," a taking of the accents away from the place they belong and putting them somewhere else. If for instance you have become accustomed to the accents on the first and fourth beats of a regular six time,

Andante Cantabile
from String Quartet in D, Op. 11
Peter Ilich Tchaikovsky
Russian (1840-1893)

1 2 3 4́ 5 6, 1 2 3 4́ 5 6, you are surprised and shocked to hear the accent on count three, 1 2 3́ 4 5 6.

Syncopation has been known and used for a long time. In recent music, however, it has been given a prominence not common in earlier years. In jazz the improvisations of the soloist will show a great deal of syncopation while the basic time is being beat on the drums.

Importance of Rhythm

Rhythm is the primary basis of music, and recognition of accent is almost universal. Even those who have no ear for melody, and cannot carry a tune, are conscious of accent and can keep time by beating the accents. Such people are often scornfully referred to as foot-listeners, and it is said that their music is *leg* music, but they have made the initial step in the enjoyment of music. It is the regular recurrence of accents that gives the music its surge, its determined onward flow. It is the accent which makes it easy and delightful to march to music. It is the steady beat of the time that makes it possible for a group to sing together or for a band to play together. It is the beat of the time that makes it easy for people to dance together.

Sometimes the accent is more important than at other times. In *America* the accent is clear, but it is not nearly so much stressed as in *Yankee Doodle* or *The Star-Spangled Banner*. When accents are stressed, the tunes are good for marching or dancing. The march and the waltz are two types that depend on the importance of the time. Play one of the Sousa marches, and notice how the accents make you want to step forward. Schubert's *Marche Militaire* is not quite so

Marche Militaire

Franz Schubert
Austrian (1797-1828)

etc.

Tales from the Vienna Woods

Johann Strauss Jr.
Austrian (1825-1899)

Waltz

etc.

200

strenuous, but it is still vigorous. For the waltz we turn first to the "waltz king" Johann Strauss in *The Blue Danube Waltz,* or the *Tales from the Vienna Woods.*

Music with a strict basis in time is almost universal. However, there are some forms of music which may be said to have free rhythms. By far the greatest examples of these both in quantity and in quality are found in the plain-song of the early Christian church. This music, which more nearly resembles present-day chant than any other form of music, is based on the free rhythms of speech. The accents follow the sense of the text instead of coming at regular intervals. Because this form of music was used in the services of the church, it came to be the church music, whereas the accented music was used for dancers. Gregorian chant is the famous example of plain-song and is still one of the greatest forms of music ever made. Fortunately Gregorian chant has been preserved and recorded by the monks of the Abbey at Solesmes in France.

TEMPO

The time or meter in which a piece of music is written has little to do with the actual speed or *tempo* of the music. Notation for time and rhythm shows the length of each note with reference to the other notes of the piece, but that is all. We can say in general that songs written with half notes as the unit of value are supposed to go more slowly than songs written in quarter notes, and songs written in eighth notes are supposed to go faster, although there is no proof that such is the case.

In general we may say the pace is slow, quick, or moderate, but more commonly we use the traditional Italian terms.

grave	grave, solemn, slow
largo	very slowly and broadly
adagio	very slowly
andante	moderately slowly
andantino	somewhat faster than andante
moderato	at a moderate tempo
allegretto	at a pace between moderato and allegro
allegro	fairly fast
presto	very fast
prestissimo	as fast as possible

These terms are made more exact by the addition of terms that indicate how the music is to be played.

assai	very
con anima	with life
con moto	with motion
con spirito	with spirit
grazioso	gracefully
maestoso	majestically
dolce	softly or sweetly
con fuoco	with fire
con brio	with vivacity or spirit
molto	much
giusto	in exact tempo
ma non troppo	but not too much
moderato	moderately
vivace	with vivacity

Generally speaking the slow tempos mean concentration, reflection, and deep feeling, whereas the quick tempos mean gayety, joy, fun, vigor, excitement. An increasing speed (*accelerando*) means increase in excitement and tension, a decreasing speed (*ritardando*) means loss of life or power, sometimes it shows relaxation and rest, sometimes exhaustion. Sudden changes often cause alarm—they alert one to danger. Always they show something out of the ordinary.

DYNAMICS

The word *dynamics* refers to the degree and variations of sonority and force with which music is played, from soft to loud. These gradations of intensity, like the terms for tempo, are traditionally indicated by Italian words, for which there are abbreviations and arbitrary symbols:

pp.	*pianissimo*	as soft as possible
p.	*piano*	soft
mp.	*mezzo piano*	somewhat soft
mf.	*mezzo forte*	somewhat loud
f.	*forte*	loud
ff.	*fortissimo*	as loud as possible
cresc.	*crescendo*	getting louder

decresc.	*decrescendo*	} getting softer
dim.	*diminuendo*	
sf.	*sforzando*	abruptly loud

MELODY AND TIMBRE

Melody and Rhythm

Melody is tune. If you sing *America,* you have produced its melody. Rhythm is thought to be older than melody, and melody is based on rhythm. To make a melody we must have, in addition to rhythm, (1) tone and timbre, and (2) pitch and scale.

Tone and Timbre. There are two kinds of sound: tone and noise. *Tone* is a pleasing sound caused by a regular series of vibrations; *noise* is an unpleasing sound caused by an irregular series of vibrations. Rhythm may be produced in noise as well as in tone, but melody demands tone. Tapping on a table with a pencil will produce rhythm, but never tune.

Tone is produced by musical instruments or by the human voice. Each voice and each instrument has its characteristic quality, called its tone color or *timbre.* We speak of the timbre of a violin as compared with that of an oboe. Since the timbre of each instrument was named in the discussion of instruments it will not be repeated here. We should remember, however, that when we have tone, we also have the timbre of the instrument or voice producing the tone.

Pitch. When we were studying rhythm we noticed that the rhythm of the first motive in *America* is repeated exactly in the second. The rhythm of "My country 'tis of thee" is the same as that of "Sweet land of liberty." But when we sing them they are not the same. "Sweet land of liberty" is higher than "My country 'tis of thee." This difference of higher or lower is called *pitch.*

To have melody there must be a change of pitch. The tune must go up or down. Beethoven repeats a single tone twelve times in the slow movement of his Seventh Symphony, but in the end he has to change. He must, however, choose his tones from a fixed series called a scale.

Tonality

A scale is a succession of tones following an established order. Scales are based on the interval called the octave. It is a natural interval

Symphony No. 7 in A major
Slow movement

Ludwig van Beethoven
German (1770-1827)

because everyone recognizes it either consciously or unconsciously. Suppose you are singing with a group of people, and the piano accompaniment is too high; you instinctively lower the tune to the "same tone" lower down. Or if the accompaniment is too low, you raise your pitch to the "same tone" higher up. This tone which we recognize as the "same tone" higher or lower is the *octave* (or eighth). It was given this name because the scale generally used has seven tones in it, and when we reach the "same tone" it is the eighth. Actually there is a simple physical reason for our recognition of this interval. The two tones are in the ratio of one to two. When middle C on the piano is vibrating 256 times per second, the C above it is vibrating just twice that number, or 512 times. And the C below it will be vibrating half that number, or 128 times.

Within the octave there are definite relations between the seven tones. Begin with C and play each white key in turn until you get to B. You feel a sense of incompleteness, that something is not finished. It is as if someone said, "This afternoon at three we will go to the" or "I put the cat in the." You are not satisfied until you play the C that follows.

The story is told that the child Mozart liked to lie in bed, and it was hard to rouse him. But his father could always get him up if he played a scale stopping on the seventh tone. The young Mozart would get up at once to complete the scale! [1]

This is what we mean by the *pull* of a tone. We feel the same kind

[1] Tovey, *Beethoven,* p. 14.

of incompleteness and the same *pull* for the right ending in tunes. Sing
the first phrase of the doxology tune, *Old Hundred:*

> Praise God from whom all blessings flow.

We cannot stop here. Go on to the second phrase,

> Praise Him all creatures here below.

The words make a good stopping place, but the music demands that
we go on, nor can we stop until we come to the last phrase, which ends
on the first tone of the scale.

> Praise Father, Son, and Holy Ghost.

Or take the last half of *America:*

> Land where my fathers died
> Land of the pilgrims' pride
> From every mountain side

we cannot stop until we reach the end,

> Let freedom ring.

The tones of the scale thus are not a disconnected series; there are
definite relationships between them just as there are between words.
The general term for these relations is *tonality.* The rules in music are
like the rules of grammar in ordinary speech. One may not know what
they are, but unless the words fit together in some sort of grammatical
relationship, they do not make sense. So, in music, the tones do not
make musical sense unless they follow the established customs or laws.

The first and most important of these laws has to do with the first
tone of the scale, the *tonic.* It is the central tone, as it were; it is the
home tone. It is usually the tone on which a composition ends.

Next to the tonic, the most important tones in a melody are the fifth
(*dominant*) and the third (*mediant*). They set the stage for the piece,
and with the tonic determine our sense for the scale. These three tones
are apt to come at the beginning of a piece, especially on the accented
notes, and they are important throughout the composition. To illustrate
this point note the tones used in the first phrase of *Drink to Me Only
with Thine Eyes.* The number refers to the place of the tone in the
scale: 1 is the first tone, 2 the second and so on.

$$3\ 3\ 3\ 4\ 4\ /\ 5\ 4\ 3\ ^2\ 3\ 4\ /\ 5\ ^1\ 4\ 3\ 2\ /\ 1\ /$$

Major and Minor Scales

The *major* is the basic scale. It is represented on the piano by the white keys beginning on C. Since each key of the piano is a half step from the keys on each side, it is easy to figure the exact intervals of the major scale.

$$\text{C \quad D \quad E \quad F \quad G \quad A \quad B \quad C}$$
$$1 \quad 1 \quad \tfrac{1}{2} \quad 1 \quad 1 \quad 1 \quad \tfrac{1}{2}$$

The *minor* scale is almost as important as the major. It may be formed by flatting (i.e., lowering a tone a half step) the third and sixth tones of the major scale.

$$\text{C \quad D \quad E♭ \quad F \quad G \quad A♭ \quad B \quad C}$$
$$1 \quad \tfrac{1}{2} \quad 1 \quad 1 \quad \tfrac{1}{2} \quad 1\tfrac{1}{2} \quad \tfrac{1}{2}$$

An important characteristic of the minor is the third note, which is one and one-half tones above the tonic, instead of two whole tones as in the major.

By using both black and white keys, a major or minor scale can be played beginning on any key on the piano. The scale which begins on C is said to be in the key of C, that which begins on A, the key of A, etc. The major and minor scales are also known as the diatonic scales.

The major lends itself to ordinary, practical, gay, happy, commonplace effects like sunlight and fresh air; it is the foundation on which most music is built. The great majority of our folk songs and hymns are in the major mode: *Drink to Me Only with Thine Eyes, Praise God from Whom All Blessings Flow*, etc.

The minor may be thought of as weird, mysterious, vague, strange, haunting. The minor, because of its expressive quality, is used largely

Symphonic Variations

César Franck
French (1822-1890)

in extended instrumental compositions. It is not a favorite for individual songs. The melody quoted earlier from the slow movement of Beethoven's Seventh Symphony is in the minor, as in the song *Go Down Moses*. The theme for the *Symphonic Variations* of César Franck is little more than a minor scale.

Other Scales

The major and the minor scales are used so nearly universally that we do not easily hear music in any other. The chief reason why music of a foreign people, such as the Chinese or the Hindus, sounds peculiar, is that it is written in a tonality other than that of the major and the minor scales. This also accounts for the strangeness of some folk songs which preserve the older scales.

Five-tone Scale. One of the early scales is the *pentatonic*, or five-tone scale. This scale may be played on the black keys of the piano. Many of the old Scotch songs are in this scale, among them *The Campbells Are Coming* and *Auld Lang Syne*. Another example is an old Appalachian tune for the ballad, *Barbara Allen*.

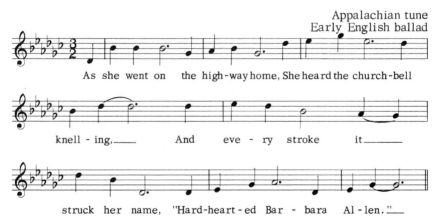

Barbara Allen

Appalachian tune
Early English ballad

As she went on the high-way home, She heard the church-bell knell-ing,___ And eve-ry stroke it___ struck her name, "Hard-heart-ed Bar-bara Al-len."___

Modes. In the diatonic, or seven-tone scale, there were originally other scales than the two that are commonly used now. These early scales are heard chiefly in songs and ballads which are said to be *modal* because they employ unusual modes or scales. A popular modal song is *Greensleeves*, a love song which is also heard with religious words: "What child is this."

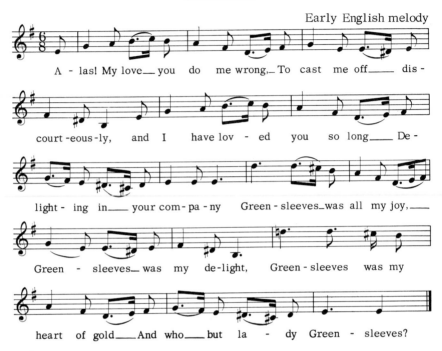

Greensleeves

Early English melody

A - las! My love__ you do me wrong,__ To cast me off____ dis -

court -eous-ly, and I have lov - ed you so long____ De -

light - ing in__ your com-pa - ny Green - sleeves__was all my joy, __

Green - sleeves__ was my de-light, Green - sleeves was my

heart of gold__And who__but la - dy Green - sleeves?

Chromatic Scale. The chromatic scale is made up of half-tone intervals. You play the chromatic scale when you sound every key on the
piano. The chromatic scale is best used in relatively short vocal numbers, as "My Heart at Thy Sweet Voice" from *Samson and Delilah,*
or "To the Evening Star" from *Tannhäuser.* One of the most popular
is the song of Carmen from Bizet's opera *Carmen.*

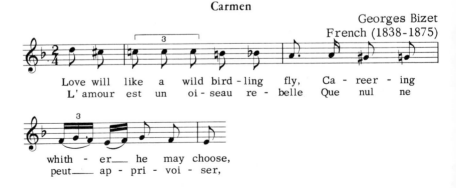

Carmen

Georges Bizet
French (1838-1875)

Love will like a wild bird-ling fly, Ca - reer - ing
L' amour est un oi - seau re - belle Que nul ne

whith - er__ he may choose,
peut__ ap - pri - voi - ser,

Whole-tone Scale. In modern music there has been considerable experimentation with modes. Debussy often used the whole-tone scale, made up, of course, of whole tones, as follows:

C   D   E   F♯   G♯   A♯   C

Quarter-tone Scale. Oriental music has long had a scale using quarter tones. We have no music using all quarter tones, but the interval is creeping into much modern music, especially jazz.

Atonality. Schönberg chose twelve tones, called a twelve-tone row, and used it as the basis for his music, a different series of tones being chosen for each piece. This is called *atonality* or no tonality.

The net effect of all the modern experiments is to break down our strong sense of major and minor, because our ears get accustomed to the new tonalities, whether whole-tone, half-tone, quarter-tone, polytonality or atonality.

Melodic Patterns

There are no rules for the making of a melody. The musician makes a tune to fit his idea and his emotion. At the same time, we do recognize certain patterns that are repeated many times. Some of them are listed below.

The Tonic Chord. Because of the importance of the tonic chord, made up of the tonic, mediant, and dominant (tones 1 − 3 − 5 of the scale), in establishing the tonality of a composition, this is one of the patterns that occurs most frequently. The bugle calls are composed entirely of these three tones.

Bugle Calls

(a) Reveille

(b) Assembly

(c) Taps

The Star-Spangled Banner begins with those three tones, first going down, then up.

Star-Spangled Banner

The hymn *Holy, Holy, Holy* repeats each tone at the beginning of the song:

Holy   Holy   Holy
1 1   3 3   5 5

Haydn begins the slow movement of his *Surprise Symphony* with the same tones to a faster tempo. Beethoven uses the three tones for the opening theme of his Third Symphony:

Symphony No. 3 in E flat major
First movement

Ludwig van Beethoven
German (1770-1827)

Because these *are* the basic tones, tunes built on them are simple, direct, natural, single-hearted.

The Scale. Another favorite pattern is the scale. The song from *Rigoletto*, "Caro nome," follows a descending scale:

Caro nome che-il mio cor
8 7 6 5   4   3 2

The hymn *Joy to the World* begins with a descending scale:

Joy to the world, the Lord is come
8 7 6   5   4   3   2   1

The Russian hymn *God the All Terrible* ends with a descending scale:

Give to us peace in our time, O Lord.
8 7 6   5   5   4   3   2   1

Wave. More often a tune follows the scale, but does not go all the way up or down. It moves around a note in a waving pattern, as in *Frère Jacques (Brother John)*:

Are you sleeping? Are you sleeping?
1   2   3   1   1   2   3   1
  Brother John? Brother John?
  3   4   5   3   4   5

or in

Merrily we   roll along
3   2 1   2   3   3   3

A favorite melody showing the wave pattern is that from the slow movement of Dvořák's Fifth Symphony, usually sung to the words "Going home." One of the loveliest of all the wave patterns is Bach's setting of the chorale *Jesu, Joy of Man's Desiring*.

Symphony No. 5 in E minor

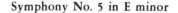

Slow movement

Antonin Dvořák
Bohemian (1841-1904)

Jesu, Joy of Man's Desiring
Chorale

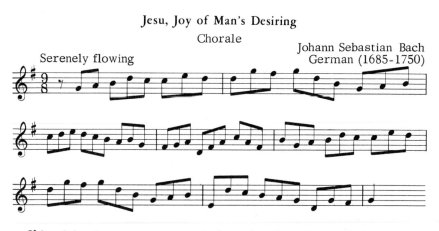

Skip. A less important pattern is the series of small steps followed by a skip, or jump. Strauss's waltz *Tales from the Vienna Woods* takes three steps down and then makes a jump up of seven (page 200). In Mozart's Symphony in G minor the jump is followed by a descending scale in the opposite direction.

Symphony in G minor
K. 550

Single Tone. The simplest pattern of all is the repetition of a single tone, the pattern we heard in the slow movement of Beethoven's Seventh Symphony. In the beautiful *Easter Hymn* from Palestrina, there is such repetition both in the refrain and in the stanza. The same tone is repeated three times at the beginning of "La donna è mobile," from *Rigoletto*.

Melodic Motives. A motive is a part of a rhythmic phrase; when the rhythmic motive is combined with series of notes of vitality it is recognized whenever it occurs. One of the most famous is the "knocking" motive which dominates the first movement of Beethoven's Fifth Symphony. Wagner uses motives in his operas to designate certain people, or places, and even ideas. The Rhine, the Rhinegold, and the sword are recognized in their motives.

Rigoletto

Act III

Giuseppe Verdi
Italian (1813-1901)

Duke: La don - na è mo - bi - le Qual piu ma al
Wo - man's as change - a - ble as an - y

ven - to Mu - ta d'ac - cen - to
fea - ther Blown by the light - est breeze

E di pen - sie - ro
heed - less and thought - less

etc.

Symphony No. 5 in C minor
First movement

Ludwig van Beethoven
German (1770-1827)

The Ring of the Nibelungs

Richard Wagner
German (1813-1883)

The Rhine

The Rhinegold

The Sword

A great deal of the beauty of what is probably the best loved Christmas carol comes from the repetition of the motive of the opening words of *Silent Night.* In work songs, often a rhythmic unit of this kind is used to mark or emphasize the special rhythm of the particular form of work. One of the best known is the Russian folk song *The Volga Boatman,* with its recurrent theme "Row, boys, row." Sea chanteys with refrains such as "Yo heave ho," and cowboy songs with calls of "Yip-ee-ti-yo," "Hi-up," or "Git along," belong to this class.

Identifying Melodies

One of the great hazards in learning music is the difficulty of remembering themes. A tune may sound familiar, yet what it is we do not know. Several ways of identifying melodies have proved useful, especially for the person not trained in music.

1. *Notes.* The best method is to know the notes as they appear on the printed page. Obviously this method can be used only for those works one studies carefully; one has the score only in the case of a small fraction of the music he hears.

2. *Words.* We have no trouble recalling the music of songs we know, because the words bring back the melody. Similarly, if any theme or motive is set to words, one remembers the music with the words. Sigmund Spaeth has been an advocate of this approach to the identification of tunes, and it is an excellent device. It serves its purpose best when it identifies the title and the composer. For example, Mr. Spaeth uses these words for the initial phrase of the *Marche Militaire.* "Marche Militaire is the name Schubert used for this." The themes used by Wagner are much more easily identified if each is sung to words, like "The sword is security" for the sword theme, or "Valhalla is the palace fair," for Valhalla.

3. *Shorthand.* For music that is not easily adapted to either of the methods already described, "shorthand" may be used. It consists of first identifying a motive that is repeated, and then making a simple notation of it. For example the "Row, boys, row" of *The Volga Boatman* might appear as _____ _____ _____ _____, the motive of *Silent Night* as _____ __ __ _____.

COUNTERPOINT

Melody is like a line drawing. The outlines are clear and distinct but there are no shadows, there is no shading. Music which consists of melody alone is today rather rare. A tune sounds bare if sounded alone. We expect additional tones which accompany and so enrich the melody. Even in the simplest songs such as hymns or folk songs, we expect an "accompaniment" which we hear along with the clear line of the melody. Ordinarily what we hear is the harmony of chords (*homophonic* music it is called), in contrast to *monophonic* music of melody alone. There is, however, a third type of music called *polyphonic* in which the melody is enriched not by accompanying chords, but by accompanying tunes.

Homophony is sometimes called vertical harmony because it is merely an enrichment to the melody, and polyphony is called horizontal harmony because it is made by the union of several different horizontal melodies. However, we usually distinguish between counterpoint and harmony, reserving the word *harmony* for all types that are not contrapuntal.

Polyphony, or *counterpoint,* which was the earliest way of embellishing a tune, developed from the habit of putting together different instruments or voices, and the discovery that some of these combinations were pleasing.

Two Types of Counterpoint

Counterpoint, the earliest form of harmony, is made by putting together two or more tunes. This is done in two ways. One is shown by putting together two separate songs, as when we sing two melodies together, like Dvořák's *Humoresque* and Foster's *Swanee River,* or *There's a Long, Long Trail* and *Keep the Home Fires Burning.* In the other type of counterpoint a tune makes its own harmony by starting at different times. This is familiar to everyone in rounds. In the round *White Coral Bells,* for instance, the first voice begins with the theme, "White coral bells upon a slender stalk," which is two measures in length. As the first voice goes on to the 3rd and 4th measures, "Lilies

Round in two parts

White cor - al bells up - on a slen - der stalk

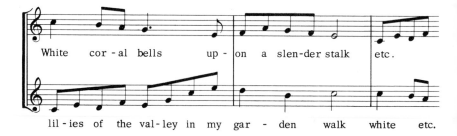

White   cor - al bells   up - on a slen-der stalk   etc.

lil - ies of the val - ley in my gar - den   walk   white   etc.

of the valley in my garden walk," the second voice is singing the first two measures, and so we have the two tunes going at the same time, with one part of the tune accompanying another part.

When one melody is played at the same time as another, it is called the countermelody, since the one is played against (Latin, *counter*, "against") the other; and this kind of writing is called *counterpoint*. (Point is an old name for note; hence counterpoint means "point against point," or "note against note.")

Imitation and Canon

When one voice repeats what has just been said by another voice, this is called *imitation*. And when one voice imitates another exactly it is said to be in *canon* (canon means strict rule). A good canon is found in the Finale of Franck's Sonata in A major for Violin and Piano, another in the F major Invention of Bach. All rounds are in canon.

Music in canon may be written for any number of voices, usually two, three, or four. The round we were just looking at, *White Coral Bells,* is for two voices. *White Sands and Grey Sands* is written for three voices, and *Row, Row, Row Your Boat* for four.

The difficulty with this type of music is that whereas it has a definite beginning, it has no definite end. It has been compared to the game of "follow the leader." It could go on forever; there is nothing to prescribe what the leader is to do, or when he must stop; the only requirement is that the others follow. Hence writing in this form tends to become garrulous unless it is kept in strict bounds by the composer, as has been done by Bach and Franck. Many of the great oratorio choruses such as the "Hallelujah Chorus" from *The Messiah* and "The Heavens are telling" from *The Creation* have polyphonic passages, though they are not polyphonic in their entirety.

Sonata in A major for Violin and Piano

Finale

César Franck
French (1822-1890)

etc.

Two-Part Invention in F major

Johann Sebastian Bach
German (1685-1750)

etc.

Round in three parts

White sands and grey sands,

White sands and grey sands, who'll buy my white sands,

White sands and grey sands, etc.

who'll buy my white sands, etc.

who'll buy my grey sands, etc.

Round in four parts

Row, row, row your boat

Row, row, row your boat gen - tly down the stream

Two Separate Melodies

The other type of counterpoint, the putting together of two separate melodies, is almost as popular a form of group singing as the round. But it too is found in formal as well as in informal music. For this type we may turn again to the slow movement of Beethoven's Seventh Symphony. It was quoted earlier as an example of the repetition of a single tone in a melody. This melody is played, first, without any accompaniment whatever. The second time the theme is presented, however, there has been a change. Our first tune is there, just as it

Symphony No. 7 in A major
Slow movement

Ludwig van Beethoven
German (1770-1827)

(later appearance)

etc.

was, but under and around it Beethoven has written another tune. It is like a vine growing on a tree; sometimes you are most conscious of the vine and sometimes of the tree, but the real pleasure is in the combination. The two tunes can be separated, for each is a good tune, but the combination is better than either.

In music since the time of Bach, the tendency has been to put together two melodies that are quite different, as has been done by Beethoven. In the great period of polyphonic music, before Bach, little emphasis is placed on the separate melodies as such. Instead, one is conscious only of the way the voices are woven together in a harmonic whole. This can be illustrated in almost any of the polyphonic music of Palestrina, who is the acknowledged master of the polyphonic period. A good example is the "Christe eleison" from the Mass, *Assumpta est Maria.*

In the past fifty years great impetus has been given to counterpoint by the development of jazz, with its emphasis on improvisation, for the jazz player's improvisation is, in reality, just a countermelody or counterpoint on the original theme.

Notes about Counterpoint

No one can hear all the melodies that are woven together in polyphonic music, but we can sharpen our ears for polyphony if we listen carefully to the melodies combined, and especially if we notice some of the characteristics which are essential in the making of counterpoint.

1. *Contrast in rhythm.* The two or more voices contrast in rhythm. In Franck's Sonata for Violin and Piano, one instrument holds a note while the other catches up, as it were. In the Two-part Invention by Bach there is no waiting of one voice for the other, but when one is slow the other tends to be fast.

2. *Contrast in the direction of the melody.* Even in a simple round such as *White Coral Bells,* when one voice is going up the other is coming down. In *White Sands and Grey Sands* the last two measures have a downward motion, whereas the others are almost horizontal.

3. *Contrast in pitch.* One voice is usually higher than the other. In *Row, Row,* the voice gets higher in each of the first three measures. In the Bach Inventions one voice is regularly put in the bass and the other in the treble. In the Beethoven Seventh Symphony the secondary melody is first lower than the primary and then is put above it.

Mass: Assumpta est Maria

Giovanni Pierluigi da Palestrina
Italian (1514 or 1515-1594)

223

HARMONY

After the great days of the polyphonic music of Palestrina and Bach, counterpoint became technical and ceased to have its original power and grandeur. Emphasis was then given to the harmony of chords, which are the simultaneous combination of tones. This is the harmony most commonly heard in hymns, songs, and music in general, and this is the harmony usually meant when one speaks of *harmony*.

How Chords Are Made

The traditional basis of harmony is the chord, a combination of alternate tones of the scale, e.g., $1-3-5$, $2-4-6$, $3-5-7$, etc. or in the key of C, $C-E-G$, $D-F-A$, $E-G-B$, etc. Chords are named from the first or root member. A chord is said to be the same, no matter how the tones are arranged, i.e., in what "position" they are, as $E-G-C$, $G-C-E$, $G-E-C$, etc. Nor does it matter if one or all of the tones are repeated.

In hearing a series of chords beginning on every tone of the scale, the student will notice that some are more pleasing than others, or we might better say that some are more stable than others. On the stable chords one can stop and rest; with other chords he wants to move on to a chord on which he can stop. In musical terminology the chord that asks us to go on is called a *dissonance* or *dissonant chord,* and it is *resolved* when one has gone on to a chord on which he can stop. Play together F and the B above it. The sound is so unstable as fairly to demand resolution by playing the tones on each side, E and C.

Of the seven possible chords, the most stable are the first, fourth, and fifth, and they are the ones that we use most commonly. Often a simple tune is harmonized with only those chords. When we want to come to the ending we use the tonic chord just as instinctively as we use the tonic note. The ending that is almost universal for any song or other musical composition is the tonic chord preceded by the dominant. This is called a *perfect cadence.* When we sing "amen" we use the tonic chord preceded by the chord of the fourth; this is called a *plagal cadence.*

Dissonance

In our study of scales we noted the "pull" of a single note, how for instance when one plays a scale to the seventh tone he has a real desire or "pull" to go on to the eighth tone. In the dissonant chord this pull is greatly increased because it combines the pull of several tones. We must resolve the chord by playing one that is consonant.

There must always be some dissonance in music; there must always be a sense of some place to go to, some point to reach. Otherwise music would be very stupid, flat, and tasteless, like sitting still all day. Amen is a satisfactory closing to a song, but you could not make an entire tune of Amens.

Not only is dissonance essential in all music, but the number of dissonances tends to increase and the time before they are resolved becomes longer. This is an inevitable result of the fact that when we become accustomed to certain kinds of dissonance we cease to be pulled by them. To get variety, the musician must then increase the amount of dissonance and the time before the dissonances are resolved. It is for this reason that each new musician is called barbarous and unmelodic, and his work compared to all the hideous noises the critic can think of. Here too belongs the explanation of some of the experiments in modern music.

The *whole-tone scale* of course has no tonality, and there is no sense of a pull in any direction. Each chord is a delightful experience but it is quite independent. The use of this scale is partly responsible for the vague impressions and strange moods that are characteristic of the work of Debussy. One is left as it were floating in the air, a delightful experience, but one begins to want solid earth under him. Ravel was another artist who used this scale. Listen to Debussy's *Nuages* (*Clouds*) and *Voiles* (*Veils*) and Ravel's *Daphnis and Chloe*.

Polytonality is strictly a matter of harmony. Imagine boys and girls singing together in different keys. Each group wants to emphasize its own tonality and to end on its tonic, but when the two groups are heard together we hear the two tonalities and are pulled in two different directions. The use of polytonality is associated with the name of Igor Stravinsky, and his *Petrouchka* is often cited as one of the more conspicuous examples. The "Petrouchka chord" used throughout the piece represents two different keys—F sharp major and C major sounded together.

Petrouchka chord

Hearing Harmony

Hearing harmonies is primarily a matter of attention. One of the best ways to begin is to listen carefully to a single voice or instrument played with an accompaniment. The solo will sing the melody while the harmonies are heard in the accompaniment. Try to hear what the accompaniment is doing. Sometimes it accompanies the melody step by step; sometimes it anticipates the melody; and sometimes it echoes it. Note what the accompaniment is doing when the solo voice is silent. Does it merely mark the time? Does it repeat the melody? Or does it go off on its own? Note also the direction of the harmony. Does it follow the line of the melody, or does the harmonic line go up when the melodic line goes down?

Are the chords largely consonant or do you hear dissonances? If there are dissonances, are they resolved? The cry of the Rhine maidens in Wagner's *Rhinegold* is simply a dissonance followed by a consonance.

The Rhinegold

Scene I

Richard Wagner

German (1813-1883)

How are the chords played? The tones of a chord may be played simultaneously as solid chords, or they may be broken or spread out in arpeggios. The arpeggio always gives a soft, smooth, flowing motion to the music, like that of the harp. In the first movement of Beethoven's *Moonlight Sonata,* the accompaniment is played in arpeggios. It is that movement which won the piece its name. The first Prelude in Bach's *Well-tempered Clavier* is in arpeggios.

Ordinarily we listen for the primary melody above the harmony, but it is not always there. In two very popular pieces, Rubenstein's Melody in F, and Liszt's *Liebestraum,* the melody first appears in the

Prelude No. 20 in C minor

Frédéric Chopin
Polish (1809-1849)

middle of the harmony. In Schumann's *Happy Farmer,* the melody
is below the harmony as in Schumann's Romance in F minor. In
Chopin's Prelude No. 6 in B minor, the air is entirely below the accompaniment. In his Prelude No. 15 in D flat major, the music is in three
distinct parts: the first and third are calm and peaceful, the second,
middle section is stormy and violent. In that section, the melody is
below heavy chords, whereas it is above the harmonies in the first and
third sections.

Finally, and in every case, one should try to determine the place of
the harmony in the total effect of the composition. Of course, the
harmony should fit the melody for which it is designed. A folk song, a
hymn, or other simple song, for example, needs a very simple, unpre-
tentious harmony. The beauty is in the tune and the harmony should
not distract from it. In the usual hymn or folk song the accompaniment
follows the melody exactly and inconspicuously.

On the other hand, the harmonies can give dignity and grandeur to
a melody as in Chopin's Prelude No. 20 in C minor. The slow movement of Beethoven's *Sonata Appassionata* begins with a theme of the
utmost loftiness and grandeur which owes its solemnity to its rich
harmonies and to their being placed in the lower register of the piano.

Sonata Op. 57
Slow movement

Ludwig van Beethoven
German (1770-1827)

Harmony can do a great deal for quite ordinary, undistinguished
tunes. Ask someone to name a common hymn with a beautiful melody,
and you will not be surprised if he names *Now the Day Is Over.* But
actually it has almost no melody; it derives what distinction it has
exclusively from its rich harmonization.

APPENDIX

Notation

Time Signature. Music is written in notes which have relative values. In writing music one decides first in what kind of notes he wants to write his music, in other words what will be the note value of each pulse, and he places a number corresponding to the value of the note at the beginning of his music. Another number is placed above it to indicate the count, or number of beats. In writing

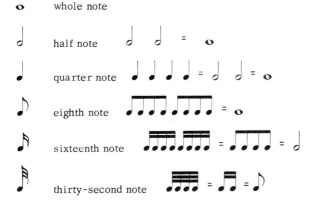

Each of these notes lasts half as long as the one preceding it, which it halves. A dot placed after a note prolongs it by half again its length; thus ♩. = ♩ + ♪, or ♩ ♩ ♩; ♩. = ♩ + ♪ or ♫♪ . Every kind of note has a corresponding kind of *rest* to indicate that nothing shall be sounded:

        ▬   whole rest

        ▬   half rest

        𝄽   quarter rest

        𝄾   eighth rest

        𝄿   sixteenth rest

        𝅀   thirty-second rest

the rhythm of *America* we might choose quarter notes, and since the count is one-two-three, we would then put the fraction 3/4 at the beginning of the music. This fraction is called the *time signature*.

In writing music, the numerator of the fraction depends upon the time, but the choice of denominator is purely arbitrary. We could write the rhythm of *America* in any notes, with 3/2, 3/4, or 3/8 time.

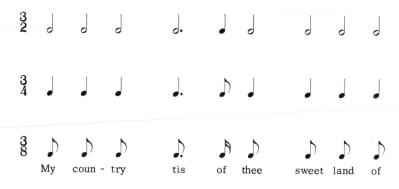

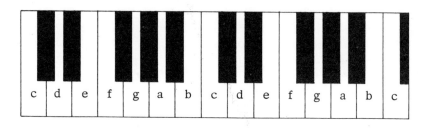

The Piano Keyboard. Each black key has two names. The black key between C and D is called C sharp (C♯) if it is thought of as a half step above C, and D flat (D♭) if it is thought of as a half step lower than D. Likewise the black key between F and G may be F♯ or G♭.

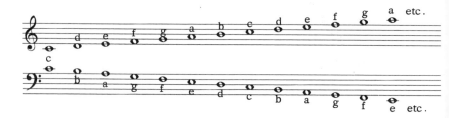

Pitch Notation. For ordinary purposes the notes are arranged on two staffs, each of which has five lines and four spaces; each line and space represents one tone of the scale.

The C in the middle represents appropriately middle C on the piano. The staff above it is called the treble clef, or more accurately the G clef, because the symbol at the left curls its tail around the letter G. The lower staff is called the bass clef, or the F clef, because the two dots by its symbol indicate the key F.

In keys which demand their use, sharps or flats are gathered at the side at the beginning of each line of music. There they serve the double purpose of telling the key in which the composition is written and of showing what keys are to be sharped or flatted.

Change of key in a composition may be indicated by a change in the key signature, or by the introduction of accidentals; that is, the note to be changed is preceded by a sign (flat, sharp, natural) to show how it is to be played. The first method is usually followed when the new key is to last for a long time, the second when it is a matter of only a few chords or measures.

FOR FURTHER EXPLORATION

1. Tap out the rhythm of a number of familiar songs. Can the song be recognized from the rhythm alone?

2. Sing a song, marking time with your feet and rhythm with your hands.

3. Write the rhythm for a song in sixteen measures, using four measures to a phrase.

4. Write a melody for the rhythm you composed. Use not more than three of the ways of making melody described in the text.

5. Sing a number of familiar songs. In how many do you recognize a rhythmic motive? a melodic motive? In each, decide whether the phrases are long or short. Indicate the tempo and dynamics of each.

6. Play the record of a symphony or sonata. Make a profile of it showing (a) rhythmic motive, (b) tempo, (c) dynamics, (d) melodic motive, (e) pattern of the melody if you recognize it, e.g., scale, wave, skip, etc.

7. Sing or play a familiar piece of music; try stopping here and there to see if you are conscious of the "pull" of its tonality.

8. Read through a collection of folk songs, such as *One Hundred Folk Songs of All Nations* or *One Hundred English Folk Songs* (in *The Musician's Library*), and see how many you can discover that are not in the ordinary major scale.

9. Write a melody that is only a rhythmical arrangement of the scale up and down. Write a melody that is only a rhythmical arrangement of the notes of a chord.

10. Study these pieces to see how much their melodies are based on scales:

    a. Grainger, *Country Gardens*

    b. Saint-Saëns, "My heart at thy sweet voice," from *Samson and Delilah*

    c. Rimsky-Korsakov, "Song of India" from *Sadko.*

11. Sing the familiar rounds *Are You Sleeping* (*Frère Jacques*), *Row, Row, Row Your Boat,* and *Three Blind Mice* for counterpoint in three and four voices. Then try singing them all simultaneously. (This will employ twelve people.)

    12. Experiment in counterpoint by singing any song as a round.

    13. Experiment in counterpoint by combining two different tunes.

    14. Listen attentively to recordings of Bach's Inventions and Fugues to hear the counterpoint.

    15. Listen to the accompaniment of each song you hear.

    16. Choose one part of the Mass, such as the Lord's Prayer (Pater Noster), and find recordings which show (*a*) no accompaniment, (*b*) counterpoint, and (*c*) harmony. For (*a*), use Gregorian chant; for (*b*), any of the great contrapuntists: Palestrina, Victoria, Josquin des Prés, etc.; and for (*c*), choose a modern Mass, as that of Brahms, or Berlioz.

CHAPTER 10

ELEMENTS OF LITERATURE

The medium of literature is words, and words, as we know, have both sound and meaning. The word *horse* stands for the sound horse and for the animal horse. The two are always associated and can be separated only by effort of the mind, yet they are quite distinct. And if we are to understand the elements of literature we must study them both. We begin with meaning.

MEANING

Grammar

Knowing a language is not just a matter of knowing words. To get the sense of a passage we must know how the words fit together as well as the meaning of each word. The rules which state how words fit together make up grammar, which is a statement of the accepted sense relationships of words. Each language has its own method of expression, its own way of putting words together to make sense, in short, its own grammar.

Those of us who have always spoken English have no difficulty with the usual simple arrangements of words. But often an author cannot express his idea clearly if he uses only the usual, simple arrangements, and so he distorts. The opening lines of *Paradise Lost* are not easy reading, but through them Milton has made us realize the magnitude of the task he has set himself, and the exalted mood in which he is beginning it.

Of Man's first disobedience, and the fruit
Of that forbidden tree whose mortal taste
Brought death into the World, and all our woe,
With loss of Eden, till one greater Man
Restore us, and regain the blissful Seat,
Sing, Heavenly Muse, that, on the secret top
Of Oreb, or of Sinai, didst inspire
That shepherd who first taught the chosen seed
In the beginning how the heavens and earth
Rose out of Chaos: or, if Sion hill
Delight thee more, and Siloa's brook that flowed
Fast by the oracle of God, I thence
Invoke thy aid to my adventurous song,
That with no middle flight intends to soar
Above the Aonian mount, while it pursues
Things unattempted yet in prose or rhyme.
—JOHN MILTON (1608–1674, English poet and essayist),
Paradise Lost, lines 1–16 (1667)

In this and in most older writings the relations between words are
always in accordance with the established rules of grammar, though it
may be hard to get the sense because of the way words and phrases
are piled on each other. In some more recent poetry the authors do not
write in complete sentences; they get emphasis by a reference here and
an exclamation there, and leave us to put them together, as E. E. Cummings does in *here's a little mouse.*

here's a little mouse) and
what does he think about,i
wonder as over this
floor(quietly with

bright eyes) drifts(nobody
can tell because
Nobody knows, or why
jerks Here &, here,
gr(oo)ving the room's Silence) this like
a littlest
poem a
(with wee ears and see?

tail frisks)

(gonE)

"mouse",
        We are not the same you and

i, since here's a little he
or is
it It
?   (or was something we saw in the mirror)?

therefore we'll kiss;for maybe
what was Disappeared
into ourselves
who   (look).   ,startled
     —E. E. CUMMINGS (1894——, American poet),
        here's a little mouse (1926)[1]

The Connotations of Words

The meanings of words are never simple. Each word has its meaning, but that meaning does not exist alone; it calls up various associations or connotations. Take for instance the various names for the male parent: father, daddy, papa, the old man, my old man, dad, pa, pop, sire, etc. In one sense all have the same meaning, but the connotations are quite different, and there are very few times when one could be substituted for another. The word *steed* has almost the same meaning as *horse* but its connotations are different. *Horse* refers to any member of the species, but the word *steed* implies a certain distinction; it is not an ordinary horse. As an illustration Professor Bradley quotes the lines from Byron:

> "Bring forth the horse!" The horse was brought:
> In truth he was a noble steed!

Interchange the words *horse* and *steed:*

> "Bring forth the steed!" The steed was brought:
> In truth he was a noble horse!

The passage has become ridiculous.

In a piece of good writing the words are chosen so well that we think no other word could have been used, and our impressions are

[1] From *Poems 1923–1954,* Harcourt, Brace and Company. Copyright 1923, 1926, 1944, 1951, 1954 by E. E. Cummings.

determined by them. Take for instance the opening lines of Wordsworth's *She Was a Phantom of Delight:*

> She was a phantom of delight
> When first she gleamed upon my sight;
> A lovely apparition, sent
> To be a moment's ornament.

To the words *phantom, gleamed,* and *apparition* we owe chiefly our
sense of the fragile, almost unearthly, beauty of the girl, and they make
us ready for the concluding lines of this stanza:

> A dancing shape, an image gay,
> To haunt, to startle, and way-lay.

In the same poem we have a glaring example of a word which to
most of us today has the wrong connotations. The last stanza begins:

> And now I see with eye serene
> The very pulse of the machine;

Wordsworth was certainly thinking of a complex organization which
was working efficiently, but the connotations are of something impersonal, cold, and mechanical.

The best way to study the connotations of a word is to substitute a
word with a similar meaning and then try to analyze the difference.
Suppose in the Wordsworth poem you read *dawned* instead of
gleamed, how does it change the meaning of the line?

Figures of Speech

Words are symbols and as symbols have no meaning in themselves;
their only meaning is what is given them by convention. Moreover, a
symbol can never be specific; it is always abstract or general. We call
words abstract or concrete as they signify abstractions or concrete
objects; we say *truth* and *honor* are abstract, *dog* and *lilac* are concrete. But these concrete words are themselves abstractions in that they
stand for a whole class of objects. The dog may be any one of a large
number of species, of any known color. And when we say *lilac,* we may
mean any variety of lilac, in any color, or any one of the other sensations concerned with lilac: its fragrance, the shape of the flower or the
leaf, the bush on which the flower grows.

This abstractness of words becomes very clear if it is compared
with the necessary concreteness of the other arts. Obviously, a sculptor

cannot carve the abstraction *dog;* he must carve a dog of certain species, age, and size. The painter cannot paint *lilac;* he must paint a white lilac or a purple lilac, a plant in full blossom, beginning to fade, in bud, or without blossoms. He cannot paint what we mean by *lilac,* for that is essentially an abstraction. In the same way, the actor or the musician can make only concrete tones, but in describing his tones the poet can use only abstractions; the poet will speak of "clear, ringing tones," but the actor or the musician must make certain definite tones, just as the sculptor must carve a certain kind of dog or the painter portray a certain species of lilac.

Because of this indefiniteness of words there have grown up certain deviations or roundabout methods of expression that attempt to make more clear the exact meaning of the words. If, for instance, Coleridge says the ice is green, he leaves it to us to imagine the shade of green; but he gives the exact shade when he says:

> And ice, mast-high, came floating by,
> As green as emerald.
> —*The Ancient Mariner*

He can make us realize more clearly the color of hair, the feeling of fear, and the sound of the departing souls by stating his point indirectly:

> Her lips were red, her looks were free,
> Her locks were yellow as gold:
> Her skin was as white as leprosy,
> The Nightmare Life-in-Death was she,
> Who thicks man's blood with cold.
>
> * * *
>
> Fear at my heart, as at a cup,
> My life-blood seemed to sip!
>
> * * *
>
> The souls did from their bodies fly,—
> They fled to bliss or woe!
> And every soul, it passed me by,
> Like the whizz of my cross-bow!
> —*The Ancient Mariner*

Such indirect methods of expression are called figures of speech.

Simile and Metaphor. The most common and therefore the most important of the figures of speech are the simile and the metaphor.

Both depend upon the comparison of one thing to another. The simile puts in the word of comparison; the metaphor leaves it out. The simile says: *The ice was as green as emerald;* the metaphor says: *The ice was emerald.* The simile says: *Fear was like a monster which sipped my blood;* the metaphor says: *Fear sipped my blood.* The simile would say: *Thou, Peter, art like a rock;* the metaphor says: *Thou art Peter, and upon this rock I will build my church* (Matt., 16:18).

The simile says:

> And he shall be like a Tree planted by the streams of water,
> That bringeth forth its fruit in its season,
> Whose leaf also doth not wither;
> And whatsoever he doeth shall prosper.
> The wicked are not so;
> But are like the Chaff which the wind driveth away.
>
> Ps. 1

The metaphor says:

> The Lord is my shepherd;
> I shall not want.
> He maketh me to lie down in green pastures:
> He leadeth me beside the still waters.
> He restoreth my soul:
> He leadeth me in the paths of righteousness for his name's sake.
>
> —Ps. 23

Tennyson uses both metaphor and simile to make us see the eagle:

> He clasps the crag with hooked hands:
> Close to the sun in lonely lands,
> Ring'd with the azure world, he stands.
>
> The wrinkled sea beneath him crawls;
> He watches from his mountain walls,
> And like a thunderbolt he falls.
>
> —ALFRED, LORD TENNYSON (1809–1892, English
> poet),
> *The Eagle* (1851)

It is metaphor when he speaks of the *hands* of the eagle and when he says the sea *crawls.* It is simile when he says the eagle falls *like a thunderbolt.*

Keats uses metaphor in the first eight lines of his sonnet *On First*

Looking into Chapman's Homer, when he identifies poetry with rich
kingdoms. In the last six lines he uses two similes as he tries to tell how
he felt when he read Chapman's translation of Homer: first he felt
like an astronomer who discovered a new planet, and second he felt
like Cortez when he discovered the Pacific.

> Much have I travell'd in the realms of gold,
> And many goodly states and kingdoms seen;
> Round many western islands have I been
> Which bards in fealty to Apollo hold.
> Oft of one wide expanse had I been told
> That deep-brow'd Homer ruled as his demesne;
> Yet did I never breathe its pure serene
> Till I heard Chapman speak out loud and bold:
> Then felt I like some watcher of the skies
> When a new planet swims into his ken;
> Or like stout Cortez when with eagle eyes
> He stared at the Pacific—and all his men
> Look'd at each other with a wild surmise—
> Silent, upon a peak in Darien.
>   —JOHN KEATS (1795–1821, English poet),
>   *On First Looking into Chapman's Homer* (1816)

Many of our most common expressions involve similes or metaphors.
We say one person has a "heart of gold" and another is as "slow as
molasses in January." Both simile and metaphor are used very commonly by all people at all times. It is hard to find a paragraph of prose
or verse that does not contain either a simile or a metaphor. From the
nature of the two, the metaphor is used most often in short, vigorous
passages, whereas the simile may be expanded to any length.

Both simile and metaphor are based on comparison. In each, comparison is made of one thing to something essentially unlike it for the
purpose of showing one point of resemblance. The power of either
figure of speech rises of course from the implications and suggestions
of the comparison. In *A Song for Simeon,* T. S. Eliot has a simile
about an old man's life,

> My life is light, waiting for the death wind,
> Like a feather on the back of my hand.[2]

---

[2] From *Collected Poems,* 1909–1935, published by Harcourt, Brace and Company, Inc.

By his comparison, Eliot emphasizes the everyday character of the scene, the sense of the nearness of death in everyday life. Another time Eliot compares an evening to a patient on an operating table.

> Let us go then, you and I
> When the evening is spread out against the sky
> Like a patient etherized upon a table.
> —T. S. Eliot (1888———, American poet),
> *The Love Song of J. Alfred Prufrock* (1917)[3]

Imagery

From the meaning and connotations of words it is but a step to the imagery of literature. Imagery is a general name for the functioning of the imagination in the formation of images; an image is a mental duplication of a sense impression. Suppose, for instance, we read the first stanza of Keats's *The Eve of St. Agnes:*

> St. Agnes' Eve—Ah, bitter chill it was!
> The owl, for all his feathers, was a-cold;
> The hare limp'd trembling through the frozen grass,
> And silent was the flock in woolly fold:
> Numb were the Beadsman's fingers, while he told
> His rosary, and while his frosted breath,
> Like pious incense from a censer old,
> Seem'd taking flight for heaven, without a death,
> Past the sweet Virgin's picture, while his prayer he saith.
> —John Keats (1795–1821, English poet),
> *The Eve of St. Agnes*, 262–270 (1820)

Not only do we understand the words and the meaning; we get a great many images; the owl hunched down in his feathers, the hare limping through the grass, the beadsman's numb fingers, the frosted breath, even the silence of the sheep. To some people these are almost like a real experience, and for everyone they have a certain vividness as they call to mind the sensations described.

Imagery is not the same as figurative language. A figure of speech usually calls up an image, and probably for this reason the word *imagery* is sometimes limited to figures of speech. As defined here, an image has reference to the sense impression evoked; a figure of speech, to the method of statement by which a sense impression may be evoked or an idea clarified. Moreover, clear images may be aroused without

[3] *Ibid.*

figurative language. In the stanza just quoted from *The Eve of St. Agnes,* the first six lines contain no figures of speech, but the images are very clear.

The Kinds of Image. Since images are duplications of sense impressions, the kinds of image are determined by the kinds of sense impression we can receive. There are obviously the impressions from the five senses: sight, sound, smell, taste, touch; and, in addition, impressions of motion, heat and cold, pain; and organic sensations such as hunger and thirst, nausea, a sense of stuffiness or its opposite; and the general vague feelings of vigor, repletion, drowsiness, discomfort, fatigue, weakness, and the like. Each of these images has as many varieties as the sensations themselves. For convenience, the more important images may be summarized in this table:

1. Images of sight—visual images
    a. Line
    b. Value
    c. Color
    d. Texture
    e. Volume
    f. Perspective
2. Images of sound—auditory images
    a. Noises
    b. Musical sounds
3. Images of motion—motor or kinesthetic images
4. Images of touch—tactile images
    a. Contact
    b. Pressure
5. Images of heat and cold—thermal images
6. Images of taste—gustatory images
7. Images of smell—olfactory images

The images of pain and the images from organic sensations are not included in this list because they occur rarely.

Many images involve more than one sense. For example, roughness or smoothness, hardness or softness, and stickiness come from touch and pressure plus motion; sharpness and bluntness, from pressure and pain; clamminess and wetness, from pressure and temperature.

Images have been listed in the order in which they are most commonly experienced; that is, the average person has visual images more readily then auditory, and auditory images more readily than motor. This does not mean, however, that there are not very wide individual differences. To the musician, auditory images are probably clearer than visual, and some people are more conscious of motor images than of either auditory or visual. In everything that has to do with imagery, the individual must be reckoned with, and it must be recognized that no two persons will have exactly the same images.

Almost all the kinds of images may be illustrated in *The Eve of St. Agnes.*

Visual images. The picture is primarily in line when Keats says:

> The carved angels, ever eager-eyed,
> Star'd, where upon their heads the cornice rests,
> With hair blown back, and wings put cross-wise on their breasts.

In the following stanza, it is in light and dark:

> Out went the taper as she hurried in;
> Its little smoke, in pallid moonshine, died:

When he describes the moonlight coming through the window of Madeline's bedroom, he uses color:

> Full on this casement shone the wintry moon,
> And threw warm gules on Madeline's fair breast,
> As down she knelt for heaven's grace and boon;
> Rose-bloom fell on her hands, together prest,
> And on her silver cross soft amethyst,
> And on her hair a glory, like a saint:
> She seem'd a splendid angel, newly drest,
> Save wings, for heaven:—

Images of sound may be images of noise or of musical tone. *Images of noise* may be found in these lines:

>   —and the thronged resort
> Of whisperers in anger, or in sport;
> He ventures in: let no buzzed whisper tell:
> Shuffling along with ivory-headed wand,

Images of musical tone

> The boisterous, midnight, festive clarion,
> The kettle-drum, and far-heard clarinet,
> The silver, snarling trumpets 'gan to chide.

We have the absence of sounds as the lovers escape from her home, except for the one sound at the end as the door turns on its hinges:

> They glide, like phantoms, into the wide hall;
> Like phantoms to the iron porch they glide;
> Where lay the Porter, in uneasy sprawl,
> With a huge empty flagon by his side:
> The wakeful bloodhound rose, and shook his hide,
> But his sagacious eye an inmate owns:
> By one, and one, the bolts full easy slide:—
> The chains lie silent on the footworn stones;—
> The key turns, and the door upon its hinges groans.

Images of motion portray any kind of movement, whether it be the stealthy escape of the lovers from the hall or the rush and bustle of preparation for a party:

> And so it chanced, for many a door was wide,
> From hurry to and fro.

Keats has fewer *images of touch* than of the other kinds. However, he does speak of Madeline

> . . . trembling in her soft and chilly nest,

and of Porphyro

> Brushing the cobwebs with his lofty plume;

and the beadsman:

> Another way he went, and soon among
> Rough ashes sat he for his soul's reprieve.

Images of heat and cold abound in all literature. The cold in *The Eve of St. Agnes* is very vividly expressed in the first stanza of the poem already quoted, as well as in the description of the little room to which Angela conducted Porphyro, where

> He found him in a little moonlight room,
> Pale, latticed, chill, and silent as a tomb,

or in the description of the bed of Madeline already quoted. This chilly bed is contrasted with the warmth as Madeline goes to sleep:

> . . . the poppied warmth of sleep oppress'd
> Her soothed limbs, and soul fatigued away.

Images of taste and smell are very close kin. The psychologists tell us that there are only four tastes that are separable from smell: sweet, sour, bitter, and salt; and some have claimed that there is no such thing as a definite image of smell in the sense in which we have clear and distinct visual images. However, one seems to get images of both taste and smell from such a stanza as this:

> And still she slept an azure-lidded sleep,
> In blanched linen, smooth, and lavendered,
> While he from forth the closet brought a heap
> Of candied apple, quince, and plum, and gourd;
> With jellies soother than the creamy curd,
> And lucent syrops, tinct with cinnamon;
> Manna and dates, in argosy transferr'd
> From Fez; and spiced dainties, every one,
> From silken Samarcand to cedared Lebanon.

Even better images of smell are found in Keats's *Ode to a Nightingale,*

> I cannot see what flowers are at my feet,
> Nor what soft incense hangs upon the boughs,
> But, in embalmed darkness, guess each sweet
> Wherewith the seasonable month endows
> The grass, the thicket, and the fruit-tree wild;
> White hawthorn, and the pastoral eglantine;
> Fast-fading violets cover'd up in leaves;
> And mid-May's eldest child,
> The coming musk-rose, full of dewy wine,
> The murmurous haunt of flies on summer eves.

It is worth while, however, to notice that many images that are carelessly considered to be images of touch, taste, and smell do not involve these sensations. With the *jellies soother than the creamy curd,* Keats is conscious primarily of touch and motion, and in the syrops, of their transparent beauty.

SOUND OF LITERATURE

Elements of Sound

The sound of words is important in making the total sense, for no two words or sounds ever have exactly the same meaning. In *The Two Gentlemen of Verona* the host sings a little song that begins:

> Who is Silvia? What is she,
>   That all our swains commend her?
> Holy, fair, and wise is she;
>   The heaven such grace did lend her,
> That she might admired be.
>> —WILLIAM SHAKESPEARE (1564–1616, English poet
>> and dramatist),
>> *The Two Gentlemen of Verona,* IV, ii, 39–43
>> (ca. 1592)

Here the name Silvia means as little as a word could mean; it is a woman's name, and nothing more. But change the name Silvia to almost any other woman's name—Alice, Peggy, Margaret, Bernice, Genevieve, Laura, Hortense—and the effect is spoiled; the charm is gone.

Or take a single line from Milton:

> And I shall shortly be with them that rest.
>> —JOHN MILTON (1608–1674, English poet and essayist),
>> *Samson Agonistes,* line 598 (1671)

Change the sound, keeping as nearly as possible the same sense: *shortly* means *soon; them* has the same meaning as *those;* and *that* as *who;* in fact, *those who* is a more common English idiom than *them that.* Make the substitutions, and the line reads:

> And I shall soon be with those who rest.

There is no appreciable difference in sense but the line is no longer poetry.

The study of literature, when considered as sound, falls into two divisions that may be illustrated by the lines just quoted. The first division is *rhythm.* Something is lost when *soon* is substituted for *shortly,* because the word of two syllables sounds better than the word of one syllable. If we say "Who is Genevieve, what is she," the smooth flow of the words is interrupted. The second division is the sound of the letters, or the combination of sounds known as *tone color* and *rhyme.* In the four lines from Shakespeare, the *s* sound of *Silvia* is repeated in *she, swains* and *grace.* And we like the rhyme in *commend her* and *lend her, she* and *be.* In the line from Milton, *s* sounds are repeated in *shall* and *shortly, t* sounds in *them* and *that.* These are followed by the combination of *s* and *t* sounds in the word *rest.*

Rhythm and tone color therefore are the headings under which literature is discussed when it is considered primarily from the point of view of sound.

Tone Color—Definition

The term *tone color* in literature is borrowed from music, because the writer gets effects somewhat comparable to those of different instruments by the sounds of the words or letters he uses. Compare Blake's Introduction to *Songs of Innocence* with the opening lines of Vachel Lindsay's *The Congo* for contrast in tone color. The first seems to have the timbre of a high-pitched, sensitive, delicate instrument, such as the violin; this matches the spirit of the piece. The second has the sound of a deep, heavy instrument like a drum or a tuba which can make a great deal of noise but is not precise; the sound alone reminds one of the untutored rhythms of savages.

> Piping down the valleys wild,
>> Piping songs of pleasant glee,
> On a cloud I saw a child,
>> And he laughing said to me:
>
> "Pipe a song about a Lamb!"
>> So I piped with merry cheer.
> "Piper, pipe that song again;"
>> So I piped; he wept to hear.
>
> "Drop thy pipe, thy happy pipe;
>> Sing thy songs of happy cheer!"
> So I sung the same again,
>> While he wept with joy to hear.
>
> "Piper, sit thee down and write
>> In a book, that all may read."
> So he vanished from my sight,
>> And I plucked a hollow reed,
>
> And I made a rural pen,
>> And I stained the water clear,
> And I wrote my happy songs
>> Every child may joy to hear.
>> —WILLIAM BLAKE (1757–1827, English poet,
>> painter, and engraver),
>> Introduction to *Songs of Innocence* (1787)

Fat black bucks in a wine-barrel room,
Barrel-house kings, with feet unstable,
Sagged and reeled and pounded on the table,
Pounded on the table,
Beat an empty barrel with the handle of a broom,
Hard as they were able,
Boom, boom, BOOM,
With a silk umbrella and the handle of a broom,
Boomlay, boomlay, boomlay, BOOM.

> —VACHEL LINDSAY (1879–1931, American poet),
> *The Congo*, opening lines (1914)[4]

Repetition of Words, Sentences, or Phrases

All effects of tone color depend on repetition. It may be repetition (1) of words, sentences, or phrases, or (2) of single sounds.

Repetition of Words. The simplest and clearest example of tone color is the repetition of words. The repetition of a word, though it may become wearisome, is one of the most effective devices in literature. In the Introduction to *Songs of Innocence,* for example, the reiteration of the word *pipe* emphasizes the childlike quality of the verse. In the famous passage from Paul's First Epistle to the Corinthians the cumulative effect produced by the repetition of the word *charity* is tremendous. All the emotion in the passage seems to be bound up in that one word.

Though I speak with the tongues of men and of angels, and have not charity, I am become as sounding brass, or a tinkling symbol. And though I have the gift of prophecy, and understand all mysteries, and all knowledge; and though I have all faith, so that I could remove mountains, and have not charity, I am nothing. And though I bestow all my goods to feed the poor, and though I give my body to be burned, and have not charity, it profiteth me nothing. Charity suffereth long, and is kind; charity envieth not; charity vaunteth not itself, is not puffed up, doth not behave itself unseemly, seeketh not her own, is not easily provoked, thinketh no evil; rejoiceth not in iniquity, but rejoiceth in the truth; beareth all things, believeth all things, hopeth all things, endureth all things. Charity never faileth; but whether there be prophecies, they shall fail; whether there be tongues, they shall cease; whether there be knowledge, it shall vanish away. For we know in part, and we prophesy in part. But when that which is perfect is come, then that which is in part shall be done away.

[4] By permission of the Macmillan Company, publishers.

When I was a child, I spake as a child, I understood as a child, I thought as a child; but when I became a man, I put away childish things. For now we see through a glass, darkly; but then face to face; now I know in part; but then shall I know even as also I am known. And now abideth faith, hope, charity, these three; but the greatest of these is charity.

—I Cor. 13

Repetition of Phrases or Sentences. Often a group of words or a sentence is repeated. In the last act of *The Merchant of Venice*, Lorenzo and Jessica have arrived at Belmont and are waiting for the return of Portia and the others. As they wait they beguile the time by playing a game in which they picture other famous lovers. Each speech begins with the words *In such a night,* the phrase serves as a musical motive and as a constant reminder of the beauty of the scene.

LORENZO:

    The moon shines bright. In such a night as this,
    When the sweet wind did gently kiss the trees
    And they did make no noise, in such a night
    Troilus methinks mounted the Troyan walls,
    And sigh'd his soul toward the Grecian tents,
    Where Cressid lay that night.

JESSICA:

            In such a night
    Did Thisbe fearfully o'ertrip the dew,
    And saw the lion's shadow ere himself
    And ran dismay'd away.

LORENZO:

            In such a night
    Stood Dido with a willow in her hand
    Upon the wild sea banks, and waft her love
    To come again to Carthage.

JESSICA:

            In such a night
    Medea gathered the enchanted herbs
    That did renew old Aeson.

LORENZO:

            In such a night
    Did Jessica steal from the wealthy Jew,
    And with an unthrift love did run from Venice
    As far as Belmont.

JESSICA:

> In such a night
> Did young Lorenzo swear he lov'd her well,
> Stealing her soul with many vows of faith
> And ne'er a true one.

LORENZO:

> In such a night
> Did pretty Jessica, like a little shrew
> Slander her love, and he forgave it her.

JESSICA:

> I would out-night you, did no body come;
> But, hark, I hear the footing of a man.
> —SHAKESPEARE,
> *Merchant of Venice,* V, i, 1–24 (ca. 1595)

In many of his poems Edgar Allan Poe is almost hypnotized by the sound effects to be obtained from repetition. In *The Raven,* the refrain comes like a tolling bell, "Nevermore." *Ulalume* is constructed with elaborate repetition; in each stanza the third line repeats and varies the second, and the last two lines repeat and vary the two lines preceding.

> The skies they were ashen and sober;
>   The leaves they were crisped and sere,
>   The leaves they were withering and sere;
> It was night in the lonesome October
>   Of my most immemorial year;
> It was hard by the dim lake of Auber,
>   In the misty mid region of Weir:
> It was down by the dank tarn of Auber,
>   In the ghoul-haunted woodland of Weir.
> —EDGAR ALLAN POE (1809–1849, American poet),
>   *Ulalume,* opening stanza (1847)

When a phrase or a sentence recurs at intervals in the same or nearly the same words, it is called a refrain. The refrain usually comes at the end of a stanza.

> Sigh no more, ladies, sigh no more,
>   Men were deceivers ever,
> One foot in sea and one on shore,
>   To one thing constant never.
> Then sigh not so, but let them go,

> And be you blithe and bonny,
> Converting all your sounds of woe
> Into Hey nonny nonny.
>
> Sing no more ditties, sing no moe,
>   Of dumps so dull and heavy;
> The fraud of men was ever so,
>   Since summer first was leafy.
> Then sigh not so, but let them go,
>   And be you blithe and bonny,
> Converting all your sounds of woe
>   Into Hey nonny nonny.
>   —SHAKESPEARE,
>   *Much Ado about Nothing,* II, iii, 64 ff. (ca.
>   ¯1599)

Alliteration, Assonance, and Consonance

More subtle examples of tone color are found when single sounds are repeated. These sounds are usually single letters. They are not always the same letters, however, for often two letters have the same sound (*c*orner, *k*ick), and a single letter has two sounds (*c*orner, *c*edar). Besides rhyme there are three types of tone color based on the repetition of single sounds: ¯alliteration, consonance, and assonance.

Alliteration. Alliteration is the repetition of accented sounds that begin words: *Peter Piper picked* a *peck* of *pickled peppers.* When used in extremes, as in the Peter Piper rhyme, alliteration may become obnoxious, but when well used it is pleasing. The use of alliteration is almost universal.

> Duncan is in his grave;
> After life's *f*itful *f*ever he sleeps well.
>   —SHAKESPEARE,
>   *Macbeth,* III, ii, 22–23 (1606)

In the short poem from *Much Ado* we have alliteration in *s*ea and *s*hore, *b*lithe and *b*onny, and also in *d*itties, *d*umps, *d*ull. Notice the alliteration in the paragraph quoted from Vachel Lindsay's *The Congo:* *b*lack, *b*ucks, *b*arrel, *b*eat, *b*room, *b*oom, *b*oomlay.

Consonance. Consonance is a general term for the effects produced by the repetition of accented consonant sounds when one of them is not at the beginning of a word. Often both consonants occur at the ends of the words, as in od*ds* and en*ds,* or bla*ck* and bu*ck*, stru*ts* and fre*ts.*

Consonance is not so nearly obvious as alliteration and is not so common, but it produces many subtle effects. When, for instance, Coriolanus greets his mother,

> My gracious silence, hail!

the repetition of the *s* sounds seems to emphasize her dignity, and his respect for her.

Assonance. Assonance is the effect obtained from the repetition of accented vowel sounds, as in f*oo*lish, cr*oo*ning; r*a*ce, m*a*ke; fr*ee* and *ea*sy; m*a*d as a h*a*tter. The effects to be gained from assonance are delicate and varied.

> Break, break, break,
> On thy cold gray stones, O Sea!
> And I would that my tongue could utter
> The thoughts that arise in me.
>   —ALFRED, LORD TENNYSON (1809–1892, English
>   poet),
>   *Break, Break, Break* (1842)

In the second line of this stanza, for example, the words do not themselves express any great grief, yet we have a sense almost of desolation. The explanation is to be found in assonance. *Oh* is universally a cry of grief and mourning; the person who cannot be consoled laments *Oh, oh, oh.* Tennyson uses the exclamation only once, but he repeats the sound two other times in the short line:

> On thy c*o*ld gray st*o*nes, O Sea!

Rhyme

Two words are said to rhyme when they are identical in sound from the vowel of the accented syllable to the end, provided the sounds that precede the accented vowel are not identical. *Cry, buy; face, place; sorrow, tomorrow; running, cunning*—these words rhyme. *Wright, write, right* do not rhyme because the letters before the accented vowel do not differ in sound. *Romantic* and *chromatic* do not rhyme because they are not identical in the syllables following the accented vowel. A rhyme is said to be "masculine" if the rhyming portion of the words is a single syllable; "feminine" if the rhyming portion is more than one syllable. *Cry, buy; face, place* are masculine rhymes; *sorrow, tomorrow; cunning, running* are feminine rhymes.

Rhyme usually comes at the end of a line and follows a set pattern. Rhyme is indicated by the letters of the alphabet, *a* being used for the first rhyming word, *b* for the second, *c* for the third, etc.

My heart leaps up when I behold	*a*
A rainbow in the sky:	*b*
So was it when my life began;	*c*
So is it now I am a man,	*c*
So be it when I shall grow old	*a*
Or let me die!	*b*
The Child is father of the Man:	*c*
And I could wish my days to be	*d*
Bound each to each by natural piety.	*d*

— WILLIAM WORDSWORTH (1770–1850, English poet),
My Heart Leaps Up (1802)

If a poem is divided into stanzas the same rhyme will usually be used in each stanza. In the Introduction to *Songs of Innocence* all the stanzas rhyme *abcb* except the first, which rhymes *abab*. In *Sigh No More, Ladies,* the verse rhymes *abab,* and the refrain *cdcd.*

There is no rhyme in the passage from Shakespeare's *Merchant of Venice* or in Lindsay's *Congo.*

Phrasing

Phrasing is found in all literature, as in all music; and it is the same in literature as in music. It is a grouping, a sense unit followed by a pause, which in literature is usually indicated by punctuation.

To a certain extent all speech is rhythmic in that it is grouped in phrases; only a child just learning to read gives the same emphasis to every word. However, some speech is more rhythmic than other speech; the term *rhythmic* is usually reserved for that speech in which the phrasing is pleasing to the ear.

Compare these examples for their rhythms. In the first, one has a disagreeable sense of being constantly jerked up; he cannot get into the swing of the sentence; there are no pauses. The other two are in contrast very rhythmic.

Mr. Davies does not let his learning cause him to treat the paintings as material only to be studied by the Egyptologist with a critical and scientific eye.

* * *

The young spirit has awakened out of Eternity, and knows not what we mean by Time; as yet Time is no fast-hurrying stream, but a sportful sunlit ocean; years to the child are as ages. . . . Sleep on, thou fair Child, for thy long rough journey is at hand! A little while, and thou too shalt sleep no more, but thy very dreams shall be mimic battles; thou too, with old Arnauld, wilt have to say in stern patience: "Rest? Rest? Shall I not have all Eternity to rest in?"

> —CARLYLE (1795–1881, English philosopher and essayist),
> *Sartor Resartus* (1833)

And as we dwell, we living things, in our isle of terror and under the imminent hand of death, God forbid it should be man the erected, the reasoner, the wise in his own eyes—God forbid it should be man that wearies in well-doing, that despairs of unrewarded effort, or utters the language of complaint. Let it be enough for faith, that the whole creation groans in mortal frailty, strives with unconquerable constancy: Surely not all in vain.

> —STEVENSON (1850–1894, Scotch poet, novelist, and essayist),
> *Pulvis et Umbra*

These examples of phrasing are all from prose, but phrasing is found in poetry as well as in prose. Often the phrase is practically synonymous with the line.

> Shall I, wasting in despair,
> Die, because a woman's fair?
> Or make pale my cheeks with care,
> 'Cause another's rosy are?
> Be she fairer than the day,
> Or the flowery meads in May!
>   If she be not so to me,
>   What care I how fair she be?
> —GEORGE WITHER (1588–1667, English poet),
> *Shall I Wasting in Despair*

More often the phrase is not synonymous with the line. It may end in the middle of a line, or it may carry over from line to line. In the last lines of *Ulysses,* note how Tennyson varies both the length of the phrase and its relation to the line:

>   Come, my friends.
> 'Tis not too late to seek a newer world.
> Push off, and sitting well in order smite

The sounding furrows; for my purpose holds
To sail beyond the sunset, and the baths
Of all the western stars, until I die.
It may be that the gulfs will wash us down;
It may be we shall touch the Happy Isles,
And see the great Achilles, whom we knew.
Tho' much is taken, much abides; and tho'
We are not now that strength which in old days
Moved earth and heaven, that which we are, we are,—
One equal temper of heroic hearts,
Made weak by time and fate, but strong in will
To strive, to seek, to find, and not to yield.

Rhythms of phrase are irregular; they cannot be traced in definite patterns. They depend on the piling up of phrase on phrase rather than on the regular recurrence of individual accents. Many attempts have been made to find definite patterns in phrase rhythms, but such attempts have largely resulted in failure. Of these points, however, we can be fairly certain:

1. Phrases are *similar,* though not identical in length.

> And as we dwell,
> we living things
>
> The young spirit has awakened out of Eternity,
> and knows not what we mean of Time

2. They are often *parallel* in structure. Similar thoughts are expressed in similar language.

> God forbid it should be man—
> God forbid it should be man
>
> To strive,
> to seek,
> to find
> and not to yield.

3. In poetry there is usually a pause or *caesura* within the line except in the case of short poems which have short lines.

4. They make frequent use of cadence. The word *cadence,* which comes from the Latin *cadere,* "to fall," refers to a "falling" sound, as when one is coming to a close. Cadence is illustrated in all the selections quoted except the first prose passage. It is especially noticeable in the quotations from Carlyle and Stevenson.

Free Verse and Hebrew Meter

Free verse is built on the rhythm of phrase. Its unit is the *strophe,* which is composed of a number of phrases subtly balanced so as to constitute a complete cadence.

> They set the slave free, striking off his chains—
> Then he was as much of a slave as ever.
> He was still chained to servility,
> He was still manacled to indolence and sloth,
> He was still bound by fear and superstition,
> By ignorance, suspicion, and savagery—
> His slavery was not in the chains,
> But in himself—
>
> They can only set free men free—
> And there is no need of that:
> Free men set themselves free.
> > —JAMES OPPENHEIM (1882–1932, American poet),
> > *The Slave* (1914)[5]

Hebrew meter is often classed with free verse; it is based on parallelism of phrases, one clause or phrase being balanced against another of similar structure. It is, of course, found most conspicuously in the Bible.

> Purge me with hyssop, and I shall be clean:
> Wash me, and I shall be whiter than snow.
> Make me to hear joy and gladness;
> That the bones which thou hast broken may rejoice.
> Hide thy face from my sins,
> And blot out all mine iniquities.
> Create in me a clean heart, O God:
> And renew a right spirit within me.
> Cast me not away from thy presence;
> And take not thy holy spirit from me.
> > —Ps. 51, 7–11

Meter

English is a language of pronounced word accent. Words of more than one syllable have at least one accent. Words such as *dismay, avoid, contend* have the accent on the second syllable. Words like *saying, duple, accent* have the accent on the first syllable. A few words

[5] Reprinted from *Songs for the New Age* by permission of Mr. Arthur B. Spingarn, Executor of the estate of James Oppenheim.

of two syllables, such as *baseball,* or *blackguard,* have accents on both syllables. *November, lemonade, vertical, butterfly* have three syllables each. In *November* the accent is on the second, in *lemonade* on the third, and in *vertical* on the first syllable. *Butterfly* has accents on the first and third syllables. *Commemorate* has four syllables, with a primary accent on the second syllable and a secondary accent on the last syllable.

Sometimes a poet puts words together so that these accents come in a regular order. Take, for instance, the lines quoted from Tennyson's *Ulysses.* The accented and unaccented syllables tend to alternate, first an unaccented, then an accented syllable. The last two lines are absolutely regular.

> Made weak by time and fate, but strong in will
> To strive, to seek, to find, and not to yield.

This pattern is not kept with absolute regularity throughout the poem, but it is sufficiently regular for us to recognize it.

Any such regular recurrence of accent is called *meter.* The meter in which an unaccented syllable is followed by an accented syllable is called *iambic.* It is so common as almost to be the universal meter of English poetry, but there are other meters. The accent may come on the first syllable instead of the second.

> Jenny kissed me when we met,
>   Jumping from the chair she sat in;
> Time, you thief, who love to get
>   Sweets into your list, put that in:
> Say I'm weary, say I'm sad,
>   Say that health and wealth have missed me,
> Say I'm growing old, but add,
>   Jenny kissed me.
>   —LEIGH HUNT (1784–1859, English journalist, essay-
>   ist, and poet),
>   *Rondeau* (1838)

Or the accent may fall on every third instead of every second syllable. It may fall on the third, sixth and ninth syllables as in *Annabel Lee,*

> It was many and many a year ago,
>   In a kingdom by the sea,
> That a maiden there lived, whom you may know

By the name of Annabel Lee;
And this maiden she lived with no other thought
Than to love and be loved by me.
                    —POE,
                    Annabel Lee (1849)

It may come on the first, fourth, and seventh syllables as in these lines:

Just for a handful of silver he left us,
    Just for a riband to stick in his coat—
Found the one gift of which fortune bereft us,
    Lost all the others she lets us devote;
        —ROBERT BROWNING (1812–1889, English poet),
        The Lost Leader (1845)

Each of these meters is identified by the pattern of accented and unaccented syllables, and the unit is called a foot.

The names and symbols of the meters may be tabulated, with *x* for an unaccented syllable, and *a* for an accented one.

iambic: x a

x   a   x   a   x   a
To strive, to seek, to find

trochaic: a x

a x   a   x
Jenny kissed me

anapestic: x x a

x x   a x x   a x x   a x a
It was many and many a year ago

dactylic: a x x

a   x x   a   x   x a   x
Just for a handful of silver

Spondee. A spondaic foot, called a *spondee,* is composed of two accented syllables. For obvious reasons the spondee cannot be used in an entire poem or even in an entire line. It is one of the important ways of introducing variety into a line. It emphasizes by slowing up the speed of the line. Milton, for instance, uses spondees in *Paradise Lost* to stress the enormous size of Satan:

So stretched out huge in length the Arch-*Fiend lay.*
                    —MILTON,
                    Paradise Lost, I, 209 (1667)

And Tennyson emphasizes the slow passage of time in *Ulysses* by substituting spondees for iambs.

> The long *day wanes;* the slow *moon climbs;* the deep
> *Moans round* with many voices.
>
> —TENNYSON,
> *Ulysses,* 55 (1842)

Line Length. The length of a line is named according to the number of feet in it.

One foot ....monometer
Two feet ....dimeter
Three feet ....trimeter
Four feet ....tetrameter
Five feet ....pentameter
Six feet ....hexameter
Seven feet ....heptameter
Eight feet ....octameter

Trimeter, tetrameter, and pentameter are the line lengths most commonly used. In the lines just quoted, *Ulysses* is in pentameter lines; *The Lost Leader* in tetrameter; *Rondeau* in tetrameter until the last line, which is dimeter; *Annabel Lee* alternates tetrameter and trimeter. Ordinarily a line is designated by the kind of foot and the number of feet in a line, as iambic tetrameter, dactylic dimeter, etc.

Verse Form

A poet usually decides on the kind of meter, the line length, and the rhyme scheme he wishes, and sticks pretty closely to that combination throughout his poem. This is called the verse form. Since the passage we read from *Ulysses* is in iambic pentameter without rhyme, we expect the entire poem to be in that verse form, and it is. And we expect Poe to have stanzas of six lines of anapestic verse alternating tetrameter and trimeter, with the even lines rhyming. A poet may make a new verse form, but usually he does not. Some forms have been used so much that they have been given names by which they may be easily identified. The number of named forms is too great for a complete list to be given here, but a few of the more common terms are included:

1. General terms
   a. *Couplet:* any stanza of two lines.
   b. *Triplet:* any stanza of three lines.
   c. *Quatrain:* any stanza of four lines.
2. Specific terms
   a. *Heroic couplet:* two lines of iambic pentameter rhymed.
      i. Closed: the two lines express a complete thought.

> Hope springs eternal in the human breast:
> Man never is, but always to be, blest.
> > —ALEXANDER POPE (1688–1744, English poet),
> > *An Essay on Man* (1733)

     ii. Open: the thought runs on from line to line.

> A thing of beauty is a joy for ever:
> Its loveliness increases; it will never
> Pass into nothingness; but still will keep
> A bower quiet for us, and a sleep
> Full of sweet dreams, and health, and quiet breathing.
> > —JOHN KEATS (1795–1821, English poet),
> > *Endymion* (1818)

   b. *Ballad meter:* four lines of iambic verse alternating tetrameter and trimeter. Rhyme *abab,* or *abcb.* Commonly used in ballads. Also called *common meter* from its use in hymns. The most popular of all quatrains.

> She dwelt among the untrodden ways
> > Beside the springs of Dove,
> A Maid whom there were none to praise
> > And very few to love:
>
> A violet by a mossy stone
> > Half hidden from the eye!
> —Fair as a star, when only one
> > Is shining in the sky.
>
> She lived unknown, and few could know
> > When Lucy ceased to be;
> But she is in her grave, and, oh,
> > The difference to me!
> > > —WILLIAM WORDSWORTH (1770–1850, English poet),
> > > *Lucy*

   c. Sonnet: fourteen lines of iambic pentameter. The sonnet is a
favorite form for short poems because of its compactness.
Ordinarily the poet states an idea in the first eight lines, the
octave, and gives an explanation or an answer in the last six,
the sestet. There are two types of sonnet which are distinguished by their rhymes.

   i. Italian: *abba abba* (octave)

            cde cde or *cdcdcd* (sestet)

> The world is too much with us: late and soon,
> Getting and spending, we lay waste our powers.
> Little we see in Nature that is ours;
> We have given our hearts away, a sordid boon!
> This Sea that bares her bosom to the moon;
> The winds that will be howling at all hours,
> And are up-gathered now like sleeping flowers;
> For this, for everything, we are out of tune;
> It moves us not.—Great God! I'd rather be
> A Pagan suckled in a creed outworn;
> So might I, standing on this pleasant lea,
> Have glimpses that would make me less forlorn;
> Have sight of Proteus rising from the sea;
> Or hear old Triton blow his wreathèd horn.
>   —WILLIAM WORDSWORTH (1770–1850, English poet),
>   *The World Is Too Much with Us* (1807)

   ii. English: three quatrains with alternating rhyme and a
      couplet.

> Let me not to the marriage of true minds
> Admit impediments. Love is not love
> Which alters when it alteration finds,
> Or bends with the remover to remove.
>
> O, no! it is an ever-fixèd mark
> That looks on tempests and is never shaken;
> It is the star to every wand'ring bark,
> Whose worth's unknown, although his height be taken.
>
> Love's not Time's fool, though rosy lips and cheeks
> Within his bending sickle's compass come;
> Love alters not with his brief hours and weeks,
> But bears it out even to the edge of doom.

If this be error and upon me proved,
I never writ, nor no man ever loved.
—SHAKESPEARE,
Sonnet 116 (publ. 1609)

d. *Spenserian stanza:* eight lines of iambic pentameter followed
by one of iambic hexameter. Rhyme *abab bcbcc.* A graceful
verse invented by Spenser for *The Fairie Queene* and often
used for longer narratives.

And more to lulle him in his slumber soft,
A trickling streame from high rock tumbling downe,
And ever-drizling raine upon the loft,
Mixt with a murmuring winde, much like the sowne
Of swarming Bees, did cast him in a swowne.
No other noyse, nor peoples troublous cryes,
As still are wont t'annoy the walled towne,
Might there be heard; but carelesse Quiet lyes
Wrapt in eternall silence farre from enimyes.
—EDMUND SPENSER (1552–1599, English poet),
The Faerie Queene, I, 1, XLI (1590)

e. *Blank verse:* unrhymed iambic pentameter.

When I see birches bend to left and right
Across the line of straighter darker trees,
I like to think some boy's been swinging them.
But swinging doesn't bend them down to stay.
—ROBERT FROST (1875——, American poet),
Birches (1916)[6]

Variety in Meter

The relation of rhythm and meter in poetry is exactly the same as
that between rhythm and time in music. Meter and time are absolutely
regular; the regular succession of accent continues inexorably like the
ticking of a clock. It may be slower or faster at one time than another,
but there is no other change.

However, a poem or a melody that followed its meter or time exactly
would become very dull and mechanical. We like it for a short time in
music, as we saw in tunes like *Yankee Doodle* and *Praise God from*

[6] From *Collected Poems of Robert Frost,* by permission of the publishers,
Henry Holt and Company, Inc.

Whom All Blessings Flow, and we like it for a short time in poems, as in this hymn:

> O God, our help in ages past,
> Our hope for years to come,
> Our shelter from the stormy blast
> And our eternal home!
> —Isaac Watts (1674–1748, English clergyman
> and poet),
> *O God, Our Help in Ages Past* (1719)

But usually we want some variety, and hence we have rhythm which accompanies the time or the meter. In poetry just as in music the regular beat of the time-meter is heard even when it is not sounded, and it gives a sense of security.

The well-known lines from Mark Antony's speech on Julius Caesar are nonsense if they are read in strict meter, and yet beneath the rhythm of the lines we hear the steady beat of the iambs.

> This was the noblest Roman of them all:
> All the conspirators, save only he,
> Did that they did in envy of great Caesar;
> He only, in a general honest thought
> And common good to all, made one of them.
> His life was gentle, and the elements
> So mix'd in him that Nature might stand up
> And say to all the world "This was a man!"
> —Shakespeare,
> *Julius Caesar,* V, v, 63–75 (1599)

FOR FURTHER EXPLORATION

1. Collect fifteen popular slogans, and analyze in each the reason for its appeal.

2. Select five of your favorite quotations; analyze them for tone color, phrasing, and rhythm.

3. For rhythm of prose, read Ecclesiastes, chapter 12; Sir Thomas Browne, *Hydriotaphia: Urn Burial,* chapter 5.

4. Rank ten passages of prose according to their rhythmic qualities, putting the most rhythmic first.

5. Do the same for ten passages of poetry.

6. Experiment with the writing of verse in different meters and verse forms.

7. Rewrite *Old Mother Hubbard* as a Shakespearean sonnet, a series of rhymed couplets, blank verse, a popular ballad, etc.

8. Imitate the rhythm of three passages of great prose.

9. Do the same for three passages of poetry.

10. Note the varying connotations of a series of familiar words such as *cow, onion, Egypt, crossword puzzle.*

11. Read a page of scientific writing. Has the author used any images or figures of speech?

12. Reduce any poem you like to a scientific statement. What is left?

13. Study a poem you like for its imagery.

14. Rupert Brooke's poem *The Great Lover* contains a list of all the things he had loved. What type of imagery prevails?

15. Make a similar list for yourself. What type of imagery do you use most commonly?

16. Notice the figures of speech used by yourself and your friends.

17. Why is it counted bad writing to use a metaphor with no thought of the comparison involved?

18. Find other poems that have symbolic meaning.

19. It has been said that any statement is symbolic. Prove or disprove.

CHAPTER 11

ORGANIZATION IN THE VISUAL ARTS

WHAT IS ORGANIZATION?

It has been said that man is most Godlike in his demand for order. He is constantly trying to find order in his surroundings, to transform his chaos into a world. The mind is confused, if not balked, when it cannot find some order. The "order" in a work of art is its organization.

In our study thus far we have been considering the separate elements that are used to make a work of art. Now we begin to put them together; to organize them so as to make a whole. For the elements are only the materials out of which an artist creates his work; he must select, arrange, and combine them to express his idea, to show his purpose, to communicate to others the meaning and form of his experiences.

The primary demands made of any organization are two: (1) it must make sense, and (2) it must be interesting. The first of these demands has to do with the arrangement of parts, the over-all design or plan of a work. In any work of art we want to feel that the parts belong together, that we are getting somewhere. We are quite unhappy if the artist seems to be rambling around without definite intent or purpose. This demand for plan is universal and instinctive. Plan might be called the skeleton of the work of art.

Plan covers the entire work—whether it be a symphony that lasts an hour or a song that is over in a minute, whether it be a novel of a thousand pages or a poem of two lines, whether it be the ceiling of a large chapel or the picture on a postage stamp. Whatever the size, we demand the orderly arrangement of the parts which reflects a plan.

The names by which we identify plans differ in the different arts. In music we speak of *forms:* rondo, sonata, fugue, etc., and in literature we talk of *types:* sonnet, novel, essay, epic. These plans are relatively simple, and many very different works will follow the same basic plan.

Plan is essential because it holds the work together, but it is not interesting as such. Two works following identical plans may differ widely in interest and value. The sonnet form has been used in very great poems, and the same form is found in poems of no value. The value of a rondo does not come from the rondo form, but from the music written in that form. In any of the arts interest comes from the way the form is used, from the elements with which the plan is fulfilled, and from their interrelations. This may be called the organic structure of the work. If the plan is compared to the skeleton, the organic structure corresponds to the flesh and blood with which the skeleton is covered.

Another analogy for this type of organization is an orchestra. The different elements play with and against each other as do the instruments of an orchestra. And so this organic structure or organic unity of a work of art is sometimes called its orchestration.

For the organic structure there is one rule that holds in all the arts, that of unity and variety. Reduced to the simplest possible terms, the rule means that the artist can use only elements that are alike or those that are different. If they are alike, we have a sense of quiet, rest, and unity. If they are unlike, there is contrast, change, variety. In most cases they are not exactly alike, nor entirely different. They are alike in some respect but different in others. In this way we have the satisfaction of the recognition of the familiar coupled with the surprise or tension of the unfamiliar. One of the most beautiful passages in Handel's *Messiah* comes in the singing of the contralto solo, "He shall feed His flock," which is followed immediately by the soprano solo, "Come unto Him, all Ye that labor." The tune is the same. The soprano sings it a fourth higher. The beauty of the soprano solo is almost unearthly. And yet with the differences in words and in pitch, not only is the song not repetitious, but few hearers even know they are hearing the same tune.

The essence of organic structure lies in the doubling of interests

Fig. 115. Raphael (Raffaello Sanzio)
(1483–1520), Italian painter. *Sistine
Madonna* (ca. 1515). (Oil on canvas.
Height: 8 feet 8½ inches. Dresden
Gallery. Photograph by Stoedtner.)

Fig. 115a. Drawing to show organization of
lines and figures in the *Sistine Madonna*.
(Drawing by Gordon Gilkey.)

such as we have in the last illustration. While we are hearing and enjoying the soprano's solo we are remembering the contralto's singing of the same tune. While we are seeing or hearing one thing, we are at the same time seeing or hearing something else, if not with the physical senses, then in memory and imagination.

BASIC PLANS IN THE VISUAL ARTS

Plan in the visual arts is simply the arrangement of the parts. In the *Sistine Madonna* (Figures 115 and 115a) the plan is made by the four units on the canvas, the Madonna and Child in the center at the top, the Pope and the saint on the sides, and the two cherubs at the bottom of the picture.

Because plan in the visual arts is obvious and essential, there are no well-established names for types of plan as in music and literature. In the visual arts we see the plan at once, and hence we do not need any assistance in determining types. There are, however, a few obvious arrangements which are used repeatedly. The two most common are the symmetrical and the pyramidal plans.

Symmetrical Plan. The two sides of the plan are similar and relatively equal. This is a favorite plan in architecture where the two sides are identical, as in the Vendramin Palace (Figure 116). It is also

FIG. 116. Pietro Lombardo (ca. 1435–1515), Italian architect. Palazzo Vendramin-Calergi (1481–1509). (Marble. Length: about 80 feet; height: about 65 feet. Venice. Photograph by Alinari.)

a favorite in painting or statues, as in the *Annunciation* by Simone
Martini (Figure 68), or the *Ludovisi Throne* (Figure 54).

Pyramid. The pyramid is almost as great a favorite in painting as
is the symmetrical plan in architecture. The broad base gives a sense
of solidity and the apex gives emphasis. It is the natural shape for a
painting of a portrait. In the portrait of *Madame Cézanne in the
Conservatory* (Figure 117), her skirts make the base of the pyramid

FIG. 117. Paul Cézanne (1839–1906), French painter. *Mme. Cézanne in the
Conservatory* (1891). (Oil on canvas. Size: 36½ by 28½ inches. Collection of
Stephen C. Clark, New York. Photograph, Museum of Modern Art.)

and her head the apex. The pyramidal plan is a favorite for the representations of the Virgin, as in Giorgione's *Castelfranco Madonna* (Figure 118). The Madonna, though dressed as a simple peasant, is seated on high at the apex of the triangle; St. Liberale and St. Francis

FIG. 119. Michelangelo (1475-1564). *Tomb of Giuliano de' Medici* (ca. 1523-1533). (Marble. Height: about 20 feet. Florence, San Lorenzo, New Sacristy. Photograph by Anderson.)

are at the corners. In the *Tomb of Giuliano de' Medici* (Figure 119), Michelangelo follows the general shape of a pyramid.

Vertical Plan. Less common plans are the vertical and the radial. The vertical plan shows a single vertical figure or other object. Monuments frequently follow this plan, as do some modern skyscrapers, the Seagram Building in New York (Figure 120), for example. It is used a great deal in sculpture, especially in statues of a single figure as in Michelangelo's *David* (Figure 27). It is not so well liked in painting as in sculpture, but it is used for full-length single figures, as in Eakins's *The Thinker* (Figure 121).

FIG. 120. Mies van der Rohe (1886——), American architect born in Germany, and Philip Johnson (1906——), American architect. The Seagram Building (1957). (Bronze. 38 stories. New York.)

FIG. 121. Thomas Eakins (1844–1916), American painter and sculptor. *The Thinker* (1900). (Oil on canvas. Height: 6 feet 10 inches. New York, courtesy of the Metropolitan Museum of Art; Kennedy Fund, 1917.)

FIG. 122. Giotto (1266–1336), Italian artist. *Death of St. Francis* (ca. 1325). (Fresco. Figures about life size. Florence, S. Croce, Bardi Chapel. Photograph by Alinari.)

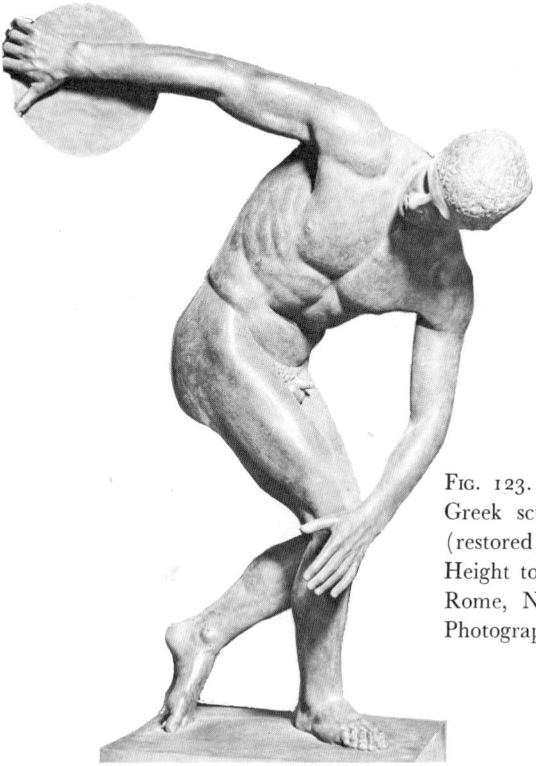

FIG. 123. Myron (fifth century B.C.), Greek sculptor. *Discus Thrower* (restored) (450 B.C.). (Bronze. Height to right shoulder: 5 feet. Rome, National Museum. Photograph by Anderson.)

Radial Plan. In the radial plan the lines of the picture form radii which meet at a point in the center. In Leonardo's *Last Supper*, all the lines of the ceiling and walls, as well as the hands and faces of the twelve disciples, point to the head of Christ. Leonardo puts his point of focus directly in the center of the picture. In the *Death of St. Francis* (Figure 122) Giotto uses a similar organization with the focal point at one side. The lines of the painting—the heads and bodies of the saint's followers, as well as lines of the banner—all converge on the head of St. Francis. The one exception is the soul of St. Francis, which looks ahead as it is being carried through the air.

There are many other plans. In the *Discus Thrower* (Figure 123) by Myron the body forms a complete half circle in the long, curved line that begins in the right hand, and goes on through the right arm and the body to the left foot. In Toulouse-Lautrec's *Circus* (Figure 124) the lady on the horse starts a movement that is completed in the man on the left with his whip.

In abstract and nonobjective art, plan is harder to see because it is not representational. The organization is based entirely on the repetition and variety of the elements. One color is balanced against another color, one line against another.

FIG. 124. Henri de Toulouse-Lautrec (1864–1901), French painter. *The Circus* (1888). (Oil on canvas. Height: 3 feet 2¾ inches. Chicago, courtesy of the Chicago Art Institute.)

Large buildings are sometimes classified according to the organization of the interior space. Some buildings like the Pantheon (Figure
147) or the Hagia Sophia (Figure 149) leave one only with a sense
of undifferentiated space. The Gothic or Romanesque cathedral, on
the other hand, is focused on the altar at one end, as in the Abbaye-
aux-Dames (Figure 155), and all the lines lead the eyes to it.

VARIETY

Architecture

The Vendramin Palace (Figure 116) at Venice is an interesting
study in repetition and variety. The famous old palace on the Grand
Canal in Venice was built by the Vendramin family at the end of the
fifteenth century. To this palace Wagner retired in 1882, and there he
died in 1883. One is impressed first by the repetition; the façade of the
building shows a single grouping of windows repeated many times.
There is, however, no lack of variety; the doorway takes the place of
the central window on the first floor, and the place of the two end
windows is left blank except for small openings. The first and second
stories are separated by a balustrade, the second and third by a
cornice. Moreover, the columns separating the windows are varied;
those on the first floor are pilasters, undecorated except for a molding
at the side; those of the second story are round and grooved; and those
of the third story are round, without grooves. The most important
device for securing variety, however, is in the arrangement of the
windows. The three central windows are grouped together, but the end
window is set off by a narrow panel with two engaged columns. This
motive, repeated at the corner of the building, brings a distinct
relief in the long line of windows; it is a breathing space, as it were,
that makes the façade seem easy and comfortable.

In a cathedral like Modena (Figure 154) we trace the many repetitions and variations of the round arch. In the Egyptian temple (Figures 49, 139), the sequence of rooms one after the other makes a
subtle progression in darkness, from the open court at the front through
the shadows of the hypostyle hall with its columns to the dark mysterious chamber of the priest.

These ways of producing variety are fairly obvious. More subtle is
the means used in the Parthenon (Figure 125). At first glance the

F<small>IG</small>. 125. Ictinus and Callicrates (fifth century B.C.), Greek architects. Parthenon (447–432 B.C.). Façade seen between columns of the Propylaea. (Pentelic marble. Height of columns: 34 feet. Athens. Photograph, courtesy Trans-World Airlines, Inc.)

building seems to show nothing but repetition, no variety except in the alternation of triglyphs and metopes in the frieze. In the Parthenon, however, are many subtle variations that do not strike the observer at once. The columns are smaller at the top than at the bottom; about one-third of the way up the shaft of the column there is a slight swell or convex curve known as the *entasis* of the column. Moreover, the columns incline at a very slight angle; it has been calculated that the columns on the two sides of the Parthenon if extended would meet more than a mile and a half above the pavement. Again, the corner columns are slightly larger than the others and are closer together. The steps and the entablature both rise in a very slight convex curve.

The idea has been expressed that in such refinements the Greeks were attempting to counteract certain optical illusions. Two long parallel lines tend to look hollow or to approach each other in a concave curve; hence the slight curve outward (entasis) was introduced in the columns. A column seen against the sky looks slighter than one seen against the background of a building; hence the corner columns were larger and nearer together. It cannot be determined, nor does it matter, whether the architects introduced these changes to correct optical illusions, or whether they introduced them merely as a means of giving variety to the building and so of improving its appearance. It is certain, however, that these changes were intentional. Similar refinements have been introduced in many buildings—St. Mark's in Venice, and the old library of Columbia University in New York City, to name only two examples. And it is certain that much of the beauty of the buildings is due to the lack of stiffness, the sense of a unified, almost breathing whole, resulting from these slight variations from the exact rule.

Sculpture and Painting

Repetition in sculpture and painting can never be the exact repetition that is characteristic of the industrial arts and architecture. In architecture, one half of a building may be, and often is, just like the other half, but in a picture or a statue the two sides cannot be the same. If, for instance, the artist wants to repeat the line of a woman's hair, he must repeat it not as hair but as cloud or tree or scarf. This kind of repetition therefore is not obvious. We see the cloud as cloud and the tree as tree, and we do not see that they are repeating the line

Fig. 126. Fra Angelico (1387–1455), Italian painter. *Annunciation* (ca. 1440). (Fresco. Figures three-fourths life size. Florence, San Marco Dormitory. Photograph by Anderson.)

of the woman's hair. In the *Annunciation* of Fra Angelico (Figures
126 and 126a), for example, the curve of the angel's body repeats the
curve of the Madonna's body. The round curve of the Virgin's halo is
repeated in the neckline of her dress, the stool on which she is
seated, and the arches above her head. The arches on the side of the
angel are seen in perspective, and they repeat the shape of the angel's
wing until the whole place seems alive with the whir of wings. To
stabilize the curves and to give variety, Fra Angelico has introduced
many straight lines in the columns, the fence, the trees, even the doorway, which has a rectangular picture showing through it.

In Vermeer's *Young Woman with a Water Jug* (Figure 127),
the composition is worked out primarily in terms of the straight lines of
the map and the slow curve which we find in the young woman's cape.
In the *Medici Tomb* (Figure 119), we find repetition of lines in the
bodies of the three figures. In the figure of Night the arm and the head
make a complete half circle, and this curve is repeated in the curves
of the body.

In *The Young Englishman* (Figure 128). Titian has made his
design primarily in the three white spots of the head and two hands.
It is, however, united in repeated circles of head, beard, and chain,
with circular lines in the lace at neck and hands. There is also an
interesting study in values.

Fig. 126a. Drawing of *Annunciation*. (Gordon Gilkey.)

Fig. 127. Jan Vermeer (1632–1675), Dutch painter. *Young Woman with a Water Jug.* (Oil on canvas. Height: 18 inches. New York, courtesy of the Metropolitan Museum of Art; gift of Henry G. Marquand, 1889.)

BALANCE

As we look at various arrangements or plans in any works we instinctively demand balance. No matter how the various parts are put together, we want that sense of equilibrium which we call balance. Some people get nervous if they see a picture hanging crooked, and most of us have little satisfaction in looking at the Leaning Tower of Pisa, though we know it has stood for centuries and will probably continue to lean long after we are dead.

Degas has a painting of two ballet girls, *Dancers Practicing at the Bar* (Figure 129). The two girls are nearly symmetrical; each is poised on one leg, and the raised legs point in opposite directions. The figures are on a diagonal line in the upper right-hand corner of the picture; all the interest points to this one spot. To balance the two dancers, Degas puts a watering can on the otherwise bare floor. This watering can is essential. If we take out the can or if we shorten the width of

FIG. 128. Titian (1480–1576), Italian painter. *The Young Englishman* (ca. 1540–1545). (Oil on canvas. Size: 43½ by 36½ inches. Florence, Palazzo Pitti. Photograph by Anderson.)

FIG. 129. Edgar Degas
(1834–1917), French painter.
Dancers Practicing at the Bar
(1877). (Oil on canvas. Size:
about 29½ by 30½ inches.
New York, courtesy of the
Metropolitan Museum of Art;
H. O. Havemeyer Collection.)

FIG. 130. Honoré Daumier
(1808–1879), French
caricaturist, lithographer, and
painter. *Strangers in Paris.*
(Lithograph. Size: 8½ by 7
inches. New York, courtesy of
the Metropolitan Museum of
Art; Rogers Fund, 1922.)

the picture, the girls are no longer secure at their bar, the plan becomes unbalanced.

One of the most important ways of getting balance is in control of the direction of lines. One line points in one direction, another in the opposite direction, and from the two we get a sense of balance. In Giotto's *Flight into Egypt* (Figure 112), for example, the entire motion of the picture is left to right until we come to the figure of St. Joseph, which stops us and turns us back. In Daumier's *Strangers in Paris* (Figure 130), the couple in the distance is moving in one direction, that in the foreground is not moving, but the direction of their heads and umbrellas is in the opposite direction. In El Greco's *Saint Jerome* (Figure 131), the eyes, head, and beard point to the right, the arms and book to the left. If the picture is cut off just below

FIG. 131. El Greco (1541–1614), Spanish painter. *St. Jerome* (ca. 1596–1600). (Oil on canvas. Size: 42½ by 34¼ inches. Copyright, The Frick Collection, New York.)

the shoulders, the beard seems to be blown as by a good breeze or a fan. With the opposing motion of the hands and book, the whole is given living, breathing balance.

Theoretically, every detail is necessary in a well-designed composition; if a balance is perfect, a change in a single detail would upset the balance of the whole. This principle is probably more theory than fact, but at the same time it is interesting to try to determine the role played by some detail of a picture. In Jan van Eyck's painting of *Jan Arnolfini and His Wife* (Figure 132), for example, we have an interesting illustration. It is obviously a portrait study. The two figures are placed side by side, the gentleman on the left, the lady on the right. Between them are the mirror on the wall, and the chandelier. The light of the window, the man's face, and his hand are balanced by the white of the lady's face, her headdress, and the long cuff to her sleeve. All is regular and as it should be except for some slippers on the floor near the man and the lady. But those slippers are necessary for the balance of the picture. Their irregular line balances the irregular line of the white trim on the lady's skirt. Both lines of white are needed to bring the eye down to the lower half of the picture. The picture is top-heavy without them. The importance of the slippers can be judged in another way also; if we cover the slippers the man seems to fall forward.

THE FRAME

In the arrangement of parts, consideration must be given to the frame and the relation of the parts to the frame. Whether we look at the façade of a building, a statue, or a painting, we have a certain area or surface that is to be filled. Within this area the space should seem neither crowded nor empty. The camera offers interesting possibilities for experimentation, for with the finder on the camera, the artist can try different types of content in different relationships to the frame. The stage illustrates another challenge; the proscenium arch offers a frame, and the problem of the director is to fill that frame agreeably with stage set, characters, and lighting. Since the theater and dancing are arts of both time and space, the director deals with a content that is constantly changing; at any moment, however, the stage is supposed to show a scene in which the frame is filled agreeably.

Since the design must fill the shape, the choice of shape partly determines the design of the picture. Moreover, the lines of the enclosing

FIG. 132. Jan van Eyck (1370?–1440?), Flemish painter. *Jan Arnolfini and His Wife* (1434). (Oil on wood. Height: 2 feet 9¼ inches. Reproduced by courtesy of the Trustees, the National Gallery, London.)

shape strengthen or oppose the lines of the design. In a picture that is
rectangular or square all the vertical or horizontal lines of the picture
are strengthened by the lines of the frame. So powerful are these lines
that an artist usually tries to cover them in some way, to fill in the
corners by the use of trees or shrubbery, or in some other way to change
the severe right angle to a more graceful curve. The square is difficult
to work with because it is all center and corners; there is no neutral
ground, as it were. We have good design in the square in the metopes
from the Parthenon (Figure 97), and in the panels of the "Gates of
Paradise" (Figure 46). But because of its difficulty the square is relatively rare in art, and the rectangle is preferred. The rectangle has the

FIG. 133. Filippo Brunelleschi (1377–1446), Italian sculptor and architect. Competition for the Gates of the Baptistery, Florence. *Sacrifice of Isaac* (1402).
(Bronze. Size: about 1½ feet square. Bargello, Florence. Photograph by Alinari.)

advantage of being in straight lines, and yet it has much free space in the middle that is neither exact center nor corner, and in this central space the design is usually placed. If it is standing on its short side it shares something of the strength of the vertical; if it is on its long side it partakes of the peace of the horizontal. Most of the illustrations in this book are rectangular, it may be noted.

Irregular shapes are not always easily filled. An illustration is found in reliefs made by Brunelleschi and Ghiberti on *The Sacrifice of Isaac* (Figures 133 and 134). Since these two reliefs were offered in a competition for the north gates of the Baptistery at Florence, they have

Fig. 134. Lorenzo Ghiberti (1378–1455), Italian goldsmith, sculptor, and painter. Competition for the Gates of the Baptistery, Florence. *Sacrifice of Isaac* (1402). (Bronze. Size: about 1½ feet square. Bargello, Florence. Photograph by Alinari.)

the same shape, the same general treatment in high relief, as well as the same subject. They have the same figures in the relief; each has Isaac kneeling on the altar, and Abraham arrested by the angel just as he is about to kill his son. In each panel are the servants of Abraham, and the ram which was the actual sacrifice. The arrangement of the figures in the two compositions is entirely different. Brunelleschi has put Isaac in the center, the other figures are crowded into the corners, and the scene is confused. Ghiberti has divided the relief in two by a diagonal line, with Abraham and Isaac on one side and the servants on the other. His plan is clearer, simpler, and better.

The circle is a difficult shape. It is always the same; the eye tends to go around and around it without stopping, and there is a general tendency for a picture to seem to roll over if it is in a circular frame. Some of the best examples may be obtained from Greek vase painting. The cylix, or drinking cup, was ordinarily ornamented on the inside; hence the Greek draftsman had many opportunities to try his hand at filling a circular shape, and he succeeded admirably. A favorite cylix painting shows two women putting away their clothes. It is attributed to Douris (Figure 135).

FIG. 135. Douris (attributed), *Two Women Putting Away Clothes* (fifth century B.C., about 470). (Red figured pottery. Ripe Archaic Style. Cylix. Size: 5 inches high, 12⅞ inches in diameter. New York, courtesy of the Metropolitan Museum of Art.)

The lunette or half-moon is largely associated with architecture and sculpture. It is found most often in the tympanum or sculptured space over a door. We studied an example in the tympanum at Chartres (Figure 23). It has the rich curve of the circle but is held steady by its horizontal base.

PROPORTION

Proportion is that phase of plan which has to do with the comparative size of the parts of a single work. It is a mathematical concept for relative length or size: it is never an absolute but always a relative matter. A picture is not too large or too small in itself but is too large for this space or too small for that. One side of a rectangle is not too long or too short except in proportion to the other. An inch is very little in computing the distance from New York City to Chicago, but it is a good deal on the end of a nose.

In the visual arts, proportion at its simplest can be seen in the arrangement of objects on an indefinite surface or field, such as wallpaper, carpets, and cloth. A plaid is nothing but a number of straight lines crossing at right angles; the interest of the plaid depends on the arrangement of these lines in relation to one another. In a polka-dotted pattern there are two elements, the size of the dot and the space between dots. Change the size of the dot or the space between them, i.e., change the proportions, and the pattern is changed radically.

Such patterns offer simple problems of proportion, because the elements are judged only by their relation one to the other. But problems in proportion are found wherever there is a question of relative size or length. In dress design, proportion determines the length of the sleeve or coat, the space between buttons. In interior decoration it governs the length of curtains, the height of the mantel, the size of the picture over it. Printed pages in books depend for their beauty largely on the proportions used in filling the page: the space at the top and the bottom, the width of the margins, the size of the type, and the space between the lines. Proportion determines also our judgments of the beauty of the human body in life and in art. Is the head too large or too small? Are the legs and arms too long? Are the hips too large? In painting, proportion determines not only the shape of the frame, its height in comparison with its width, but also the placing of the subject in the frame, whether the center of interest be high or low, right or left.

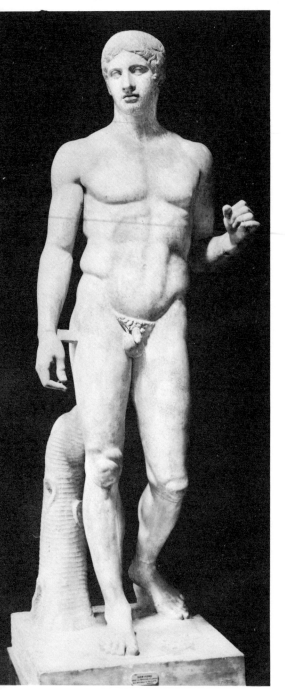

What are good proportions, and what are bad? This is like asking when is a steak cooked enough or what is a long walk. People do not agree. The critic gives the ultimate answer: that is good which seems good, that is in good proportion which we find pleasing. But people have always wanted to know definite rules; accordingly, various people have tried to make exact formulas for pleasing proportions.

Polyclitus, a Greek sculptor of the fifth century B.C., wrote a treatise on the proportions for the ideal human figure, which he called *The Canon* or *The Rule*. Then he made a statue to illustrate his principles, called also *The Canon*. It is not certain just what this statue was, but it is believed to have been the *Doryphorus*, or *Spear Bearer* (Figure 136). Unfortunately, the original, probably in bronze, is lost, and the stone copy that is in the museum at Naples is not good; the copyist has had to make certain additions because of the weight of the stone, a tree stump to support the legs, and a bar between the hips and the right arm. Nevertheless, one can see the general proportions

FIG. 136. Polyclitus (fifth century B.C.), Greek sculptor. *Doryphorus* (ca. 440 B.C.). (Roman copy in marble of bronze original. Height: 7 feet. Naples, Museum. Photograph by Alinari.)

of the original. Polyclitus had a mathematical formula for the figure: the head is one-seventh the height of the entire body and all details are worked out in terms of a fixed ratio.

A century later Lysippus introduced a new canon with a smaller head and a slimmer body, the head being only one-eighth the height of the body. The statue that has been most commonly associated with these new proportions is the *Apoxyomenos,* or *Strigil Bearer* (Figure 137), a figure of a young athlete holding the strigil, a curved scraper which athletes used to remove oil and dust from the body after exercise.

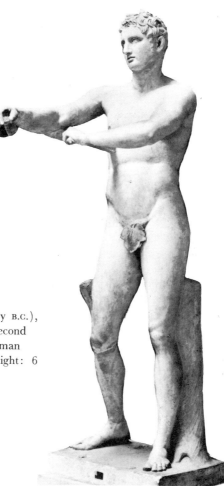

Fig. 137. Lysippus (fourth century B.C.), Greek sculptor. *Apoxyomenos* (second half of fourth century B.C.). (Roman marble after bronze original. Height: 6 feet 8½ inches. Rome, Vatican. Photograph by Alinari.)

Another proportion that has received great attention is that known variously as the "section," the "divine section," the "golden section," "phi proportion," and "extreme and mean ratio." This ratio has been recognized through the ages as one creating a good proportion. It more nearly reaches the goal of a perfect ratio than any that has been discovered, and works of art that are not made in that ratio approximate it.

This ratio divides a line so that the shorter segment is to the longer as the longer segment is to the entire line.

A	B	C

In the line AC, the segment AB bears the same relation to BC as BC does to AC. The proportion is given approximately in the figures 3–5–8, 5–8–13, 8–13–21, etc. If one side of a rectangle is five feet, the other side should measure three or eight. A living room that measures thirteen by twenty-one will be in more beautiful proportion than one that measures fifteen by twenty. Various measurements have been made to illustrate the universality of this ratio. Curious people have measured buildings, statues, and paintings to prove the universality of the rule, and they come forth with interesting results. In the *Birth of Venus* (Figure 28), for example, the height of the horizon line is exactly in extreme and mean proportion with the top and bottom of the picture. And if the measurements are reversed so that the smaller section comes at the bottom of the picture, the top of the shell is in extreme and mean proportion with the top and bottom of the picture. In Titian's *Bacchus and Ariadne* (Figure 31), if a horizontal line is drawn measuring extreme and mean proportion from top and bottom of the picture, and a vertical line is drawn showing the same proportion in the sides of the picture, the two lines cross at the shadow just under the head of Bacchus, the most important point in the picture.

Discoveries of this kind always raise again the question of the artist and the rule. Did Botticelli and Titian consciously follow the rule, and are the paintings good because they follow the rule? The answers here, as always, are in the negative. Botticelli and Titian probably knew the rule, and may have deliberately measured the distances; however, they used the proportion not because it was the rule but because they had found it good. And the result is good not because it follows the rule but because we find it agreeable.

FOR FURTHER EXPLORATION

1. Study the arrangement of the articles on a mantel, the top of a dresser, the side of a wall. Distinguish the skeletal and the organic structure.

2. Try to find the plan in songs, stories, pictures.

3. Test in your experience the truth of the statement that we do not like art if it seems to us without plan. Study, in this connection, the essays of Emerson and Bacon, the poems of Walt Whitman, the music of Prokofiev and Honegger, the paintings of Klee and Kandinski.

4. Study early criticisms of some accepted masterpieces to see how often new work is branded "formless."

5. Begin listening for melodies in music. How are they repeated and varied?

6. Trace the variants of a single motive in an automobile, a pattern of dress goods, a piece of furniture.

7. Do the same for the exterior of a building.

8. Do the same for a statue or a painting.

9. Listen to Bach's Passacaglia and Fugue in C minor. Notice how the same melody is repeated over and over with different accompaniments.

10. Choose six different shapes; try to fit the same design into each. How does the frame change the effect of the design?

11. Study a volume devoted to Raphael. Do you find that he favored any certain plans?

12. Select one painting by Raphael. What repetitions do you find? Cover any one detail; is the balance upset?

13. Do the same for any other artist you like.

14. Turn a painting on its side and upside down. How important is right and left balance?

15. Make a thorough analysis of one building, one statue, one painting to show the plan, the emphasis on certain elements, the organic structure, and balance.

16. Construct six polka-dotted patterns for cloth; do not vary the size of the dot.

17. Experiment with the common problems of proportion named in the second section, e.g., the length of the curtains or the sides of a picture frame.

18. Measure the bodies of your friends for their conformance to the ideal proportions of Polyclitus or Lysippus.

19. Select any door, picture, or other object that seems to you to have good proportions. Measure it. How nearly does it conform to the extreme and mean ratio?

20. Compare two houses which have the same general arrangement and the same number of windows, but differ in proportions.

CHAPTER 12

ORGANIZATION IN ARCHITECTURE

Because of its size and complexity architecture needs separate treatment for the study of its design and organization. In this chapter the historical approach is used as the one best suited to make clear the various designs or styles of building.

EGYPTIAN ARCHITECTURE

Egyptian architecture is closely bound up with religion. The *ka,* or "vital force," was dependent upon the body for its life; if the body was destroyed, the ka ceased to exist. Hence pyramids were built to preserve the body, that the ka might be safe. The most striking group of pyramids is at Giza, where there are the great pyramids Khufu, Khafre, and Menkure (Figure 138).

Great as were the pyramids, however, they did not protect their dead from robbers and marauders, and later tombs were cut in rocky cliffs. A temple adjoined each tomb, and, as the tombs were made more inaccessible, these temples developed independently. The great temples are those at Karnak, Edfu, and Luxor. They followed the same basic plan. First was the *pylon* (Figure 139), a huge gateway covering the entire front of the building. The temple itself, as we have said when discussing the adaptation of plan to function, was composed of a series of halls. In one of these halls the roof was supported by rows of columns (hypostyle). In the temple at Karnak and in some of the other temples, the center columns are higher than those next to the wall, thus making a clerestory for the light to enter (Figure 140).

Egyptian columns are primarily of two types, the flower and the

FIG. 138. Pyramids of Giza seen from the air. (ca. 2700–ca. 2200 B.C.). (Photograph, courtesy Trans-World Airlines, Inc.)

FIG. 139. Temple of Horus, pylon seen from first court (started by Ptolemy III, third century B.C.). (Sandstone. Height: about 100 feet. Edfu, Egypt. Photograph by Stoedtner.)

flower + bud

bud. In the flower columns the flower makes a wide bell-shaped capital. In the bud columns the uppermost part of the capital is smaller than the lower, like the bud of a flower. The model of the hypostyle hall at Karnak shows the clerestory and the columns; the central columns have flower capitals, the aisle columns, bud.

Fig. 140. Temple of Amon (ca. 1300 B.C.). Hypostyle Hall. (Red-brown sandstone. Height of columns in middle aisle: 69 feet; width of capital at top: 22 feet; height of columns in side aisles: 42½ feet. Karnak, Egypt. Model in Metropolitan Museum, New York. Photograph, courtesy of the Metropolitan Museum of Art.)

An outstanding characteristic of Egyptian art is its size. This is probably due to the nature of the country, for in the desert everything is swallowed up, and only the very large stands out in the wide stretches of sand. But even with this warning one can hardly grasp the enormous size of Egyptian buildings. The columns of the Great Hall at Karnak are large enough for a hundred men to stand on top of the capital.[1] The Great Hall at Karnak is 338 feet wide and 170 feet deep, furnishing a floor area about equal to that of the cathedral of Notre Dame in Paris, although this is only a single hall of the temple.[2] The pyramid of Khufu at Giza is 480 feet in length and covers about 13 acres.[3]

[1] James Henry Breasted, *The Conquest of Civilization*, Plate IX, p. 98. Harpers, 1926.

[2] *Ibid.*, Fig. 61, p. 96.

[3] *Ibid.*, p. 64.

MESOPOTAMIAN ARCHITECTURE

Of all the great palaces and temples of the Mesopotamians, Chaldeans, Babylonians, and Assyrians, very few examples are left; the brick, either unbaked or only partially baked, has crumbled away. The distinguishing characteristic is the *ziggurat,* or tower, built at successive levels, with ramps leading from one platform to the next. In many respects the ziggurat is like the modern building with setbacks.

GREEK ARCHITECTURE

Greek architecture in its most characteristic form is found in the temple, a low building in post-and-lintel construction as was the Egyptian temple. In this type of construction, two upright pieces, *posts,* are surmounted by a horizontal piece, *lintel,* long enough to reach from one to the other. This is the simplest and earliest type of construction, and it is more commonly used than any other. Barns are good examples, since the beams are exposed and can be seen. Post-and-lintel construction is well adapted to wood, because wooden beams are strong and are able to uphold the weight of the roof; at the same time they are long, and a large building may be erected. However, wooden

Fig. 141. Temple of Apollo (sixth century B.C.). (Porous limestone, originally covered with stucco. Height of columns: 23⅔ feet. Old Corinth. Photograph, courtesy Royal Greek Embassy.)

beams are not permanent; they burn, they rot, and they are eaten by insects. Stone lintels, in comparison, are enduring, but they cannot be obtained in as great lengths, and they stand much less weight than wood; therefore, in stone buildings the distance between posts must be small. A typical example of post-and-lintel construction is found in the ruins of the Temple of Apollo at Old Corinth (Figure 141).

The typical Greek temple had columns in front and often at the back also. Sometimes the entire building was surrounded by a row of columns, making a double row of columns in the front and back of the building and a single row at the side. The Parthenon belongs to this class. In the pure Greek style all columns are fluted.

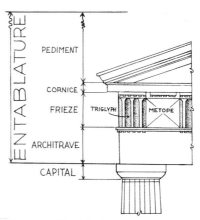

There are three styles of Greek architecture, Doric, Ionic, and Corinthian. The *Doric* (Figure 142) is seen in the Temple of Apollo at Old Corinth, and in the Parthenon (Figure 125), one of the greatest temples ever built. The Doric column has no base, the bottom of

Fig. 142. The Doric Order (Drawing by Thad Suits).

the column rests on the top step. The capital is very plain; a flat block, or slab, is joined to the column by a simple curve looking something like a cushion. The frieze is divided into *triglyphs* and *metopes;* the triglyph is a square slab having two vertical grooves (or glyphs) in the middle and a half groove at each end; the metope, which alternates with the triglyph, is also square. Metopes are often carved, as in the Parthenon (Figure 97).

The *Ionic* column is taller and slenderer than the Doric. It has a base, and the capital is ornamented with scrolls, or volutes, on each side. In the Ionic order the frieze is continuous instead of being divided into triglyphs and metopes. The architrave below the frieze is stepped; that is, it is divided horizontally into three parts, each being set in slightly. The greatest example of the Ionic order is the Erechtheum (Figure 10), which is unfinished and, unlike most Greek temples, is irregular in shape; but, like all examples of the Ionic order in general, it is characterized by great elegance and grace. The Ionic

FIG. 143. Callicrates (?). Temple of Athena Niké (ca. 423 B.C.). (Pentelic marble. Size: 18½ by 27 feet. Athens. Photograph, courtesy of Royal Greek Embassy.)

FIG. 144. Temple of Olympian Zeus (174 B.C.–A.D. 130). (Pentelic marble. Height of column: 56½ feet. Athens. Photograph, courtesy of Royal Greek Embassy.)

column is found also in the little temple of Athena Niké at Athens (Figure 143).

The *Corinthian* column is distinguished from the Ionic by still greater height and by its capital, which shows two rows of acanthus leaves with volutes rising from them. The Corinthian, although an authentic Greek order, was last in point of development and was not so much used as the Doric and the Ionic. The late-second-century Temple of Zeus at Athens has Corinthian capitals (Figure 144).

ROMAN ARCHITECTURE

Roman architecture follows the general lines of the Greek with significant changes. The temple is no longer the typical building; equally important are civic buildings, baths, law courts, amphitheaters, aqueducts, and bridges.

Structurally the most important innovation of the Romans is the arch, which was widely used though it was not invented by them. Next to the post-and-lintel, arch construction is historically of greatest

Fig. 145. Segovia Aqueduct (first century A.D.). (Granite. Length: 2,700 feet; height: 102 feet. Segovia. Photograph, courtesy of the Spanish National Tourist Office.)

Fig. 146. Pantheon (A.D. 120–124). Portico A.D. 202. (Brick, mortar, and concrete, originally faced on the exterior with Pentelic marble and stucco. Height of columns: 46½ feet. Rome. Photograph, courtesy of the Italian State Tourist Office.)

Fig. 147. Pantheon (A.D. 120–124), interior. (Cement dome; wall decoration and pavement of marble and porphyry. Diameter of rotunda: 142 feet. Rome. Photograph by Alinari.)

importance. An arch is made of wedge-shaped stones that are arranged with the small side of the wedge turned down toward the opening. When the stones have been put in place by means of scaffolding or centering, their shape keeps them from falling, as we can see in the aqueduct of Segovia (Figure 145). Each stone of the arch, by its weight, exerts constant pressure on the stones on each side, and the arch is held in position only by an exact balancing of these pressures. If that balance is upset, the arch collapses. As the old Arabic proverb has it, "an arch never sleeps."

Another characteristic of Roman architecture is the flat round dome *dome* that covers an entire building as in the Pantheon (Figures 146 and 147).

When the Romans used the same designs as the Greeks, they did not use them in just the same way. The columns are taller and thinner, and often, as in the Pantheon, the columns are not fluted. The Corinthian column is used extensively, as is the composite column, an invention of the Romans made by combining the Ionic volutes with the Corinthian acanthus-circled bell. The orders are not kept separate, but are stacked or superimposed, as in the Colosseum (Figure 148). Those on the first

FIG. 148. Colosseum (A.D. 72–82), travertine exterior. (Restorations in brick. Length: 620 feet; width: 513 feet; height: 157 feet. Rome. Photograph, courtesy of the Trans-World Airlines, Inc.)

floor are Doric, on the second Ionic, and on the third Corinthian. Moreover, the elements borrowed from the Greeks are sometimes used only as ornaments, whereas with the Greeks they were used structurally. In the Colosseum, again, the columns between the arches and the entablature above them are not essential to the structure of the building; this is seen in that part of the building from which the outer layer of concrete has been torn away; the columns are missing, but the arches stand as before.

BYZANTINE ARCHITECTURE

During the Middle Ages, religion again took an important place, and the most important buildings were the church and the cathedral. But architecture developed on different lines in the East and in the West.

Eastern or Byzantine architecture takes its name from Byzantium, later called Constantinople and now called Istanbul. Byzantine archi-

FIG. 149. Anthemius of Tralles and Isidorus of Miletus, architects. Hagia Sophia interior (A.D. 532–537, restored A.D. 558, 975). (Width of nave: 108 feet; height of central dome: 180 feet. Istanbul. Photograph, Bettmann Archive.)

tecture is characterized by a great central dome with half domes grouped around it. The dome, which is rather flat, reminds one of the Pantheon, but is fitted to the building in a different way. In the Pantheon the round dome just covers the round building. In the Byzantine building the dome has to be fitted to a square area, and the space between the arches and the dome is filled by curved triangles (pendentives) on which the dome rests. This gives greater height and makes the interior more spacious and inspiring. A dome supported in this way is called a *dome on pendentives* (Figure 149).

The greatest example of Byzantine architecture is the Hagia Sophia, or Church of the Divine Wisdom, in Istanbul. The Byzantine type has been widely used for the national church of Russia, for Mohammedan mosques, and for Jewish synagogues.

WESTERN ARCHITECTURE IN THE MIDDLE AGES

During the medieval period Western architecture passed through three stages of development in the three styles known as early Christian, Romanesque, and Gothic. These developed one out of the other; the Romanesque was an outgrowth of the early Christian, and the Gothic of the Romanesque. As in all such cases, there is never any sharp line to be drawn between one style and the other; there is never a time when one can say definitely that all buildings before that time are one style and after that time they are another. Accordingly we shall attempt to trace the development of the styles in their prominent characteristics.

The Basilica. In basic plan the three Western styles follow the general type of the Roman basilica, a long rectangular building divided by pillars into a central nave and aisles (Figure 150). Sometimes there is one aisle on each side of the nave; sometimes there are two. Often the nave is higher than the aisles, and, therefore, there is opportunity for clerestory lighting. Between the clerestory windows and the columns there is necessarily a space in which there can be no windows because of the roof over the aisles. This space, which was later used for the *triforium,* was decorated differently in different periods and is one of the significant features in determining the style of a building. At one end was a semicircular *apse,* which was used for the high altar. It was traditionally at the east, and that part of the church was known as the choir.

In the early churches the building was the one simple rectangle with apse. Later the plan was adapted to the shape of a cross by the addition of cross aisles between the nave and the choir. The arms thus made are known as *transepts*. Directly opposite the high altar, i.e., at the west, was the main entrance.

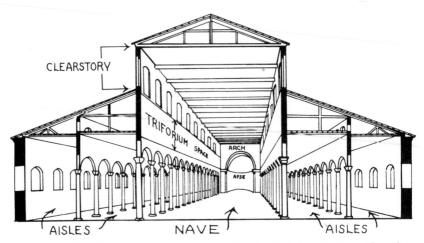

Fig. 150. Basilica. Perspective cross section of early Christian Basilica. (Drawing by Thad Suits after Dorothy Shea in Sewall, *A History of Western Art,* p. 281. Henry Holt and Company.)

Early Christian Architecture

The early Christian church, of which Sant' Apollinare in Classe at Ravenna (Figure 151) is an example, does not have transepts; the clerestory is heavy and the windows are small. The columns separating the nave from the aisles follow the Roman orders with flat lintels or round arches between them. The interiors are often decorated with elaborate mosaics as in Sant' Apollinare (Figure 152).

ROMANESQUE ARCHITECTURE

Romanesque architecture differs from early Christian in many ways. One of the most important is its use of the arch. In shape it was the round arch employed by the Romans, but when it was introduced into Romanesque building, it took on several different forms. First is the *recessed arch.* An opening, especially if it be a door, is made of a series of arches, each slightly farther back than the preceding, so that the

FIG. 151. Sant' Apollinare in Classe (second quarter of sixth century). Interior looking toward apse. (Marble, mosaic, and plaster; wooden roofing. Length: 150 feet; width: 98 feet. Ravenna. Photograph by Anderson.)

FIG. 152. Sant' Apollinare in Classe. Detail of interior looking toward apse. (Mosaic. Ravenna. Photograph, courtesy of the Italian State Tourist Office.)

305

door or window is deeply recessed. Often, as in the door at Aulnay (Figure 153), each recess is decorated with carvings. In this way the opening gains greatly in weight and massiveness. The arch, also, is combined with one or two other arches under one large arch and becomes a _compound arch_. In the cathedral at Modena (Figure 154) we have two small arches combined under one large arch which is recessed. Between the small arches is a small column, or _colonnette_. The colonnette is very light and unsubstantial, largely ornamental. In the doorway at Aulnay we notice that each of the recesses ends with a colonnette. Often the small arches are combined to form an arcade as in the cathedral at Pisa (Figure 156). In the façade at Modena we see a round window above the main doorway. Such a window, called a _rose window_, becomes usual in the Gothic adaptation of this style. Towers are another feature that made a first appearance in Romanesque architecture.

In the interior of the Abbaye-aux-Dames at Caen (Figure 155) the triforium space is no longer empty but is filled with small arches. There are recessed arches between the pillars of the nave. Most im-

Fɪɢ. 153. St. Pierre, portal of South Transept (twelfth century). (Stone. Aulnay, Foto Marburg.)

portant is the ceiling. When the principle of the arch was used in the covering of large buildings, the first result was the barrel vault. It was simply a succession of arches. The groin vault was next made by cutting the barrel vault at right angles (Figure 155a). Later it was discovered that diagonal arches or ribs could be built that would support the entire weight of the roof. The space between the ribs could then be filled in with lighter material. This system, known as "ribbed

FIG. 154. Cathedral (1099–1106). Modena. (Photograph by Anderson.)

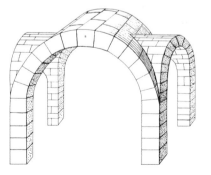

Fig. 155. Abbaye-aux-Dames, or La Trinité. Interior, looking toward choir (ca. second half of eleventh century, remodeled twelfth century). (Stone. Average width of middle aisle: ca. 26 feet; height: ca. 52 feet. Caen. Photograph by Stoedtner.)

Fig. 155a. Groin Vault (Drawing by Thad Suits).

vaulting," is the chief characteristic of Romanesque and Gothic architecture. This construction also made a change in the columns; the ribs of the ceiling had to be supported at the base and were, therefore, carried down to the floor. A number of these ribs made a pier or column.

GOTHIC ARCHITECTURE

As the Gothic developed from the Romanesque, the buildings became larger and taller, the change having been made possible by the use of the pointed arch. The thrust of an arch changes with its shape (Figure 155b). In general, the flatter the arch the greater the thrust, and the steeper the arch the more nearly the thrust is absorbed in the vertical wall. With the pointed arch, therefore, the buildings could be made higher than with the round arch.

With the higher buildings came a new type of buttress. The general shape of the exterior of a cathedral can be clearly seen in the cathedral of Pisa (Figure 156), with its central nave rising above the aisles on each side. In the early churches, as at Pisa, no extra support was needed for the central section, but as the churches grew larger and taller, it was found necessary to reinforce this part of the building. If a solid buttress were put up, it would cut off the aisles below. Accordingly the plan was devised of making a buttress at the aisle wall from which a half arch was stretched out over the aisle to support the roof of the nave. Sometimes just one such arch was sufficient; sometimes, as at Amiens (Figures 156a and 157), two were used, one above the other. These are called *flying buttresses*. The photograph of Notre Dame at Paris (Figure 158) shows the flying buttresses as they are

FIG. 155b. Direction of thrust in round and pointed arch. (W. D. Richmond, from Sewall, *A History of Western Art*, p. 191. Drawing by Thad Suits. Henry Holt and Company.)

FIG. 156. Busketus and Rainaldus, architects. Cathedral and Leaning Tower (1063–1100). (White, black, and colored marbles and some stone. Length: 312 feet; width, 106 feet. Pisa. Photograph, courtesy of the Italian State Tourist Office.)

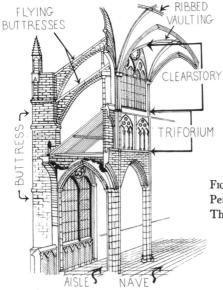

FLYING BUTTRESSES

RIBBED VAULTING

CLEARSTORY

TRIFORIUM

BUTTRESS

AISLE   NAVE

FIG. 156a. Amiens Cathedral. Perspective cross-section. (Drawing by Thad Suits after Viollet-le-Duc.)

actually seen. More than any other characteristic of Gothic architecture, they seem to create its mood of soaring aspiration.

In the Romanesque cathedral, several small windows were combined in a compound arch; in the Gothic, this process was continued until the arches appear only as stone tracery. Eventually the windows

Fig. 157. Cathedral of Notre Dame (begun 1220), interior. (Stone. Height: 147 feet; width of middle aisle: 43 feet. Amiens. Photograph, Clarence Ward.)

FIG. 158. Cathedral of Notre Dame (twelfth and thirteenth centuries). View of apse, showing the flying buttresses. (Length: about 415 feet; height of fleche: about 310 feet. Paris. Photograph, Clarence Ward.)

became so large that the walls ceased to have any function as walls; the roof was supported by the huge buttresses and the entire wall space filled with stained-glass windows. The triforium space was regularly filled with small arches, and the rose window became large and important. The doorways changed too. In the Romanesque church the façade sometimes had one doorway, sometimes three. The Gothic façade regularly had three doorways. Each was made with multiple orders, like the Romanesque, though the arch, of course, was pointed. The decorations, also, were much more elaborate. In the

Romanesque they were relatively simple moldings, with or without carvings of conventional designs, figures, animals, or fruit. In the Gothic the human figure became the characteristic decoration, a doorway being filled with rows of saints or kings.

In general shape the façade is a rectangle resting on the short side, and the great height is emphasized by the two towers that usually complete the design. In Notre Dame at Paris (Figure 159) and in the cathedrals at Amiens (Figure 171) and Reims, the towers are square and relatively short, but in many other cathedrals, such as Cologne (Figure 176) and Chartres, the towers are tall and pointed.

The Gothic cathedral often took centuries to build, and the same style was not used throughout. Part of a building may be in Romanesque, part in early Gothic, and another part in late Gothic. As the ideas of architecture changed the building itself was changed. In the Chartres Cathedral, one of the greatest of all cathedrals, the towers are

FIG. 159. Cathedral of Notre Dame (twelfth and thirteenth centuries). (Stone. Diameter of rose window: 42 feet; height of towers: 223 feet. Paris. Photograph, courtesy of the Trans-World Airlines, Inc.)

not the same; the older tower is shorter, more solid, and more substantial than its younger brother.

RENAISSANCE ARCHITECTURE

In Renaissance architecture the cathedral or temple is no longer the typical building; secular architecture comes to the fore as in Roman times. Although Renaissance architecture is a return to the ideals of the Greeks and Romans, it is not a slavish imitation, but rather a free use of the materials found in classic architecture. The designers got their ideas from Greece and Rome, but they used these suggestions freely, according to their own tastes, in a way that was original. For example, in the Medici-Riccardi Palace at Florence (Figure 48), designed by Michelozzo, we find the round arches of the Romans. On the first floor a single arch occupies the space of two arches on the second and third floors. In the upper floors, moreover, the window space is filled with the compound arch of the Romanesque. At the top of this building there is a large cornice, heavy enough to crown the

Fig. 160. Michelangelo (1475–1564), Italian painter, sculptor, and poet. Palace of the Senate (begun 1538). Rome. (Photograph by Anderson.)

whole mass of the building. There is also a molding or *stringcourse* that separates one story from the other.

In the Palace of the Senate at Rome (Figure 160), designed by Michelangelo, we find the stringcourse and the cornice, this time surmounted by a balustrade. In addition, each large window has its own post-and-lintel system. The windows are decorated with pediments; some are triangular, some are rounded. The classical rule would have been one pediment, one building, and the pediment would have been in scale with the building. Between the windows are flat columns called *pilasters.*

The overhanging cornice, the stringcourse, the pilaster, and the ornamental pediment are characteristic features of the Renaissance style. Another is the dome on a drum. The Roman dome was so low that it could hardly be seen from the outside. In Renaissance architecture the dome was made small, and it was raised high on a circular drum and surmounted with a lantern. The curve of the dome was changed, too; it was made much steeper, and its sides were ribbed, as we see in the dome of St. Peter's (Figure 161).

FIG. 161. Michelangelo (1475–1564). St. Peter's Cathedral, apse and dome (1547–1564). (Stone. Height of dome: 435 feet. Rome. Photograph by Stoedtner.)

In the smaller building, whether residence, church, or store, the Renaissance produced a type of symmetrical building of great simplicity and beauty. In England it is known as the Georgian style, and in the United States as the American colonial.

NINETEENTH CENTURY ARCHITECTURE

The nineteenth century in architecture is known as a period of *eclecticism*. Eclecticism means freedom of choice; in architecture it means the freedom to choose from the styles of the past. In former times architects had used the style of the period because that was the way things were being done. But in the nineteenth century both architects and clients became style-conscious, and they deliberately chose to make a building in one style or another. Hence it happens that we have in almost any American city examples of all the historical styles from the Greek down. This self-consciousness about choice of style has produced some good and some bad results. The Gothic motive in the Brooklyn Bridge is well suited to the tall pillars of that bridge. On the other hand it is love for the Gothic that is responsible for the "gingerbread" and scroll decorations on many houses.

The interest in various styles has resulted in the adoption of certain styles as suitable for certain types of building: Gothic for churches, Baroque for theaters, Renaissance for government buildings, and so on.

The real objection to eclecticism is philosophical. In the course of historical development, each of the major styles has been evolved to meet the needs of its own age and to express its philosophy. To go back to the style of a previous age is essentially false.

MODERN ARCHITECTURE

Skeleton Construction

Skeleton construction is a development of modern times, and on it most of our great modern structures depend. But skeleton construction in its turn was made possible by the development of two new materials: structural steel and reinforced concrete.

Structural steel dates back to 1855 when Bessemer invented his process for the mass production of steel. As the advantages of steel became apparent it gradually superseded cast iron. These advantages are primarily that it is resilient, strong, and reliable.

Concrete is composed of sand, crushed stone or gravel, water, and cement. When mixed it is a semifluid which, owing to the cement, dries into a hard, stonelike substance. Forms are made just the size and shape desired. The fluid concrete is poured into them; when dry it forms a solid substance of just that form and shape. Concrete is very strong, and it will stand great weight, but it will not stand strain or tension. At the end of the last century, some French engineers discovered that by adding steel rods to concrete they could give it the lacking tensile strength; in other words, it would withstand strain. Reinforced concrete, as the new material is called, is thus the combination of concrete and steel. It has the strength of concrete, and like concrete it can readily be made into any shape. At the same time it will withstand strain as does steel. It is also much cheaper than steel and lighter in weight.

In skeleton construction, strong but slender beams of steel or reinforced concrete make the framework of a building, and on it all the other parts are placed or hung. This type of construction has opened many new possibilities in building. First, it has made possible tall buildings, because the skeletons are strong but light. The walls which are hung from the skeleton are merely curtains to keep out cold and air. They may be made entirely of glass. They have no weight to speak of, and they are not essential to the strength of the building. A modern

Fig. 162. Skidmore, Owings, and Merrill, American architects. The Inland Steel Building (1958). (Steel and glass. Main building 19 stories, tower 25 stories. Chicago, Illinois. Photograph, Bill Hedrich, Hedrich-Blessing, Chicago.)

skyscraper, if built of masonry in the old fashion, would need to have the first floors of solid stone to support the weight of the upper stories. In the building of the Inland Steel Company (Figure 162) in Chicago, the columns which carry the weight of the building are on the outside. As a result, the entire space on any floor is free of posts or pillars and, if it is desired, can be used as a single room.

Moreover, with skeleton construction the building may be set up off the ground on posts so that the ground floor may be used for outdoor living or for garage and driveway. Another important result of this type of construction is the fact that an opening of any size may be spanned. Lintels of stone are necessarily short, since stone cannot be cut in great lengths and stone will not bear strain. Lintels of wood are longer, but they are obviously limited. Since steel may be made of any length and strength, a door or a window may be of any desired width.

Skeleton construction also allows freedom in the shape of the house. Concrete is a fluid material and can take any shape. Buildings of wood, brick, or stone tend to be rectangular, partly because of the difficulty of putting a roof on any but a rectangular building. Now, buildings may be made of any shape: circular, round, or square. In the Guggenheim Museum in New York City the galleries mount in a continuous spiral. In the State Fair Arena (Figure 163) at Raleigh, North Carolina, the walls are two opposing parabolas of glass and concrete, with their open ends joined on the ground and their arches rising out-

FIG. 163. Matthew Nowicki (1910–1950) and William Henley Deitrick, American architects. State Fair Arena, 1953. (Width of interior: 300 feet. Raleigh, North Carolina. Photograph, State Advertising Division, Raleigh, N. C.)

ward from each other. The arena measures eight hundred feet across in all directions and there is not a single column to obstruct the view. The building seats about nine thousand.

Cantilever Construction

Cantilever is a special form of steel and reinforced concrete construction. *Cantilever* has reference to any member or unit of an architectural design which projects beyond its support. The cantilever principle is often seen in bridges, where each half of the bridge

FIG. 164. Frank Lloyd Wright (1869–1959), American architect. Research and Development Tower of S. C. Johnson and Son, Inc. (1947–1950). (Brick and concrete with walls of glass tubing. Height of tower: 156 feet [50 feet underground]; each floor 40 feet square; each alternate floor 38 feet in diameter. Racine, Wisconsin. Photograph, courtesy of Johnson Wax.)

is supported on one side only. The two halves meet in the center to form the bridge, but each half is entirely independent of the other. In most airplanes the wings are attached to the body in a cantilever construction. We see the principle in buildings when the upper story juts out beyond the lower. The two essentials of cantilever construction are first, that the material used be able to stand the strain (i.e., have the tensile strength), and second, that it be fastened securely at the side where it is supported. This principle, which is very old, has been much used in recent years, because the piece that projects can be larger in steel and reinforced concrete than in older materials.

The cantilever was used rather widely by the American architect Frank Lloyd Wright. In a number of houses he used the cantilever in a veranda, so that the roof projects over the porch with no columns or pillars to hold it up. In one case he had a house projecting over a waterfall by means of cantilevered balconies. For the research building of the Johnson Wax Company (Figure 164), Mr. Wright erected a tall building in which all the floors are cantilevered from one central column. The floors are alternately square and round. The whole is enclosed in glass. The central column contains elevators and tubes for air conditioning besides all the passages for the machinery of the building, electric controls, etc.

Organic Architecture

The boast of modern architecture is that it is organic. Eclectic architecture, as we saw, was primarily decorative. The architect and his client chose a certain façade or a certain treatment of the material because they liked the looks of it, and often it had little if any relation to the actual structure of the house. House plans were frequently presented as floor plans with the exterior to be finished in Gothic, classic, American colonial, or what have you. But when we say modern architecture is organic, we mean that there is organic unity in planning, structure, materials, and site; all are designed to meet exact needs. The needs of the age are many and various: factories, office buildings, laboratories, railroad stations, schools, hospitals, mass housing, airports, broadcasting stations, theaters, churches, homes, dormitories. The demands of each must be studied and met if the building is to be good.

To study in detail one example of a building designed for a special need, we will take the chapel at Stephens College, designed by Eero Saarinen. The chapel was intended primarily as a place for private

Fig. 165. Eero Saarinen, architect. Chapel, Stephens College (finished 1956). (Brick. 70 feet by 70 feet. Columbia, Missouri.)

worship. It was presumed that small functions might be held there, like a wedding, a baptism, or an occasional concert, but such occasions were not to be frequent enough to interfere with private devotions. Moreover, the chapel was dedicated to the One God, the one maker and ruler of the universe, whether the form of worship were that of Jew, Mohammedan, Buddhist, or Christian. No one was to feel a stranger or unwelcome. Therefore, there were to be no symbols of any one faith such as the cross, or the star of David: all symbols were to be large and general.

The building as designed by Mr. Saarinen is square, foursquare, close to the earth; walls and roof make one unit, clinging to the ground and at the same time pointing up and ending in the central steeple. The walls are not interrupted by any windows, but at the entrance in the center of each side is a portico of stained glass, serving, as Mr. Saarinen said, as a small lantern leading to the chapel (Figures 165 and 166).

The interior is simple and direct. If one were to draw diagonals from the four corners of the building, he would obtain four equal triangles. One of these is designed for the organ and choir, the other three for the audience. In the exact center of the room is the altar, a plain square block. The chief light comes from the base of the spire and falls directly on the altar.

Fig. 166. Stephens College Chapel. Interior of Fig. 165.

An ambulatory around the entire auditorium is separated from the main chapel by a screen of interlaced brick, which makes a division but at the same time gives a view of the interior and the stained-glass doors beyond. The organ and choir are set behind a screen of wooden pieces, light brown and black. The ceiling is of wood in a square design.

The general effect is of simplicity and greatness. The place is small but one has vistas of vast spaces; the room is intimate, but its many vistas are conducive to thoughts of the distant and the far away. It is the kind of place where one can get away from the perplexities of everyday in the contemplation of the infinite.

FOR FURTHER EXPLORATION

The study of styles in architecture should enable the student to recognize the various styles in historical buildings and to identify elements of older styles in modern buildings. Work with pictures of buildings is valuable chiefly as a prelude to the recognition of details in actual buildings. For this no specific questions can be asked.

The student may identify styles or details of styles in the buildings of his home town. Again, the teacher may name certain buildings as examples of specific styles, and ask the student to name the characteristics by which the style is identified.

CHAPTER 13

FORM IN MUSIC

FORMS BASED ON THE ORGANIZATION OF THE MUSIC

It has been said that the problem of form in music is primarily that of making music last; a short tune may be very beautiful, but it takes only a few seconds to play or sing, and if repeated many times, soon becomes monotonous. A song with many verses will account for a number of repetitions, but even then it lasts only a few minutes; the music must stop, or some way must be found to keep it going. Hence there have been developed various ways of combining or varying short tunes so as to make music of greater stature. In general, these may be classified into two groups as (1) those that depend primarily on the use of one melody, and (2) those that employ contrasting melodies. Those that employ one melody are the variation form and the fugue. Those that depend on contrast of melody are binary form, song form, minuet and trio, rondo, first-movement form, suite, and sonata.

The Variation Form

The first step in hearing form is to listen for themes or phrases which are repeated; sometimes they are identical and sometimes they are changed. The next step is to plot, or make a map of, the tunes you hear. For this work the letters of the alphabet are commonly employed. In Chopin's Prelude No. 7 in A major, one phrase is repeated eight times. The first and fifth are exactly alike, but all the others are slightly different. It could be diagrammed:

$$A \quad A^1 \quad A^2 \quad A^3 \quad A \quad A^4 \quad A^5 \quad A^6$$

Prelude No. 7 in A major

Frédéric Chopin
Polish (1809-1849)

The music divides into two units of four phrases each. The first measure gives the theme itself, the second goes higher and the third and fourth fall back. The statement in the second half follows the same general plan, but the phrases go higher. The climax comes in the sixth measure, when the music seems to make a great effort to rise only to fall again.

The opening phrases of Verdi's "Caro nome" from *Rigoletto* repeat the same theme four times. In this case the second and fourth versions are the same, the first is slightly higher, and the third is the highest of the three. Later this air is changed in a different way by additions that indicate the fluttering of the girl's heart.

Rigoletto, Act II
Caro nome

Giuseppi Verdi
Italian (1813-1901)

Ca - ro no - me che il mio cor fe - sti
pri - mo pal - pi tar, le de - li - zie del - l'a -
mor mi dêi sem - pre ram - men- - tar! Col pen-sier il mio de -
sir a te sem - pre___ vo - le - rà, etc.

This kind of repetition forms the basis for the *variation form*. A charming example is found in Schubert's Quintet in A major for Piano and Strings, Op. 114. This quintet is usually called *The Trout* because Schubert uses as his basic theme a song he had written earlier about a trout. The words of the song describe the way the trout was caught, while the accompaniment portrays in realistic style the darting movements of the fish in the water. In the fourth movement of his Quintet, Schubert has a series of variations on this air. It is played first on the violin; then the different instruments take the lead.

Variation 1   Piano
Variation 2   Viola
Variation 3   Bass
Variation 4   All instruments (a fragment given to each)
Variation 5   Cello
Variation 6   Violin

"Schoolboys love the variations in which the tune can always be heard with such slight but delicious alteration," writes A. J. B. Hutchings,[1] "and old boys who do not love them are advancing in sin, as well as in years."

In the slow movement of Haydn's *Surprise Symphony* there are four variations on the theme. The theme itself is a very simple folk tune, one to which we sometimes sing the alphabet. The "surprise" comes in a loud chord after the theme has been heard twice.

Surprise Symphony
Second movement

Franz J. Haydn
Austrian (1732-1809)

1. The first variation repeats the main theme with a counterpoint on the violins.

2. In the second variation the eighth notes are changed to six-teenths, with a "bouncing" effect. This variation starts very loud and becomes softer. It is repeated in a minor key. The two halves are treated differently.

3. The strings and wood winds play together while the flute sings a new melody.

4. This variation shows large chords and a broad swing with a good deal of running around.

In Handel's Harpsichord Suite in E major, which is usually known under the name *The Harmonious Blacksmith*, there are five variations. The air is serene and tranquil even if it does sound a bit like a black-smith beating on his forge. In the variations, the pace remains the same, but the number of tones to a measure is increased each time the melody is repeated.

Sometimes the composer makes very free use of the original theme. For example, in Elgar's *Enigma Variations* the theme describes the

---

[1] Slip case of the Columbia recording.

artist, and each of the variations pictures one of his friends. The initial air pervades the music, but it is a variation more in spirit than in exact repetition of tones.

Passacaglia. The *passacaglia* is a special example of the theme and variation form. The theme is played over and over in the bass, while many contrapuntal variations are played above and against it. The most famous *passacaglia* is that of Bach, Passacaglia and Fugue in C minor for Organ. It has been transcribed for orchestra by Stokowski. The theme is a very simple one. First we hear this theme alone as played by the low strings, next it is accompanied by the high strings, then by wood winds and French horn, and so on for twenty variations. The contrapuntal variations become more and more complicated until the end, when there is a fugue.

Passacaglia and Fugue in C minor

J. S. Bach
German (1685-1750)

The Fugue

The fugue is a contrapuntal form. The word *fugue* means flight, as the voices seem to flee one from the other. The fugue may be described briefly as an elaborate and intricate round. The first voice begins singing the theme, called the *subject,* and as soon as it has finished, the second voice begins. The first voice, however, does not stop when the second voice enters, but begins singing a new melody, called a *counter-subject,* or *answer.* In this way, all the voices come in, one by one.

In a round, all voices enter at the same pitch. In a fugue the voices show the normal range of *soprano, contralto, tenor,* and *bass.* Obviously the four voices do not sing at the same pitch; the contralto sings a fourth below the soprano, the tenor an octave below the soprano, and the bass an octave below the contralto. A fugue is not, however, limited to four voices, nor do the voices always enter in this order. Yet whatever the number of voices or the order of entrance, the distinction in pitch is regularly found. The number of voices is usually stated in the title of the composition, as a fugue in three voices, etc. Most fugues have from three to five voices.

An excellent example of a fugue is Bach's Fugue in G minor, often called the "Little G minor Fugue" to distinguish it from the "Great" or longer fugue in G minor. This fugue was written for the organ, but it has been transcribed for the orchestra by Stokowski. It is easier to follow the theme in the transcription than in the original, since a different instrument is used for each voice. There are four voices. The first voice, soprano, is played on the oboe; the second, contralto, on the English horn; the third and fourth, tenor and bass, are played on the bassoon and contrabassoon. Before the third voice enters, there is a short transition played by the oboe and English horn. In each case, the voice continues singing, so that when the fourth voice enters with the main theme, the other three voices are singing the countersubject.

Little Fugue in G Minor

J. S. Bach
German (1685-1750)

etc.

The introduction, where each voice states the theme, is called the *exposition*. In the remainder of the fugue, called the *development*, the themes are presented in a great variety of ways. No rules can be given but we may notice three devices by which the composer seeks to avoid monotony:

(1) *Episode.* He may introduce new material, known as the episode. It is often found near the beginning of the development, just after all the voices have been introduced, and before the subject and counter-subject are heard again. Throughout the middle section, subjects and episodes may be said to alternate.

(2) *Stretto.* Often the voices are made to overlap as though the answer could not wait for the subject to finish and were treading on its toes. This device called *stretto* greatly increases the excitement.

(3) *Pedal point.* One tone is held for a long time. It increases tension because it creates dissonance and demands resolution.

A fugue ends with a climax in which there is a last full-bodied presentation of the subject.

Another favorite Bach fugue is the one in C minor, from *The Well-tempered Clavier.*

Fugue in C Minor

J. S. Bach
German (1685-1750)

Contrast of Theme

Various forms are built on a contrast of themes.

Binary Form. In the melody of "The Harmonious Blacksmith," from Handel's Harpsichord Suite in E major, the music is in two parts which are not the same. As someone has said, it is as though you walk up a hill, rest a short time, and then walk down again. We may map this melody as A B in form.

Harpsichord Suite in E major

Air: "The Harmonious Blacksmith"

Georg Friedrich Handel
German (1685-1759)

Another example is Brahm's *Lullaby* "Hushabye and goodnight."

America must also be plotted as A B, the A part ending with "Of thee I sing," and the B part finishing the song. This form, often called *binary form,* was very popular in the seventeenth and eighteenth centuries and can be found at its best in the music of Couperin and Scarlatti.

Lullaby

Johannes Brahms
German (1833-1897)

Drink to Me Only with Thine Eyes

Ben Jonson, "To Celia"
Music traditional

First phrase - A

Drink to me on - ly with thine eyes, And I will pledge with

Second phrase, same as first - A

mine; Or leave a kiss but in the cup And I'll not look for

Third phrase - B

wine. The thirst that from the soul doth rise Doth

Fourth phrase, same as first - A

ask a drink di - vine; But might I of Jove's

nec - tar sup, I would not change for thine.

330

Song Form. *Ternary form* states a theme, A, then a contrasting theme, B, and concludes with a return to the initial theme. In the folk song *Drink to Me Only with Thine Eyes,* we have four phrases. The first, A, is repeated; then a contrasting theme, B, is introduced; and then we go back to the A theme, making a pattern A A B A. This is exactly the pattern of the "Ode to Joy" in the last movement of Beethoven's Ninth Symphony. It is the pattern found in the *Blue Bells of Scotland,* quoted earlier. This form is so much used for hymns, folk songs, and all simple songs that it is frequently distinguished by name as *song form,* or four-part song form.

Minuet and Trio. The minuet-trio form makes an easy introduction to the group of larger forms that use the A B A pattern. The first melody, which is a *minuet,* is followed by a second, called a *trio,* and then the first is repeated again. This form may be expressed as an A B A form, each letter representing a complete unit. The minuet and trio of Mozart's *Eine kleine Nachtmusik* are reproduced here.

This form is regularly used for the third movement of a sonata or symphony. In the work of Mozart, this movement is usually minuet —

Serenade in G major

Eine kleine Nachtmusik

Minuet

Wolfgang Amadeus Mozart
German (1756-1791)

Trio

trio – minuet, as in the early symphonies of Beethoven. In Beethoven's later symphonies, the minuet is changed to a scherzo, and we have scherzo – trio – scherzo.

Rondo. In the *rondo,* the theme remains the same, but it is alternated with other tunes: A B A C, etc. The rondo is thus in essence an extension of the A B A design. Two, three, or more melodies are combined. The first or A melody is the important one and it occurs after every other tune. Typical forms for rondo are A B A C A, or A B A C A B A. The second movement of Mozart's *Eine kleine Nachtmusik* is a rondo in the pattern A B A C A and coda.

In strict rondo form it is not necessary to have any change or any development in the melodies. The A theme is exactly the same every time it appears. The repetition may become monotonous, and for this reason themes are often varied or developed slightly. They can never be varied a great deal, or we lose the distinguishing characteristic of the form, which is the constant return of the initial theme.

Serenade in G major

Eine kleine Nachtmusik

Slow movement

Wolfgang Amadeus Mozart
German (1756-1791)

First theme - A

Andante

Second theme - B

after which theme A is repeated

Third theme - C

after which theme A is repeated, leading to the Coda

First-Movement Form

The *first-movement form* is a complicated composition in what is essentially a ternary form, since it is made of three sections, the third repeating the first. These are known as exposition, development, and recapitulation.

The *exposition* contains two contrasting groups or themes. There may be an introductory theme, there will certainly be a transition theme between the two groups, and there will be some kind of concluding theme or transition to the development. In the *development*, the two groups of themes are broken down and developed in any way the composer desires. Ordinarily, the main emphasis is put on the first of the two themes, but this is by no means a rule. After the development section, the exposition is repeated in the *recapitulation*. The two groups which appeared first in contrasting keys now are in the same key. Otherwise there are few changes. The composition usually ends with a *coda*. The plan may be mapped as follows:

Exposition
    Theme A, in tonic
        Transition to theme B
    Theme B in key of dominant or other related key
        Transition
Development
    Varied use of themes A and/or B in many keys
Recapitulation or restatement
    Theme A in original key
        Transition to theme B
    Theme B in original key of theme A

Transition
Coda

Mozart's *Eine kleine Nachtmusik* illustrates the first-movement form
admirably.

Serenade in G major

Eine kleine Nachtmusik

First movement

Theme B, in dominant

repetition of second half of Theme B

Transition

the dominant

DEVELOPMENT: Theme A in D major, modulating to

C major for second half of Theme B

modulating variously and

leading to a

transitional passage

RECAPITULATION:

Theme A, in original key

337

Theme B, in tonic

Transition

CODA

The first movement of Beethoven's Fifth Symphony is another clear example of the form. In the exposition, the first theme is built on the famous "knocking" motive (p. 213). This theme is primarily rhythmic, with little interest in melody. The second theme therefore offers great contrast, since it is primarily melodic. The development uses chiefly the knocking theme, and the recapitulation repeats the two themes. The coda uses both themes, with emphasis on the first.

Symphony No. 5 in C minor
First Movement
First movement   Ludwig van Beethoven
Second theme   German (1770-1827)

Second Theme

The Suite

One of the earliest efforts in the attempt to make music of stature was the *suite,* a collection of dances. In the seventeenth and eighteenth centuries there were usually four dances, in the same key: (1) the *allemande,* a rather slow dance, (2) the *courante,* a dance of simple rhythms and running passages, (3) the *saraband,* a slow, stately ceremonial dance, and (4) the *gigue,* a fast, lively dance, kin to the English jig. Other dances could be and were added, even pieces not in dance form. In Bach's Suite No. 2, in B minor, for flute and strings, there are a rondo, saraband, *bourrée,* polonaise, and minuet. Furthermore, the suite opens with an overture, and ends with a section called "Badinerie," a bit of playfulness and mischief.

The modern suite has no necessary connection with dance forms. It is a collection of separate pieces which have been put together for some reason. Bizet, for instance, puts together excerpts from the opera in his *Carmen* suite. Ravel tries to evoke the spirit of former times in his suite *Le Tombeau de Couperin (The Tomb of Couperin).* Rimsky-Korsakov based his symphonic suite *Scheherazade* on the Arabian Nights. Prokofiev has written a suite on the adventures of the imaginary hero, Lieutenant Kiji.

Sonata

The *sonata* was developed after the suite. It is like the suite in that it is a series of independent compositions, each one of which may be and is played without any of the others. However, these are not all in the same key as are the dances in a suite. Traditionally, the sonata is made up of three or four compositions called *movements,* and there are very definite traditions about each. The first, which is the longest and most important, is usually a bright, gay piece; ordinarily it is marked *allegro.* In contrast, the second movement is slow and tuneful, *andante, adagio,* or even *lento.* The third is a dance; in the earlier sonatas the minuet was used, but in Beethoven's time the scherzo replaced the minuet. It is usually the shortest of the four movements, and when a sonata has only three movements, it is the third which is omitted. The fourth movement is again a bright, gay, fast movement, *allegro, presto.* Thus we have in the four movements of a sonata the contrasts in mood and speed which were characteristic of the suite, the sonata being successively fast, slow, dance, fast.

There are definite traditions, also, about the form of each movement. The first is usually in first-movement form; in fact, that form gets its name because it is the first movement of a sonata. It is sometimes called *sonata form* because it is the characteristic movement of a sonata. The third, or dance movement, if there be one, is always in the minuet-trio, or scherzo-trio form. For the second and fourth movements, the composer may use any form he wishes. Since the second movement is slow and melodious, the variation form is a favorite; and because it is fast, the rondo is often found in the last movement.

Sonata form has become very popular; in fact, it is now the form most widely used for long, serious compositions. It is played on different instruments and with different combinations of instruments. However, it is given different names, according to the instruments used. The word *sonata* is used when one instrument is involved. The *symphony,* written for and played by a symphony orchestra, calls for all the varied timbres and dynamics of the orchestra. The *trio, quartet,* and *quintet* are used for combinations of three, four, or five instruments. The strings usually form the backbone of the group, and such groups are always designated as string quartet, piano quintet (for strings and piano), etc. The *concerto* is played by a solo instrument with an orchestra, and is designated by the name of the solo instrument as violin concerto, etc. In the concerto the music is designed to show off the solo instrument, and hence it is usually music that demands technical dexterity. Sometimes the concerto is thought of primarily as a means for the exhibition of the brilliant technique of the solo performer, but that is hardly fair. The essential contrast is between the timbre, and even more the volume, of the solo instrument and the orchestra.

Formless Forms

Since music goes on in time, and it is never possible to see it or compare its members all at once, there can also be musical compositions without specific form, music with no set design. The more usual of these are listed here.

The *prelude* originally meant something designed to be played before something else, as the Preludes and Fugues of Bach, the Prelude to *Lohengrin,* etc. But the word has become less definite; the twenty-four preludes of Chopin are not preludes to anything; they are pieces in themselves. The word now enjoys both meanings: a piece to be played before something else, and a separate piece.

The *ballade* is an extended piece professing to be narrative. The only formal characteristic that can be discerned is that the ballades of Chopin are all in compound time.

The *impromptu* is a contradiction in terms, for it purports to be extemporaneous, which it obviously cannot be, being written down and published. However, it has connotations of spontaneity and of rather slight organization.

The *nocturne* professes that its atmosphere is suggested by the connotations of night. The nocturnes of Chopin are usually meditative or elegiac.

The *capriccio* is a capricious piece and the *intermezzo* should be an interval in some larger whole. Brahms uses these two titles in his piano works for his more lively and more reflective pieces respectively.

The *étude,* a technical study, became important in music at the time of Chopin and Liszt. The *toccata* is earlier; its name conveys a display of keyboard skill.

FORMS BASED ON SUBJECT OR FUNCTION

It is a temptation to say that in this section we will examine the forms in music that are not musical! For there is a definite and legitimate distinction between the points of view in the two parts of the chapter. In the first section those forms were discussed in which the determining factor was the organization of the music, as in the rondo or the fugue. In the present section, the forms discussed all have to do with subject, and the name of the composition is determined by that reference, not by the organization of the music. Sometimes the words of the subject are sung, as in a song or an opera; sometimes the subject forms the imaginative impetus only. But in either case, the music is trying to express the emotions and ideas of the subject, and it may use any musical form that seems fitting.

Program Music

In chapter 2, program music was defined as music with subject, and little needs to be added to that discussion. However, we may note that program music generally falls into three classes: the imitative, the descriptive, and the narrative.

Imitative music imitates the actual sound of the subject, as in Rimsky-Korsakov's *Flight of the Bumblebee.*

Descriptive music is typified in Beethoven's Sixth Symphony, the *Pastoral.* It describes a day in the country, with a festive gathering of country people. Their pleasure is interrupted by a storm which soon subsides, and the festivities are resumed. Beethoven's own notes, usually printed with the symphony, are as follows:

Pastoral Symphony, or a recollection of country life (more an expression of feeling than a portrayal)

1. *Allegro ma non troppo*—The cheerful feelings aroused by arrival in the country
2. *Andante molte moto*—Scene by the brook
3. *Allegro*—Peasants' merrymaking
4. *Allegro*—Storm
5. *Allegretto*—Shepherds' song: glad and thankful feelings after the storm

In this class too belong compositions which try to distill the feeling or essence of a scene, for example, the moonlight evoked in Debussy's *Clair de Lune.*

Narrative music tells a story. Dukas in *The Sorcerer's Apprentice* tells the old story of the person who starts a magic charm going and cannot stop it. His immediate source is a ballad by Goethe, *Der Zauberlehrling (The Sorcerer's Apprentice).* The apprentice has often heard his master utter a charm and order a broomstick to do his work. Left alone one day, he tries his hand, repeats the charm, and tells the broomstick to draw water for him. But when he has all the water he wants, he realizes that he has forgotten the word to stop the broom from bringing water. In desperation he seizes an axe, cuts the broomstick in two, only to have each half hauling water! Just when the flood is getting out of control the master returns, speaks the correct formula, the broomstick retires to its corner, and the deluge ceases.

Folk Song and Art Song

A song in the broadest sense is anything sung. Songs are easily divided into two classes: folk song and art song. *Folk songs* are the songs of the folk. They are communal in that they are the property of the community and express the life of the community. Everybody knows them and everybody sings them. No one knows, and no one cares, who wrote them. They show no trace of individual authorship, or if they ever did, these traces have been lost throughout long ages of singing.

An *art song* is the work of an individual composer and as such shows his individuality. Some of the greatest writers of art songs are Schubert, Schumann, Brahms, Wolf, and Grieg. Each composer tries to make the music of his song fit the words, but his song is nevertheless characteristic of himself. One of Schumann's songs is not like one of Schubert's. On the other hand, certain songs by known composers have so much of the simplicity and spontaneity of folk songs that they are accepted and sung by the people as their songs. Such songs are rightly classed as folk songs and are usually found in volumes of folk songs. Examples are the American *Dixie* and *Swanee River,* and the Bohemian *Songs My Mother Taught Me.* The person who sings one of Schubert's songs is usually conscious that the song is by Schubert; at any rate he thinks of it as an art song, and could look up the composer if he wished. But the Southerner who applauds *Dixie* almost certainly never heard of its composer, Dan Emmett; and he might dispute the point if he were told it was written by a Northerner. Or, if he did know these facts, he would be indifferent to them. *Dixie,* to him, is not a song like Schubert's *Serenade.* It is the expression of community spirit; it is the song of the South.

Folk songs are often classified according to subject as hunting songs (*John Peel*), cowboy songs (*Home on the Range*), spirituals (*Nobody Knows de Trouble I See*), etc. They are also classified according to the country from which they come: the *Volga Boatman* is Russian, *Auld Lang Syne* is Scotch, etc.

The *Christmas Carol* is the folk song of the Christmas season. Many are very old. The *Angelic Hymn,* with the refrain "Gloria, in Excelsis Deo," is supposed to be the one referred to by the Bishop of Rome in

A.D. 129, the first Christian hymn as well as the first carol. The melody of *Adeste Fideles* (*O Come, All Ye Faithful*) is attributed to Saint Bonaventura (13th century). It is thought to be an old Latin carol. The *Coventry Carol* ("Lullay, thou little tiny child") originated in the fifteenth century Coventry play, probably around 1591. Composed carols include: *O Little Town of Bethlehem*, by Lewis Redner, and *Silent Night*, by Franz Grüber.

Strophic Form and Continuous Form

Another classification of songs has to do with the form of the music, whether it be strophic or continuous. In *strophic form* the same music is repeated for each stanza. In *Barbara Allen*, for example, the same music is used, no matter whether one is singing of the "Merry month of May," of Barbara's scornful words to her lover, or her death. The only differences that can be introduced are in tempo, dynamics, and general expressiveness.

In *continuous form* the music is adapted to the words. Schubert's *Erlking* is a classic example. The story is well known.

Wer reitet so spät durch Nacht und Wind?
Es ist der Vater mit seinem Kind.
Er hat den Knaben wohl in dem Arm,
Er fasst ihn sicher, er hält ihn warm.

Mein Sohn, was birgst du so bang dein Gesicht?
Siehst, Vater, du den Erlkönig nicht?
Den Erlenkönig mit Kron' und Schweif?—
Mein Sohn, es ist ein Nebelstreif.

"Du liebes Kind, komm, geh mit mir!
Gar schöne Spiele spiel' ich mit dir.
Manch' bunte Blumen sind an dem Strand,
Meine Mutter hat manch gülden Gewand."

Mein Vater, mein Vater, und hörest du nicht,
Was Erlenkönig mir leise verspricht?—
Sei ruhig, bleibe ruhig, mein Kind:
In dürren Blättern säuselt der Wind.—

"Willst, feiner Knabe, du mit mir gehn?
Meine Töchter sollen dich warten schön;
Meine Töchter führen den nächtlichen Reihn
Und wiegen und tanzen und singen dich ein."

Mein Vater, mein Vater, und siehst du nicht dort
Erlkönigs Töchter am düstern Ort?—
Mein Sohn, mein Sohn, ich seh' es genau:
Es scheinen die alten Weiden so grau.—

"Ich liebe dich, mich reizt deine schöne Gestalt;
Und bist du nicht willig, so brauch' ich Gewalt."
Mein Vater, mein Vater, jetzt fasst er mich an!
Erlkönig hat mir ein Leids getan!—

Dem Vater grauset's, er reitet geschwind,
Er hält in den Armen das ächzende Kind,
Erreicht den Hof mit Mühe und Not—
In seinen Armen das Kind war tot.
    —JOHANN WOLFGANG VON GOETHE (1749–1832, German
       poet, dramatist, and novelist),
      Der Erlkönig

*   *   *

Who gallops so late through wind and night?
A father bearing his son in flight;
He holds him tightly, breasting the storm,
To bear him safely and keep him warm.

"My son, why bury your face thus in fear?"
"Don't you see, father, the Erl-King draw near,
The king of spirits, with crown and with shroud?"
"My son, it is a wisp of cloud."

"My darling child, come, go with me!
I'll play the finest games with thee.
The brightest flowers grow on the shore;
My mother has clothes of gold in store."

"My father, my father, but surely you heard
The Erl-King's whisp'ring, promising word?"
"Be quiet; there is nothing to fear:
The wind is rustling through thickets sere."

"Wilt thou come with me, my boy, away
Where my daughters play with thee night and day?
For my daughters shall come in the night if thou weep
And rock thee and dance thee and sing thee to sleep."

"My father, my father, but do you not see
His daughters lurking by yon dark tree?"

"My son, my son, it is only the light
Of old willows gleaming gray through the night."

"I love thee so, thy beauty leaves no other course,
And if thou'rt not willing, I'll take thee by force."
"My father, my father, he drags me from you;
Erl-King has seized me, and hurts me too."

The father shudders; he spurs through the wild.
His arms strain closer the weak, moaning child.
He gains his home with toil and dread—
Clasped in his arms there, the child was dead.

                                        —Translated by Calvin Brown [2]

In Schubert's music we hear the galloping of the horse, and the thunder of the storm. The voices of the three characters are carefully differentiated. The father's voice is low, calm, assured; that of the child is high-pitched, afraid, curious, wondering; the erlking's voice is pleading and ingratiating, until he announces he will take the child by force, when it becomes brusque and harsh. At the end of the song the galloping and thunder, which have been continued throughout, suddenly cease as the father stops at his home and finds that the boy is dead.

Another song in continuous form is Schubert's *Gretchen at the Spinning Wheel*. Gretchen is singing a sad song that begins "Meine Ruh' ist hin, mein Herz ist schwer" ("My peace is gone, my heart is heavy"), as she mentally passes in review all the hours she has spent with her lover. Throughout, the song is accompanied by the ceaseless turning of the spinning wheel until she recalls the time of his kiss; then she stops work and the spinning sound is broken off abruptly. Later it is resumed slowly, but finally it gets back to its usual swift speed.

All folk songs are in strophic form, frequently though not always in the A A B A quatrain. Art songs may be in either strophic or continuous form. We have cited two of Schubert's songs as examples of continuous form. His *Serenade* and *Hedgeroses* are in strophic form.

The *aria* is a set piece for solo voice from an opera, oratorio, or cantata; usually it has the association of technical difficulty, although this is not essential. However, in many respects the aria is only a song. It is not usually in strophic form.

2 *Music and Literature,* pp. 71–72. Courtesy of Mr. Brown and the University of Georgia Press.

Madrigal, Motet, Anthem, Hymn

The *madrigal* and the *motet* are generally considered to be a product of the fifteenth, sixteenth, and seventeenth centuries. The madrigal and the motet are alike in that they are designed for unaccompanied voices and are usually polyphonic. They differ in that the madrigal is secular and the motet is sacred. The English madrigal school (Byrd, Morley, Gibbons, Weelkes, Wilbye) is the glory of English music and, indeed, one of the peaks in the whole history of the art. An example is Gibbons's *The Silver Swan*.

The *anthem* is the Protestant successor to the motet, though as time goes on, it is losing all the distinguishing characteristics of its predecessor. Anthems may be accompanied; they are not necessarily polyphonic, and they are being written today. But in the anthem we can still see vestiges of its polyphonic origin in the motet.

The *hymn* is a sacred strophic song; it is most often of four related phrases and is usually several stanzas in length, intended for community singing. The hymns of the German Lutheran church, especially those dating from the period between the Reformation and the time of Bach, have the special name of *chorals* or *chorales*. In these is to be found what is probably the highest level of hymn tunes. Examples are Luther's *A Mighty Fortress*, and the *Passion Chorale*, harmonized by Bach, and usually sung to the words *O Sacred Head Now Wounded*.

Opera

Opera is drama set to music: the words are sung instead of spoken. Like drama, opera uses the resources of acting, costuming, and staging. In short, there are three different elements in opera: (1) drama, (2) spectacle, and (3) music. Each has its own interests and each has at times been dominant. All are present in the standard opera. The drama tells the story which is the occasion for the performance. Spectacle is seen in the setting and costume, especially when they involve strange places and exotic effects: Egypt in *Aïda*, Japan in *Madame Butterfly*, Spain and gypsies in *Carmen*, and so on. In opera music is considered more important than either spectacle or drama. We think of opera as music, and in the final analysis opera stands or falls by its music.

Opera started in an attempt to reproduce the effect of the Greek drama in a kind of musical speech called *recitative*. The voices followed the accents of speech, but in musical tones. This recitative is more like chant than any other form of music today. The first operas, which were entirely composed of recitatives, must have been very tedious. Accordingly, songs were added to break the monotony: solos, duets, trios, quartets, choruses, etc. For a time the drama lost its importance, and the music was everything. At this time Gluck came along. He is known as the great reformer of opera, because he brought the drama back into prominence and insisted that the singers take their places in the plot. At the same time he continued to stress recitative and had many set and separable songs and choruses. This concept of opera is to be seen in the great operas of Verdi and Mozart. Drama is emphasized, but the music still contains recitative, and the great arias, duets, and choruses are set pieces which can be detached from the drama. We all know the arias "Caro nome," "Celeste Aïda," "Toreador's Song," as well as the "Soldier's Chorus" from *Faust*, and the sextette from *Lucia*.

A new and different type of opera was inaugurated by Wagner. He attempted to make a more unified work, with music and drama of equal importance, and therefore he called his works *music dramas*. The voices and the music combine to tell the story. In this way the orchestra is made important, and the music is continuous. In short, the music is not interrupted for set arias and ensembles by the singers; the vocal line is treated as one of the orchestral lines, and often the voices are subordinated to the orchestra. The action, too, is continuous; there is no pause from the beginning of an act to the fall of the curtain.

In addition, Wagner devised a new type of musical development based on themes. Each character and many of the important objects and places in the play have a musical motive, or theme: the "sword," the "rainbow," the "ring," the "Rhine," and even such abstractions as "fate." The entrance of a character is announced by his theme in the orchestra, and often the music tells us what the characters do not know. In the *Valkyrie*, for instance, when Siegmund is lying in Hunding's house, desolate because he has no sword, the music fairly shouts the sword theme, calling *our* attention, if not his, to the sword in the tree beside him.

Oratorio

Oratorio, like grand opera, is an extended piece of music employing the resources of orchestra, chorus, and individual singers. It differs from opera in many ways.

Subject. The subject of grand opera is usually serious, but it may be on any subject; in many of the great operas it is a love story. In oratorio the subject is usually biblical, and in many of the great oratorios the words are taken directly from the Bible. Handel's *Messiah* and Mendelssohn's *Elijah* are outstanding examples.

Performance. Operas are enacted on the stage, and oratorios are sung in a concert, without costume, stage setting, or lighting. The chorus and the soloists are on the stage, each rises when he is to perform, but there is no acting or taking of parts.

Use of recitative. In the oratorios, the recitative is of greater importance than in contemporary opera. Each aria is preceded by its recitative. We may cite from *The Messiah* the recitative, "Then shall the eyes of the blind be opened," preceding the aria, "He shall feed His flock like a shepherd."

Choruses. The choruses of an oratorio tend to be polyphonic in structure and, as befitting the subject, are weighty and solemn and powerful, like the "Hallelujah Chorus" from the *Messiah,* or "The Heavens are telling," from *The Creation.* The usual opera, probably telling a love story, has no like occasion. Accordingly, the choruses from opera are apt to sound cheap and tawdry in comparison with the choruses of oratorio. We can see this in the "Soldier's Chorus" from *Faust,* the "Anvil Chorus" from *Il Trovatore,* and even the "Triumphal March" from *Aïda.*

Cantata and passion are special forms of the oratorio. A *cantata* is a small oratorio. It may also be secular in subject. The subject of a *passion,* as the subject implies, is the death of Jesus. The words follow the text as found in one of the gospels. Passions are not numerous. Two of the greatest are Bach's *The Passion According to St. John,* and *The Passion According to St. Matthew.* A passion introduces singing by the audience from time to time. Otherwise a passion corresponds closely to an oratorio.

Mass

The *Mass* has been discussed earlier as an essential part of the liturgy of the Catholic church, and its five parts were named in chapter 3. From very early times the Mass has been set to music, and some of the greatest music of the world has been that composed for the Mass. In its music we find illustrations of the three great periods in music history. From the earliest period before the time of harmony or counterpoint, we have the Gregorian chant, which is simple, unaccompanied melody. Disembodied, aspiring, and unworldly, these Masses are absolutely cut off from any secular consideration. In the polyphonic period we have the great Masses of Josquin and Palestrina. In the later periods we have the Masses of Beethoven and Mozart.

The *Requiem* is celebrated for the repose of the dead. It gets its name from the first words of the text: "Requiem aeternam dona eis, Domine" (Give to them, O Lord, eternal rest.) Among Requiems we may mention those of Brahms, Bizet, and Mozart.

FOR FURTHER EXPLORATION

1. Suppose that you were going to write a set of variations on *Swanee River?* How many ways of changing the theme can you think of?

2. What are the characteristic rhythms of the usual dances? Of the fox trot, tango, *rumba*, polka?

3. If you have friends who are dancers, ask them to show you the pavan and the minuet.

4. Listen to some pieces in binary form, such as the *French Suites* of Bach. Would you be contented if the piece ended at the first half? If not, why not?

5. Take two small pieces, such as two waltzes by Schubert, and put them together to make A B A form. Take three or four, and construct a rondo.

6. Compare the first movement of Tchaikovsky's Fifth Symphony with the first movement of his Sixth Symphony. In the Sixth, the second theme is unmistakable but does not occur in the development. In the Fifth there are four distinct themes, apart from the introduction. Are they all used in the development?

7. Compare Mozart's Symphony in G minor with César Franck's Symphony in D minor. Does Mozart carry the same themes over from movement to movement? Does Franck? Which themes?

8. Listen to Tchaikovsky's Fifth Symphony, and observe how the theme of the introduction occurs in all the movements. How does the composer alter it in each case?

9. Listen to some piano pieces without knowing their titles. What type names would you give them?

10. Listen to the last movements of these sonatas and symphonies to see whether you can tell their form:

Haydn, *Surprise Symphony*
Haydn, *Clock Symphony*
Mozart, Symphony in G minor
Mozart, *Haffner Symphony*
Beethoven, *Pathétique Sonata,* Op. 13
Beethoven, *Waldstein Sonata,* Op. 53
Beethoven, *Appassionata Sonata,* Op. 57
Beethoven, Symphony No. 1 in C major
Beethoven, Symphony No. 2 in D major

11. Recite the words of some familiar songs, and then sing them. Does the music ever contradict the natural accentuation of the words?

12. Compare two translations of a song or air from a foreign language. Which is closer to the sense of the original? Which goes better with the music?

13. Do you know any folk songs characteristic of your part of the country? Compare the songs of your friends from the Southwest with those of your friends from Missouri and Kentucky.

14. Take a story, and consider how you would set about making an opera out of it. To what kinds of voice would you assign the main roles? At what points would you have the music interrupt the action? What episodes would you omit as being unsuitable for operatic treatment?

15. Examine the hymns commonly sung in your church. Which have music that is really beautiful, or devout in itself? Which are sung only because their words are familiar?

16. Compare the nature and order of the music at a Protestant and a Roman Catholic church service. What languages do they use? How much does the clergyman participate? How much does the congregation participate?

17. If possible, attend a Requiem Mass at a Roman Catholic church that employs Gregorian chant.

18. Invent words or tags to fit the subjects of these fugues by Bach, and see how readily you can detect their subsequent entries in the fugue:

a. Organ Fugue in G minor, the "little"
b. Organ Fugue in G minor, the "great"
c. Organ Fugue in F minor
d. Fugue in C minor from *The Well-tempered Clavier.*

CHAPTER 14

TYPES OF LITERATURE

LOGICAL ORGANIZATION OF LITERATURE

Organization in music and literature is largely a matter of memory and anticipation. We remember what we have heard, and on the basis of that, we anticipate what is to come. In music, we know when we hear a theme that we have or have not heard that theme, but we can rarely be very definite about it. We do not recall the themes and arrangements of music easily. Hence our memories and anticipations are not very clearly formulated. In literature, on the other hand, we remember the events and the ideas of a work clearly and exactly, and we retain the entire organization in our minds with very little difficulty. Therefore we know the organization of literature much better than we do that of music. And we demand in literature a logical organization. Take, for instance, this sonnet of Shakespeare's:

> When, in disgrace with Fortune and men's eyes,
> I all alone beweep my outcast state,
> And trouble deaf heaven with my bootless cries,
> And look upon myself and curse my fate,
>
> Wishing me like to one more rich in hope,
> Featur'd like him, like him with friends possess'd,
> Desiring this man's art, and that man's scope,
> With what I most enjoy contented least;
>
> Yet in these thoughts myself almost despising,
> Haply I think on thee; and then my state,
> Like to the lark at break of day arising
> From sullen earth, sings hymns at heaven's gate;

For thy sweet love rememb'red such wealth brings
That then I scorn to change my state with kings.
—WILLIAM SHAKESPEARE (1564–1616, English poet and
dramatist),
Sonnet 29 (publ. 1609)

There is a big break between the octave and the sestet. The octave, the
first eight lines, says that the poet is in a bad mood, discouraged, and
blue. The sestet, the last six lines, says that he cheers up when he
thinks of his lady-love. Nor is that all; the two quatrains of the octave
are clearly differentiated. The first states the trouble in general, the
second gives details. In the sestet the quatrain relates his change of
spirit when he thinks of the lady, and the couplet at the end sums up
the whole matter.

There are as many logical ways of ordering the content of a work of
literature as there are of thinking. Sometimes a writer begins with the
least important and goes on to the more important. Sometimes he
begins with the simple and goes on to the difficult or complicated.
Cause usually precedes effect. In Milton's sonnet *On His Blindness*,
the octave asks a question and the sestet gives the answer. In the
Shakespearean sonnet just quoted, there is the statement of a difficulty
and its solution. The writer arranges his ideas in the manner that will
make them say what he wants them to say. It is not necessary that the
author follow any one particular plan; it is only necessary that there be
a logical plan and that it be clear.

EXPOSITION

Traditionally there are three forms or general types of literature:
exposition, lyric, narrative. Exposition is explanation.

The *essay* is the outstanding type of expository writing. In an essay
the author sets out to explain something. In other words, he is trying
to make clear something that is not generally known. It is, therefore,
something that the author thinks needs explanation and is worth
explaining. He chooses a single subject and centers his attention on
that subject. He organizes his material to make his understanding of it
clear. Even if he writes in story form, his object is still the explanation
of his subject. The essay may be on any subject: religion, politics,
science, or literature. It is always short, about the length of a magazine article.

The *familiar essay* is a special type. It is short and personal, often whimsical, and seemingly trivial or fantastic. Cowper, for instance, writes about a card table, and Lamb about roast pig. The author is always calm and philosophical.

There are many books that share the essential character of the essay though they are not classed as essays. Among them are books of political ideas such as the *Republic* of Plato, or *The Prince* of Machiavelli; statements of philosophy such as the noble truths of Buddha or the *Dialogues* of Plato; and statements of practical wisdom, as the *Meditations* of Marcus Aurelius and the sayings of Epictetus. To this class also belong books of devotion such as the *Confessions* of St. Augustine or *The Imitation of Christ* by Thomas à Kempis.

History is usually counted as narrative in which the events are recorded as they actually happened; in a better sense, it belongs with expository writings. The main business of the historian is the same as that of the writer of essays. He must find just what events did take place, and select from all that are known those that have a direct relation to the main current of the time. Memoirs, biographies, autobiographies, and reminiscences are all types of history.

THE LYRIC

The lyric is a poem which expresses a single emotion. It is frequently short, like Landor's four-line poem *On Death:*

> Death stands above me, whispering low
> I know not what into my ear:
> Of his strange language all I know
> Is, there is not a word of fear.
> —WALTER SAVAGE LANDOR (1775–1864, English
> poet, literary critic, and prose writer)

Or it may be a poem of several pages like Wordsworth's *Ode on Intimations of Immortality.*

Sometimes the emotional quality is preserved in what is only a fragment, not a complete poem at all, as in these lines from Sappho:

> Before the lovely queen each night
> The stars in shyness hide their face
> As all the earth swims soft and bright
> And the full moon rides in her place.
> —SAPPHO (about 600 B.C., Greek lyric poet)

Love and death are the two favorite subjects, though any subject
may be used. Dylan Thomas tells of his reasons for writing poetry:

> In my craft or sullen art
> Exercised in the still night
> When only the moon rages
> And the lovers lie abed
> With all their griefs in their arms,
> I labour by singing light
> Not for ambition or bread
> Or the strut and trade of charms
> On the ivory stages
> But for the common wages
> Of their most secret heart.
>
> Not for the proud man apart
> From the raging moon I write
> On these spindrift pages
> Nor for the towering dead
> With their nightingales and psalms
> But for the lovers, their arms
> Round the griefs of the ages,
> Who pay no praise or wages
> Nor heed my craft or art.
>
> —DYLAN THOMAS (1914–1953, British poet),
> *In My Craft or Sullen Art* [1]

And Hopkins writes of the grandeur of God:

> The World is charged with the Grandeur of God.
> It will flame out, like shining from shook foil;
> It gathers to a greatness, like the ooze of oil
> Crushed. Why do men then now not reck his rod?
> Generations have trod, have trod;
> And all is seared with trade; bleared, smeared with toil;
> And wears man's smudge and shares man's smell: the soil
> Is bare now, nor can foot feel, being shod.
> And for all this, nature is never spent;
> There lives the dearest freshness deep down things;
> And though the last lights off the black West went
> Oh, morning, at the brown brink eastward, springs—

[1] From *The Collected Poems of Dylan Thomas*, copyright 1953, by Dylan
Thomas, and reprinted by permission of the publisher, New Directions, and
J. M. Dent & Sons, Ltd.

Because the Holy Ghost over the bent
World broods with warm breast and with ah! bright wings.
—GERARD MANLEY HOPKINS (1844–1889, English poet),
God's Grandeur

Whatever the subject, the lyric is timeless. Once it is written the song becomes universal. The poem may be very personal, as when a lover is telling of his love, but once it is said it becomes a song for all lovers, just as Dylan Thomas's poem becomes the statement for all poets.

NARRATIVE

Narrative is story. The essentials of narrative are the essentials of every story. The first is *plot;* something must happen. The second is *characters;* it must happen to certain people. The third is *setting;* it must happen in a definite place at a definite time. The fourth is *idea;* the author tells his story with some idea or purpose in mind. These four—plot, characters, setting, and idea—are essential to every narrative.

There is no plot without *conflict,* for unless there is some kind of conflict nothing happens. The action is usually analyzed in three parts: first, the conflict arises; second, there is a time when it is uncertain which side of the conflict will be victorious; third, the ending returns to a state of calm. The turning point, when it becomes clear which side is to be victorious, is called the *crisis.* It does not matter what the nature of the conflict, the narrative follows this general plan. In the subplot of *Much Ado about Nothing,* for example, when the play opens, Beatrice and Benedick are each calm in their expressed dislike of the other sex. The conflict starts when their friends plot to make them fall in love with each other. The conflict ends when they admit they are in love and marry.

The conflict may be of any kind. It may be a conflict of man against man, as in the Beatrice-Benedick story. It may be of man against nature, as in Stephen Crane's *The Open Boat,* where the survivors of a shipwreck are left for days in an open boat on rough seas. It may be a struggle of man against society, as in Ibsen's *An Enemy of the People,* where a doctor discovers the city water supply is polluted; he tries to make known and correct this state of affairs, but the people in control realize that it would hurt business if the fact were known, and the doctor himself is driven out of town as "an enemy of the people." It may be a struggle against fate as in the story of Oedipus, when his father and mother try to see that the prophecy of the oracle is not fulfilled. Or it may be a struggle of man against himself, as in *Hamlet,* when Hamlet debates what he should do. In one sense, most plots have an element of this last kind of conflict, because it is more interesting to see a man growing and changing than to see purely external struggle. Whatever the nature of the struggle, it must work out to some definite end, some meaning or lack of meaning which the author wants to make clear.

WAYS OF TELLING A STORY

Within the general framework of the narrative there are many ways of telling a story and hence of changing the plan. Ordinarily a narrative starts at the beginning and goes through to the end. *Pride and Prejudice* begins when strangers move into the community and Elizabeth and Darcy have a chance to meet each other, and it continues through many different events until they are safely married at the end. *Vanity Fair* begins when Becky Sharp leaves boarding school as a young girl, and it carries her through all her adventures until she is an old woman.

This is the method followed in the ballad *Sir Patrick Spence.* The story is presented in three scenes: The first is at the court when the king and the old knight are discussing plans for the trip; the second is on the seashore when Sir Patrick hears the message and suspects foul play; the third jumps to the ending after the lords and their ship have gone down. Except for the third stanza, however, there are no connecting links between one part and the other; the reader must guess from the context what has happened.

> The king sits in Dumferling toune,
>   Drinking the blude-reid wine:
> "O whar will I get a guid sailor,
>   To sail this schip of mine?"
>
> Up and spake an eldern knicht,
>   Sat at the kings richt kne:
> "Sir Patrick Spence is the best sailor,
>   That sails upon the se."

The king has written a braid letter,
    And signd it wi his hand,
And sent it to Sir Patrick Spence,
    Was walking on the sand.

The first line that Sir Patrick red,
    A loud lauch lauched he;
The next line that Sir Patrick red,
    The teir blinded his ee.

"O wha is this has don this deid,
    This ill deid don to me,
To send me out this time o' the yeir,
    To sail upon the se!

"Mak hast, mak hast, my mirry men all,
    Our guid schip sails the morne:"
"O say na sae, my master deir,
    For I feir a deadlie storme.

"Late late yestreen I saw the new moone,
    Wi the auld moone in her arme,
And I feir, I feir, my deir master,
    That we will cum to harme."

O our Scots nobles wer richt laith
    To weet their cork-heild schoone;
But lang owre a' the play wer playd,
    Thair hats they swam aboone.

O lang, lang may their ladies sit,
    Wi thair fans into their hand,
Or eir they se Sir Patrick Spence
    Cum sailing to the land.

O lang, lang may the ladies stand,
    Wi thair gold kems in their hair,
Waiting for thair ain deir lords,
    For they'll se thame na mair.

Haf owre, haf owre to Aberdour,
    It's fiftie fadom deip,
And thair lies guid Sir Patrick Spence,
    Wi the Scots lords at his feit.
            —ANON.,
              Sir Patrick Spence

Again, the story may be related a long time after the events have
taken place. This is the method followed by Conrad in *Youth*. Mar-
lowe, an old man, tells about the experiences of his youth. This method
is used by T. S. Eliot in *The Journey of the Magi*, when one of the
wise men remembers his trip to Bethlehem. One of the advantages of
this plan is that the narrator can intersperse comments and explanations, criticisms and evaluations.

Sometimes we see one character through the eyes of another, and
our understanding of that character changes as our informant learns
to know him. In Henry James's *Portrait of a Lady* we see one of the
main characters, Madame Merle, through the eyes of the heroine,
Isabel Archer. At first Madame Merle is glamorous; then as Isabel
begins to see her more clearly, we learn of her faults and shortcomings.

Another favorite way of telling a story is to begin the story when the
action is ended. This is essentially the method of Greek tragedy. In
Sophocles's *Oedipus the King*, for example, the story begins before
Oedipus was born. His parents, the king and queen of Thebes, con-
sulted the oracle and were told that the son to be born would kill his
father and marry his mother. To avoid this catastrophe, the parents
gave their baby to a shepherd, with directions that he was to be left
to die on the mountains. Instead the child was given to the king of
Corinth, at whose home he was reared. When he was a young man he
learned that he was to kill his father and marry his mother; to avoid
this crime he ran away from Corinth and went to Thebes. On the way,
he got into a quarrel with a stranger and killed him, not knowing it
was his father, the king of Thebes. Then he went on to Thebes. Just
outside the city was a sphinx, half woman and half lion, who
destroyed everyone who could not answer the riddle: "What animal
is it that walks on four feet in the morning, two at noon and three in
the evening?" Oedipus gave the right answer: Man crawls as a baby,
walks erect in the greater part of this life, and in his old age walks with
a cane. When her riddle was guessed, the sphinx destroyed herself and
Oedipus entered the town as its hero. The people were so grateful to
him they made him their king and gave him Jocasta, their queen (his
mother), as his wife. And so the oracle was fulfilled.

The play by Sophocles begins many years after all these events.
Oedipus has ruled as king for a long time; his children are grown.
Then a plague falls on the country. Oedipus sends to the oracle to
find out the cause of the trouble. Here the play begins. First is the

answer of the oracle that he must get rid of the unclean thing in their midst; then comes the message that Oedipus is himself the unclean thing. One by one the various strands of the story are unwound: Oedipus learns for the first time that the man he killed before he reached Thebes was the king, and then that he was the child exposed on the mountaintop. Jocasta sees the ending before Oedipus does, and when Oedipus goes to tell her his news he finds she has hanged herself. He then puts out his eyes with her breastpin, saying that one like him should not look on the light of day. He is led away to exile by his daughters.

In recent years there has been much emphasis on a new type of narrative—the "stream of consciousness" novel—in which all matters are presented in an uninterrupted flow of ideas, sensations, memories, and associations, as they would be presented to the consciousness of any one individual. James Joyce and Virginia Woolf are but two of a large number of contemporary writers who have used this method of writing.

In another recent type of narrative, there is not one sequence of events; instead events are presented in a kaleidoscopic series of pictures focusing on different occurrences of the story. In *John Brown's Body,* for instance, Stephen Vincent Benét paints a picture of the Civil War by giving short scenes that tell what was happening to various people at various times. There is no attempt to make a connection between one of these scenes and another, but they all fit together into a clear composite of the whole.

PROSE FICTION

The more important types of narrative are prose fiction, which is always in prose; drama, which may be in prose or verse; the epic and the ballad, which are always in verse.

Prose fiction, as the name indicates, is always in prose, and it is always fiction, always make-believe. A story in verse does not qualify; neither does a history. Historical fiction straddles the fence, because the novelist does not pretend that he is stating literal truth at all times, even though he is talking about events and people that are historical. Fiction is always told in the past tense. The events have happened and we look back on them.

Prose fiction is found chiefly in the short story and the novel. In the short story it is not only length that is indicated by the adjective *short;* because of its length the short story is limited in its analysis of character, and it is usually concerned with a single crisis. Technically the novel is supposed to designate only those works which emphasize characterization, but the name is used for all types of prose fiction. Some of the types of novel are:

Romance: sometimes distinguished from novel in that the novel puts emphasis on characterization, the romance on plot, e.g., the *novels* of Galsworthy and Jane Austen, and the *romances* of Scott and Stevenson.

Historical novel: a novel with a definite historical setting which is not limited to verifiable fact. The author invents characters, events, and conversations which seem to him in the spirit of the time he is portraying (Mitchell, *Gone with the Wind*).

Psychological novel: a novel in which the chief interest is in the minds of the characters—what they think and why (Conrad, *Lord Jim*).

Stream-of-consciousness novel: a novel in which the author tries to present every thought that passes through the mind of the central character (James Joyce, *Ulysses*).

Problem novel: a novel which deals with some special problem of the day (John Steinbeck, *The Grapes of Wrath*).

DRAMA

Drama differs from other forms of narrative, not in content or in organization, but in manner of presentation. All information must be conveyed to the audience through dialogue, except for what can be told through costume, the stage set, and the movements and gestures of the actors.

The story is further limited by the time of performance and by the greater necessity for clearness. The actors cannot repeat what the audience did not get on the first hearing, and hence the story must be clear enough for the audience to grasp the first time. The length of a play is determined by the capacity of the audience to enjoy it at one sitting. The critic may be reading a book for two weeks but he sees a play through at one time. Within these limitations, any type of narrative subject may be presented in dramatic form.

Drama may be either in prose or in verse. Modern drama is predominantly prose, but the drama of the three great periods of the theater—the Greek, the Elizabethan English, and the classical French —was in verse.

Drama may be further classified as classic, romantic, or social. The *classic drama* is the type defined by the Greeks. In form it is distinguished by the chorus and by its observance of the three unities. The *chorus* is a group of people, men or women, whose function it is to comment on the action or supply details not given by the actors. The three unities are time, place, and action. The *unity of time* demands that the action of the play should not take more than twenty-four hours; the *unity of place,* that it be in a single place; and the *unity of action,* that there be but one plot. Furthermore, in the classic play there is no violent action on the stage. Murders and deaths take place off stage.

The play of *Medea* by Euripides has been freely but admirably adapted for modern use by Robinson Jeffers. In it the entire action takes place in the square before the house of Medea. The play begins in the morning and ends that day, and the only subject is the revenge of Medea for her treatment by Jason. The chorus is composed of three Greek women who speak usually as individuals, not in chorus. The various events of the play are enacted as one or another of the characters comes to see Medea before her house. Medea sends the poisoned robe to Creüsa, and is told of her death by the nurse. Medea herself kills her two children within the house, but brings out their bodies to show Jason what she has done.

The *romantic drama,* as typified by the plays of Shakespeare, follows none of the unities. The time of the play may extend over a number of years, the scene is moved from one place to another, and there is usually more than one plot. In *King Lear,* the scene takes place in the palaces of the principal characters, on the battlefield, and on the heath. The time extends over months if not years. And there are scenes of the greatest horror such as the blinding of Gloucester. Moreover, the main plot of Lear and his daughters is contrasted with the subplot of Gloucester and his sons.

The *social drama* of the nineteenth century and after is not distinguished by its form but by its content. It treats of some social condition or situation with a view to its improvement. Ibsen, for instance, writes of problems of heredity in *Ghosts,* and of woman's position in society in *A Doll's House.*

EPIC

Of all the types of narrative, the epic is one of the most distinct as well as the rarest. An epic is a long, dignified poem in lofty style; its hero is of more than ordinary strength, and his deeds are of consequence to the entire nation. The authentic or natural epic is the product of an age of heroes, of a people just emerging from barbarism, when the individual, as an individual, performed deeds that were or seemed to be superhuman. In the *Iliad,* Achilles and Hector fight side by side with the gods, and are by no means inferior to them. Beowulf, in a foreign country, hears of the damage being done by the monster Grendel and goes across the sea to fight him.

The authentic epic probably originated as a series of songs in praise of the hero, which were later joined into one poem. The author, or authors, are not known, or, if a name such as Homer is given, it is merely a name, for the poetry does not reflect the personality of the poet. Because it is the product of a stage of civilization that lasted for only a short time, the authentic epic is extremely rare. The *Iliad,* the *Odyssey, Beowulf,* the *Song of Roland, Le Cid,* and the *Nibelungenlied* almost complete the list for Western literature.

The literary or artificial epic is the work of a single, conscious literary artist. We would expect it to be more common than the authentic epic, but it is not. The *Aeneid* of Vergil and *Paradise Lost* of Milton are two that are given the title without dispute. The literary epic also has a conscious purpose. Vergil is trying to arouse in the people a greater reverence for the gods, the country, and the family. Milton is trying to "justify the ways of God to man."

THE BALLAD

The ballad is a story told in song. The folk ballad is the story of an important event, told dramatically for popular singing. The subject may be any conspicuous event: the death of a suitor, the betrayal of a sister, the hunting of the cheviot, or the adventure of a hero.

As in all folk songs, the author is of no importance, and hence he is not usually known. A famous ballad has to do with Lord Randal.

"O where ha'e ye been, Lord Randal, my son?
O where ha'e ye been, my handsome young man?"
"I ha'e been to the wildwood; mother, make my bed soon,
For I'm weary wi' hunting, and fain would lie down."

"Where gat ye your dinner, Lord Randal, my son?
Where gat ye your dinner, my handsome young man?"
"I dined wi' my true-love; mother, make my bed soon,
For I'm weary wi' hunting, and fain would lie down."

"What gat ye to your dinner, Lord Randal, my son?
What gat ye to your dinner, my handsome young man?"
"I gat eels boiled in brew; mother, make my bed soon,
For I'm weary wi' hunting, and fain would lie down."

"What became of your bloodhounds, Lord Randal, my son?
What became of your bloodhounds, my handsome young man?"
"O they swelled and they died; mother, make my bed soon,
For I'm weary wi' hunting, and fain would lie down."

"O I fear ye are poisoned, Lord Randal, my son!
O I fear ye are poisoned, my handsome young man!"
"O yes, I am poisoned; mother, make my bed soon,
For I'm sick at the heart, and I fain would lie down."

—ANON.,
Lord Randal

In most ballads, as in this one, there is a great deal of repetition, probably because it made the singing easier. This repetition is not exact; each recurrence of a phrase carries the story forward a little. Each question adds to our knowledge of Lord Randal's day until we know the truth in the last stanza. The ballad seldom tells a story directly from beginning to end. In *Lord Randal* we begin at the end and learn by degrees what had happened earlier. The ballad form is also used by literary artists; with them it approximates the folk song more or less closely, as in Coleridge's *Ancient Mariner*.

UNITY AND VARIETY IN LITERATURE

The use of unity and variety in the fabric of literature has been so well illustrated in our discussion of the elements and types of literature, it needs little if any emphasis now. The only point we need to stress here is that in literature, as in all the arts, there is no place for surplus baggage. Every detail is necessary. Every incident is important, every allusion or figure of speech is needed for the effect of the whole. If a man is seen on the stage cleaning a gun when the curtain goes up, that gun must be used before the play is over. To know the fabric of any work of literature, one must study it until he knows what elements are combined, how they are repeated and varied, and why.

As an experiment let us examine the first two lines of a poem by E. E. Cummings.

> pity this busy monster, manunkind,
> not. Progress is a comfortable disease.[2]
> —*Pity This Busy Monster, Manunkind*

Probably the first thing we notice is the word *manunkind;* we are all familiar with the word *mankind,* but this is *manunkind.* He is called a monster—not a cruel or tyrannical monster, just *busy.* The word *busy* coupled with the word *monster* gives a great sense that this is not a good way of being busy, just a foolish, time-consuming, effete "busyness." The monster thereby becomes rather little and foolish. He has no evil purpose, he does what he does in being unkind just because he is busy; he does not know he is unkind or monstrous.

Notice the sound of the first line. You cannot read it fast or smoothly. It is like walking through deep mud, or like trying to do something with your hands when you have honey on your fingers. In contrast the *not* which begins the second line is like a pistol shot—clear, direct, simple. It is put at the beginning of the line to get emphasis, to hit in the head the foolish busyness of *manunkind.* The remainder of the line is a comfortable jog trot. Progress is comfortable even though it is a disease. In fact we are so comfortable we refuse to admit it is a disease.

The complete poem continues to show how man is deceived with the "bigness of his littleness," but the two lines above have given the "feel" of the complaint.

FOR FURTHER EXPLORATION

1. Make an outline of one of Shakespeare's plays; show what part each act serves in the play as a whole.

2. In any narrative, choose the moment you are conscious of the beginning of conflict, the moment you are conscious of a turn in the action (crisis).

[2] From *Poems 1923–1954,* Harcourt, Brace and Company, Inc. Copyright 1923, 1926, 1944, 1951, 1954 by E. E. Cummings.

3. In a number of short stories name the exact nature of the conflict.

4. Take any one of the narratives referred to in this section, and imagine the difference if another plan had been followed. For instance, imagine *Lord Randal* as told by the mother or the ladylove twenty years after Randal's death. Imagine *Vanity Fair* as a Greek play with all the plot focused on one scene near the end of Becky's life.

5. Try to set down all the ideas and impressions that pass through your mind in ten minutes. What are the advantages of the "stream of consciousness" method of writing?

6. Can you find any reason for the fact that the long series of stories, like the *Canterbury Tales,* is not so much liked now as it used to be? For a modern audience, what is the superiority of a plan like that of *The Ring and the Book,* or *The Bridge of San Luis Rey?*

PART FOUR

STYLE AND JUDGMENT

CHAPTER 15

STYLE

DEFINITION OF STYLE

. . . I remember myself, years ago, sketching with two well-known men, artists who were great friends, great cronies, asking each other all the time, how to do this and how to do that; but absolutely different in the texture of their minds and in the result that they wished to obtain, so far as the pictures and drawings by which they were well known to the public were concerned.

What we made, or rather, I should say, what we wished to note, was merely a memorandum of a passing effect upon the hills that lay before us. We had no idea of expressing ourselves, or of studying in any way the subject for any future use. We merely had the intention to note this affair rapidly, and we had all used the same words to express to each other what we liked in it. There were big clouds rolling over hills, sky clearing above, dots of trees and water and meadow-land below, and the ground fell away suddenly before us. Well, our three sketches were, in the first place, different in shape; either from our physical differences, or from a habit of drawing certain shapes of a picture, which itself usually indicates—as you know, or ought to know—whether we are looking far or near. Two were oblong, but of different proportions; one was more nearly a square; the distance taken in to the right and left was smaller in the latter case, and on the contrary, the height up and down—that is to say the portion of land beneath and the portion of sky above—was greater. In each picture the distance bore a different relation to the foreground. In each picture the clouds were treated with different precision and different attention. In one picture the open sky above was the main intention of the picture. In two pictures the upper sky was of no consequence—it was the clouds and the mountains that were insisted upon. The drawing was the same, that is to

371

say, the general make of things; but each man had involuntarily looked upon what was most interesting to him in the whole sight; and though the whole sight was what he meant to represent, he had unconsciously preferred a beauty or an interest of things different from what his neighbor liked.

The colour of each painting was different—the vivacity of colour and tone, the distinctness of each part in relation to the whole; and each picture would have been recognized anywhere as a specimen of work by each one of us, characteristic of our names. And we spent on the whole affair perhaps twenty minutes.

I wish you to understand, again, that we each thought and felt as if we had been photographing the matter before us. We had not the first desire of expressing *ourselves,* and I think would have been very much worried had we not felt that each one was true to nature. And we were each one true to nature.

> —JOHN LA FARGE (1855–1910, American artist),
> *Considerations on Painting,* pp. 71–73 [1]

This account of a sketching expedition as told by the artist John La Farge is dramatic because of the wide variety in the results. La Farge and his friends had decided together what they wanted to accomplish and how they expected to get it done. Each felt he was merely carrying out the assignment agreed on, and yet each painting showed clearly the individuality of the painter. The fact underlying this experience however is familiar to everyone; no two people do anything in the same way. No matter what they are doing or how carefully they plan to do it the same way, the results are different.

Or we may compare two paintings of nudes. Giorgione made a beautiful study of a reclining figure in his *Sleeping Venus* (Figure 167). Two centuries later Manet tried his hand at the same figure, *Olympia* (Figure 168). Giorgione puts his figure out of doors and presents her sleeping. Manet opens her eyes and makes her more erect in posture. The effect of the paintings is very different. Giorgione's is calm and idyllic, whereas Manet's is realistic, a frank picture of a courtesan, hard and cold-blooded as her profession.

We find the same difference in words even when they have almost the same meaning. In Longfellow's line, "Learn to labor and to wait," the meaning is almost the same as in Milton's verse, "They also serve who only stand and wait." But the first lacks the dignity and reserve

[1] Reprinted by permission of The Macmillan Company, publishers.

FIG. 167. Giorgione (ca. 1478–1510); landscape by Titian (1480?–1576), Italian painters. *Sleeping Venus* (ca. 1505). (Oil on canvas. Height: 3 feet 6¾ inches. Dresden, Gallery. Photograph by Alinari.)

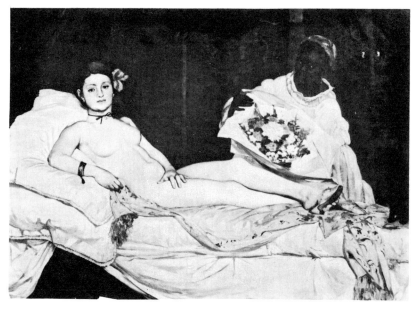

FIG. 168. Edouard Manet (1832–1883), French painter. *Olympia* (1863). (Oil on canvas. Height: 4 feet 2 inches. Paris, Louvre. Photograph by Stoedtner.)

of the second. When two people set the same words to music, or even
when they sing the same song, there is a difference. No two conductors
with the same orchestra playing the same tones make the same music.
Even in a chorus of ballet girls, where costume and training have done
their utmost to make all the members exactly alike, there are subtle
differences between one girl and another. No matter what we are
doing or how we do it, no two people accomplish exactly the same
results.

These differences are what are known as differences in style. Each
of the artists painting the scene in La Farge's account had his own
style. Manet's style is different ,from Giorgione's, and Longfellow's
from Milton's. Differences in style are very quickly and easily seen
and felt, but they are not easily described. We can all see that there is
a difference between Longfellow's line and Milton's, between Giorgione's painting and Manet's, but we do not know how to put that
difference into words, and we tend to speak of the difference in terms
of the personality of the artist. La Farge says that he and his two
fellow artists were "different in the texture of their minds." Manet and
Giorgione felt differently about their subjects. Longfellow did not have
the same outlook as Milton.

Differences in style are primarily differences in the man behind the
work of art, and the best definitions identify style with personality.
This is essentially the famous definition of Buffon: "The style is the
man." Or we may say style is the personality of the artist showing
through medium, elements, and organization.

STYLE AND STYLES

In the last analysis, style is always individual. It is the way some one
person living at some one time does some one thing. And just as no
one person is ever an exact duplicate of any other person, the style of
any one person is not exactly like that of any other person.

At the same time, people are alike in a great many respects, and we
soon begin grouping them together under certain headings to show
their kinship one with the other. Accordingly we have various styles:
a British or an American style, a classic or a romantic style, a medieval
or a Renaissance style. In this sense a style is a recognition of certain
qualities in which the work of one individual is like that of others. The

various styles may be grouped under two major headings. (1) Those that reflect the time and the place in which the artist lived—these are the historical styles; and (2) those that express similar attitudes toward life—the more important of these are the classic and romantic styles, and the comic and tragic styles.

HISTORICAL STYLES

The historical styles derive from the similarities of people living together. A man lives with other people in a certain place at a certain time. They speak the same language, they dress alike, they have the same manners and customs. What the artist does and thinks is conditioned by those people, that place, and that time. If La Farge had been Chinese, and had gone sketching with two Chinese friends, we would expect individual differences between the works of the three, in that each would express his own personality, but their paintings would be Chinese paintings, in the Chinese manner, on a Chinese subject.

As the centuries have passed, certain periods have become known for their characteristic ways of knowing and interpreting the world. Historians do not always agree on exact dates, but the following is a list of the major periods and approximate dates.

Oriental
1. Chinese, from ca. 3000 B.C.
2. Japanese, from ca. A.D. 500
3. Indian, from ca. 3300 B.C.
4. Persian, from ca. 500 B.C.
    Mohammedan Persian, from ca. A.D. 600

Ancient
1. Near East
    Egyptian, from ca. 4000 B.C.
    Mesopotamian, from ca. 4000 B.C.
    Hebrew, from ca. 2000 B.C.
2. Greek
    Aegean, ca. 3000–1100 B.C.
    Archaic and Golden Age of Greece, ca. 1100–400 B.C.
    Hellenistic, ca. 400 B.C. to first century B.C.
3. Roman, ca. 750 B.C. to A.D. 500

Medieval
1. Early Christian, to ca. A.D. 500
2. Byzantine, ca. A.D. 300–1453
3. Romanesque, ca. A.D. 500–1150
4. Gothic, ca. A.D. 1150–1550

Modern
1. Renaissance—Reformation, A.D. 1300–1700
2. Democratic revolt, nineteenth century
3. Contemporary, twentieth century

A study of the historical styles helps us to know and understand the conditions that produced each work of art, and the influence of one artist on another. Some of the obvious differences between one style and another are familiar, and within limits the styles are recognized by name as Greek, Egyptian, Gothic, etc. To this end the date and nationality of each example have been given. It is not, however, the province of this book to consider the historical development of art. Our study is limited to those styles which reflect the attitudes of people: the classic and romantic, the tragic and comic.

FIG. 169. *Hegeso Stele* (late fifth century B.C.). (Pentelic marble. Height: 4 feet 10½ inches. Athens, National Museum. Photograph by Alinari.)

THE CLASSIC AND THE ROMANTIC

The qualities that characterize *classicism* are clarity, simplicity, restraint, objectivity, and balance. The qualities that characterize *romanticism* are love of the remote and the indefinite, escape from reality, lack of restraint in form and emotions, preference for picturesqueness or grandeur or passion. Classicism and romanticism are fundamentally in opposition; what is classic is not romantic, and what is romantic is not classic. The classic is restrained; the romantic is not restrained. The classic is finished, perfect; it has great beauty of form; the romantic is unfinished, imperfect, and often it is careless of form. The classic is simple, the romantic is complex; the classic is objective, the romantic is subjective; the classic is finite, concerned only with projects that can be realized and accomplished; the romantic is infinite, concerned with plans that can never be realized, affecting "thoughts coequal with the clouds."

The difference between the two can be seen most clearly in the great art of each type. Mozart is a typical composer of the classic school. His music is calm, restrained, reasonable; the melodies and harmonies are clear and perfect. The emotions are subordinated to the forms used.

FIG. 170. Augustus Saint-Gaudens (1848–1907), American sculptor. *Adams Memorial* (ca. 1891). (Bronze figure, granite setting. Height of figure: 4 feet 1 inch. Washington, D.C., Rock Creek Cemetery.)

Beethoven followed Mozart in his early works; and his early symphonies, notably the second and the fourth, are classic. But his more characteristic symphonies, such as the fifth and the ninth, are romantic. The music is personal and emotional;

it expresses the struggles of the composer as he sought to find peace and calm. It is not contained and perfect, but exuberant, exultant, and free.

The difference, again, is clearly demonstrated if we take two pieces of sculpture, the Greek *Hegeso Stele* (Figure 169), and the American *Adams Memorial* by Saint-Gaudens (Figure 170). Both are tombstones. The Greek stele shows us Hegeso with her servant; the two are watching intently as Hegeso lifts a jewel from the box. It is a simple scene of everyday life, quiet and impersonal in its treatment. On the other hand, the Adams monument wraps us at once in mystery and questioning. A robed and hooded figure is seated before a severe granite slab. Is it man or woman? What does it mean? Is it supposed to symbolize Death? Or Grief? Moreover, our attention is no longer centered on the object itself, as it was with the stele of Hegeso; the object now serves as a point of departure for our emotions and questionings.

The Greek temple is classic and the medieval cathedral is romantic. Both are religious edifices, but they show a difference in the attitudes that created them, a difference far deeper than the dissimilarities of construction and mechanics. The Greek temple is hard, bright, exact, calm, and complete; the walls and the columns are no higher than will stand of their own strength; the lintels and the roof are simple, sane, and sensible. Nothing more is attempted than can be accomplished, and the result is a perfect building, finished and finite. Anyone can understand its main construction at a glance (Figure 125).

The Gothic cathedral, on the other hand, is built on the principle of tension. The openings are not made with lintels but are arched. One stone is held in place only by its relation to the other stones. The walls will not stand alone; they must be buttressed. As the walls go higher the arches become more pointed, the roof becomes steeper, and the buttresses are strengthened with flying buttresses, the whole so carefully and cleverly balanced that a fault in one part might cause a wall or even the entire building to collapse. The whole cannot be grasped at a glance; one is conscious only of its great complexity, its infinite variety, its striving upward and beyond (Figure 171).

The Greek temple might be as solid as a statue, for all the feeling we have of its interior; it has no more character than the inside of a box. But with the Gothic cathedral, on the other hand, the outside sends us inevitably within. The inside is as complicated and diverse as the outside, with its aisles and arches, and the light coming in

FIG. 171. Cathedral of Notre Dame (begun 1220; towers from 1288). (Stone.
Height of north tower: 224 feet. Amiens, Façade. Photograph, Clarence Ward.)

through stained-glass windows. One can never see the whole, but vistas like that in a corner of Chartres (Figure 172) open up, and these change as the light changes. It is a mystery in light and dark, an experience of unlimited space, and it is of the essence of romanticism.

The difference of attitude is illustrated again in two love poems, the first, which is classic, by Landor, and the second, which is romantic, by Shelley. The first is calm and restrained, with great precision of form. The second is passionate, exuberant, and exaggerated.

> Ah, what avails the sceptred race,
>   Ah, what the form divine!
> What every virtue, every grace!
>   Rose Aylmer, all were thine,
> Rose Aylmer, whom these wakeful eyes
>   May weep, but never see,
> A night of memories and of sighs
>   I consecrate to thee.
>   —WALTER SAVAGE LANDOR (1775–1864, English
>   poet, literary critic, and prose writer),
>   *Rose Aylmer* (1806)

FIG. 172. View of the ambulatory from the south transept, Cathedral, Chartres. (Photograph, Harry H. Hilberry.)

I arise from dreams of thee
In the first sweet sleep of night,
When the winds are breathing low,
And the stars are shining bright:
I arise from dreams of thee,
And a spirit in my feet
Hath led me—who knows how?
To thy chamber window, Sweet!

The wandering airs they faint
On the dark, the silent stream—
The Champak odours fail
Like sweet thoughts in a dream;
The nightingale's complaint,
It dies upon her heart;—
As I must on thine,
Oh! beloved as thou art!

Oh lift me from the grass!
I die! I faint! I fail!
Let thy love in kisses rain
On my lips and eyelids pale.
My cheek is cold and white, alas!
My heart beats loud and fast;—
Oh! press it to thine own again,
Where it will break at last.
                —PERCY BYSSHE SHELLEY (1792–1822, English
                poet),
                The Indian Serenade (1822)

Many years ago an excellent example of the classic spirit in acting
was given when Sarah Bernhardt was starring in Racine's *Phèdre*.
The play tells the story of Theseus, who in his old age married a
beautiful young woman named Phaedra. She fell in love with her
husband's son, Hippolytus, who combined all the virtues of his father
with youth and beauty that matched her own. Hippolytus, though he
returned the love of Phaedra, would have nothing to do with his
father's wife. In one scene Phaedra (Sarah Bernhardt) makes passionate love to Hippolytus. Hippolytus stood unmoved through the
time that Phaedra was wooing him; at last she turned away in desperation, and as she turned Hippolytus took one step forward, his arms
outstretched, showing in this one movement the love which honor had

kept him from making known. If this gesture of Hippolytus is compared with what we may call the usual romantic portrayal of love, we see again the difference between the classic and the romantic. It is not a difference in the degree of feeling that is expressed, but in the manner of expression.

Between the extremes of classicism and romanticism there are many gradations, and as the pendulum swings from one to the other the greatest artists are always found near the center: Shakespeare, Bach, Michelangelo.

It may be noted however that some periods lean toward classicism or romanticism. The Greek period was primarily classic, and the Gothic romantic. In the same way some arts are essentially more classic or romantic than others. Figure painting may be classic or romantic, but landscape painting is romantic. The distant view, by its nature, leads one on and on; one wants to know what is over the river, beyond the tree, on the other side of the hill.

Sculpture is traditionally exact, precise, well-defined, and balanced. The effects most natural to it are therefore classic, and a people of marked classic tendencies like the Greeks find in sculpture one of their best means of expression. It can however be romantic, as we have seen in the *Adams Memorial*. Nevertheless the classic seems the more appropriate style for sculpture, and most sculpture tends to be classic in feeling. Music, on the other hand, is by nature vague, elusive, evocative, emotional. The effects most natural for it are therefore romantic, and music can express in a few bars all the yearning and poignancy that it takes the profoundest efforts of the other arts to express.

Finally, we should perhaps insert a word of warning that classicism and romanticism are not in themselves good or bad; they merely reflect different points of view and must be judged on their own merits. The good in the classic is poised, serene, and balanced; the bad in the classic is cold, overformal, and lifeless. The good in the romantic is rich and full of emotion; the bad in the romantic is gushing and undisciplined.

FOR FURTHER EXPLORATION

1. Have you ever tried to assume the style of another? What was your experience?

2. Choose a group of two or three congenial people and set out to do the same thing. It may be writing a sonnet, making a picture, singing a song, arranging the ornaments on a mantel, saying the same speech. Do you get the same results? Can you see the personality of each person in his results?

3. Study in detail any one work of an artist.

4. Is there any painter whose work you can identify from his style?

5. Turn the radio to the first music you happen to get. How long before you can identify it as jazz, folk song, or classical music?

6. Try the same experiment by having someone read to you from an anthology.

CHAPTER 16

THE TRAGIC AND THE COMIC

THE KINSHIP OF TRAGEDY AND COMEDY

It has been said that tragedy is life viewed close at hand, and comedy is life viewed at a distance. It has also been said that life is comedy to the man who thinks and tragedy to the one who feels. In other words, the same situation may seem tragic to one and comic to another, or tragic at one time and comic at another. Pieter Brueghel has painted a picture illustrating the parable of Jesus: "Can the blind lead the blind? Shall they not both fall into the ditch?" (Figure 173). The old men in this picture might be inmates of any workhouse or poor farm. Each is trying to keep in touch with the one in front of him by holding to his shoulder and by touching him with his stick. But the one in front has stumbled and the others are falling. To some the grotesque positions they assume as they try to keep balance are comic; to others they are tragic.

The close connection between the comic and the tragic is very well illustrated in characters that formerly were considered comic but now are counted tragic. There is no question but that Shylock, in *The Merchant of Venice,* was originally considered a comic character; now he is tragic. We feel only sympathy for the old man when we hear him say:

> In the Rialto you have rated me
> About my moneys and my usances.
> Still have I borne it with a patient shrug,
> For suff'rance is the badge of all our tribe.
> You call me misbeliever, cut-throat dog,

Fig. 173. Pieter Brueghel, the Elder (ca. 1525–1569), Dutch painter. *Parable of the Blind* (1568). (Tempera on canvas. Height: 2 feet 10 inches. Naples, National Museum. Photograph by Anderson.)

And spit upon my Jewish gaberdine,
And all for use of that which is mine own.
Well then, it now appears you need my help.
Go to, then! You come to me, and you say,
"Shylock, we would have moneys;" you say so—
You, that did void your rheum upon my beard
And foot me as you spurn a stranger cur
Over your threshold; moneys is your suit.
What should I say to you? Should I not say,
"Hath a dog money? Is it possible
A cur can lend three thousand ducats?" Or
Shall I bend low and in a bondsman's key,
With bated breath and whisp'ring humbleness,
Say this:
"Fair sir, you spat on me on Wednesday last;
You spurn'd me such a day; another time
You call'd me dog; and for these courtesies
I'll lend you thus much moneys"?
    —William Shakespeare (1564–1616, English poet
      and dramatist),
      The Merchant of Venice, I, iii, 108–130 (ca. 1595)

THE FUNDAMENTAL TYPES

The fundamental types of comedy and tragedy are seen in the attitudes toward the old joke in which a person about to sit down has the chair pulled out from under him. There are, in general, four possibilities: (1) The person sits on the floor, and we laugh. It is comic, but it is a comedy of situation only; we are amused because the person on the floor is in a situation in which he did not expect to be. (2) The person sitting on the floor breaks his back. This is obviously not comedy but tragedy, but again it is a tragedy of situation because the person is in an unfortunate situation. It does not matter in either of these cases who the person is; it is the situation that gives the scene its character. (3) We laugh when the chair is pulled out from under someone, but we laugh not at the person who sits on the floor but at the man who pulls out the chair. We are amused that anyone should think such a thing is funny. We are laughing, in this case, not at a situation but at a man; in other words, this is comedy of character rather than of situation. (4) From comedy of character to tragedy of character is only a step. Instead of laughing at the person who has such a depraved sense of humor we feel it is tragic that anyone who is living in a civilized community should find such a trick amusing.

Comedy and tragedy of situation are also called *low comedy* and *low tragedy;* comedy and tragedy of character, *high comedy* and *high tragedy*. Low comedy is the basis for slapstick comedy and farce—the comedy that results from the throwing of custard pies or from the big feet of Charlie Chaplin. Low tragedy is the essence of melodrama. One is interested in the events that occur because they are exciting—a train wreck, an explosion, a race, the hunt for a criminal. In low comedy and low tragedy the characters are not individuals but types—the hero, the heroine, the villain, etc. In high comedy and high tragedy the people are individuals.

Shakespeare's *Comedy of Errors* is comedy of situation. As everyone knows, the play deals with twin masters who have twins for their servants. To make the confusion worse both the masters are named Antipholus and both the servants are named Dromio. The masters, who had been separated at birth, find themselves in Ephesus, and naturally there are many amusing situations as masters and servants are mixed up, until at last their identity is discovered and their relationship established. There is nothing comic in the twin masters or in the twin servants as such. The comedy lies in the situations which arise because they are confused one with the other.

The French comedy of Molière and the English comedy of Ben Jonson present comedy of character almost without comedy of situation. For example, the miser Volpone, in Ben Jonson's play of that name, pretends to be very ill; his miserly friends bring rich gifts, each one hoping to ingratiate himself so as to be the sick man's heir. When Volpone has got all their gifts, he resumes his usual state of health. There is nothing comic in this situation; we are amused only by the characters.

Ordinarily a dramatist uses elements of both high and low drama; the preponderance of one or the other determines the character of the play. In *Hamlet,* for instance, many elements of the plot are frankly melodramatic. To enumerate: the guards are watching at midnight when they see a ghost; the hero kills a man through a curtain; there is a fight in an open grave; drinks are poisoned and the wrong person gets the poison; swords are exchanged and a man is killed with his own poisoned sword. All this is melodrama. The real tragedy is concerned with what takes place in the minds of the people. But so great is this interest that we are surprised when we realize how much melodrama the play contains.

Shakespeare's comedies, in general, are not comedies in the strict sense of the word, in that the plot is not itself a comic plot. The plot is a pleasant, gay story which does not take life too seriously. In *Twelfth Night,* for instance, the plot tells how Olivia, learning that she is near the estate of a duke (Orsino) of whom she has heard much, decides to assume the guise of a boy, and enter the duke's service in the hope that she may win him and marry him. She does both. It is a pleasant tale, not a comic one. In the development of the story, however, Shakespeare uses both comedy of character and comedy of situation.

BASIS OF COMEDY

The chief source of the comic is the incongruous, the unexpected. We expect one thing and we find another. If one man pulls a chair out from under another, the joke lies in the fact that the second sits on the floor when he expected to sit on the chair.

It is the unexpectedness of the speech that makes for comedy in the reply of the nurse in *Romeo and Juliet:*

Your love says, like an honest gentleman, and a courteous, and a kind,
and a handsome, and I warrant, a virtuous,——Where is your Mother?

—II, v, 56–59

Juliet has sent the nurse to find out from Romeo whether she is to be
married that day. The nurse has returned with the news, and Juliet
wants to know. But the nurse is hot and tired and out of humor because of the long trip she has had. At last she begins to tell the message
from Romeo, but when she comes to the word *virtuous*, she is re-
minded of the nature of the alliance she is promoting and she breaks
off with the question "Where is your mother?" It is the contrast
between what we expect and what we receive that is comic.

In comedy of character it is the difference between what a person
thinks he is and the person we think him to be that is funny. In the
famous passage from *Much Ado about Nothing* when Dogberry is
swearing in the watch, there is nothing funny in the situation. The
comedy comes from the fact that Dogberry is pompous; he thinks he is
better than he is.

> DOGBERRY: Are you good men and true?
> VERGES: Yea, or else it were pity but they should suffer salvation, body
> and soul.
> DOGBERRY: Nay, that were a punishment too good for them, if they
> should have any allegiance in them, being chosen for the Prince's
> watch.
> VERGES: Well, give them their charge, neighbour Dogberry.
> DOGBERRY: First, who think you the most desartless man to be con-
> stable?
> FIRST WATCH: Hugh Oatcake, sir, or George Seacole; for they can
> write and read.
> DOGBERRY: Come hither, neighbour Seacole. God hath bless'd you with
> a good name. To be a well-favoured man is the gift of fortune,
> but to write and read comes by nature.
> —SHAKESPEARE,
> *Much Ado about Nothing*, III, iii, 1–22 (ca. 1599)

Comedy thus implies a norm or a standard; the actual is measured
by this norm, and the comic arises in the difference between the actual
and the norm. It is normal for a man to be taller than a woman, for a
man to sit in a chair rather than on the floor, for a girl to get an
intelligible answer when her messenger returns from an important
errand. It is in this sense that the unexpected is comic. The unexpected

is not, as such, comic; there is nothing comic in having an unexpected attack of ptomaine poisoning, or in getting a letter one has not expected; but if one is expecting to learn whether one is to be married, and hears the question "Where is your mother?" the difference between what one expects and what one hears *is* comic. Sometimes the standard is given; more often it is implied; but in any case we expect a standard, and hence we find it amusing when the actual deviates from it.

It is this measurement against a standard which has ind iced us to think of the abnormal as funny. Deformity, insanity, and pain used to be considered comic and were regularly introduced for low-comedy effects. The fool, the hunchback, and the midget were accepted as comic characters of the court; as such they are prominent in Velázquez's paintings of court scenes. In the Elizabethan drama choruses of madmen were sometimes introduced for comic effects. Drunkenness, until a few years ago, was considered a cause of laughter and is still so considered in many cases. Children laugh if they see a cat having fits. In these cases the abnormal is measured against the standard of the normal and found funny.

CHARACTERISTICS OF THE COMIC

Comedy is primarily intellectual. The perception of the comic depends on the recognition of the difference between the normal and the actual. If one does not know the standard, or if he does not perceive the deviation from the standard, he does not find it funny. It is for this reason that jokes are tricky and that there are so many limitations on them. For comedy is highly specialized in its appeal. The people of one country do not like the jokes of another country. There is the American joke, the English joke, the French joke, the German joke. Even the sexes differ in their appreciation of comedy; women do not appreciate all the jokes of men, nor do men appreciate all the jokes of women.

Comedy, moreover, is detached. No one can laugh at anything that is very close to him. Even when one laughs at himself he must, as it were, get away from himself in order to laugh. When one is suffering from puppy love he cannot laugh at himself, but when he has recovered from the attack he can join with others in the laugh. There is thus something impersonal about the comic. And it implies a degree of insensibility on the part of the audience; we cannot sympathize too much if we are going to laugh. If we are distressed about the nurse's fatigue or her concern over Romeo's being a virtuous young man, we cannot laugh when she interrupts her tale, "Your love says . . . Where is your mother?"

Because comedy is detached, we laugh at all sorts of things in the world of comedy that we do not find funny in everyday life: the man who does not pay his bills, the woman who deceives her husband, the young boy suffering from puppy love. In *Arsenic and Old Lace,* one of the most delightful of recent comedies, two gentle old ladies are in the habit of administering arsenic in elderberry wine to the lonely old men they meet, because they feel sorry for them. The men are then buried in the basement by a brother who thinks he is Teddy Roosevelt and counts this digging as part of the work on the Panama Canal. In real life we would demand that something be done; it would be no excuse that the old ladies are slightly insane. Nor would it be possible to keep the whole thing quiet as is done in the play. In short there would be consequences. In the play there are none; the situations are hilariously funny, but the plot takes place, as it were, in a vacuum. Evil in comedy is not evil but something to be laughed at.

Because comedy is intellectual and depends on perception, the comic always has in it a feeling of superiority. The person who sees the joke feels superior to the one who does not, and frequently he is patronizing. There is a bond of union between people who like the same joke. But feeling superior is a tightrope for one to walk on. The artist usually veers to one side or the other; and he takes sides for or against the people who are the subject of his comedy. He is either sympathetic or critical. If he is sympathetic, his writing becomes humorous; if he is critical, it becomes satirical.

HUMOR AND SATIRE

Humor is a matter of spirit rather than of words. It is kindly; it is sympathetic. Usually it has in it something of extravagance, and the author, looking at the extravagant person, smiles with tolerant indulgence. In this way we love Falstaff while we smile at the extravagance of his statements:

Bardolph, am I not fallen away vilely since this last action? do I not bate? do I not dwindle? Why, my skin hangs about me like an old lady's loose gown; I am withered like an old apple-john. Well, I'll repent, and that suddenly, while I am in some liking; I shall be out of heart shortly, and then I shall have no strength to repent. An I have not forgotten what the inside of a church is made of, I am a peppercorn, a brewer's horse. The inside of a church! Company, villainous company, hath been the spoil of me.

—SHAKESPEARE,
Henry IV, Part I, III, iii, 1–11 (1592)

When Orlando, in *As You Like It,* protests that he will die if he does not win Rosalind, she reminds him of famous lovers, none of whom died of love: the brains of Troilus were beaten out with a club; Leander died of a cramp while swimming the Hellespont, and so on. She ends with a summary for all time:

But these are all lies: men have died from time to time, and worms have eaten them, but not for love.

—IV, i, 106–108

Because we know Rosalind, and realize how much she is in love with Orlando, and how gallantly and cleverly she is carrying on her game with him, we find the words humorous, but had they been spoken by another we might have found them cynical.

Satire aims, or at least pretends to aim, at improvement. The satirist sees the vices and faults of the human race, and exposes them in a comic manner in order to call the matter to attention for correction. To this end, the satirist may use any device. Swift uses allegory in *Gulliver's Travels,* where he is satirizing the littleness of men. On his first voyage Gulliver goes into the land of the Lilliputians, a people who are only a few inches in height. Here he is amazed at the cunning and the foolishness of the little people. The test of the politician's ability to hold office is his skill in walking a rope. The Lilliputians are in a great agony of disagreement and even fight a war to decide at which end an egg should be broken. Some who believe it should be broken at the big end are called the Big-endians; others, who are just as strong in their faith that it should be broken at the little end, are called the Little-endians.

WIT

Wit is a general name for those forms of the comic which have to do with words. Like all other forms of the comic, it is based on incongruity. We expect one word and we hear another.

Under the heading of wit come spoonerisms, malapropisms, puns, epigrams, and parody.

The *spoonerism,* named from one of its most distinguished makers, the Reverend W. A. Spooner of Oxford, is the accidental transposition of the initial letters of two or more words. One says he has just received a "blushing crow," when he means a "crushing blow." The English poets Keats and Shelley become, by juxtaposition, Sheets and Kelly.

The *malapropism,* named for Mrs. Malaprop in *The Rivals,* is the ludicrous misuse of a word for one resembling it, for example, "contagious countries" for "contiguous countries."

Observe me, Sir Anthony. I would by no means wish a daughter of mine to be a progeny of learning; I don't think so much learning becomes a young woman. For instance, I would never let her meddle with Greek, or Hebrew, or Algebra, or simony, or fluxions, or paradoxes, or such inflammatory branches of learning—neither would it be necessary for her to handle any of your mathematical, astronomical, diabolical instruments.— But Sir Anthony, I would send her, at nine years old, to a boarding-school in order to learn a little ingenuity and artifice. Then, sir, she should have supercilious knowledge in accounts; and as she grew up, I would have her instructed in geometry, that she might know something of the contagious countries;—but above all, Sir Anthony, she should be mistress of orthodoxy, that she might not misspell and mispronounce words so shamefully as girls usually do; and likewise that she might reprehend the true meaning of what she is saying.—This, Sir Anthony, is what I would have a woman know; and I don't think there is a superstitious article in it.
   —Richard Sheridan (1751–1816, Irish-born English playwright),
   The Rivals (1775)

A *pun* is a play on words which have the same sound or similar sounds but different meanings. One of the more serious puns is that on "grave" in Mercutio's speech in *Romeo and Juliet:*

Romeo: Courage, man; the hurt cannot be much.
Mercutio: No, 'tis not so deep as a well, nor so wide as a church-door; but 'tis enough, 'twill serve. Ask for me tomorrow, and you shall find me a grave man. I am pepper'd, I warrant, for this world.
   —Shakespeare,
   Romeo and Juliet, III, i, 99–102 (ca. 1593)

James Joyce made a delightful pun in "Lawn Tennyson"; the word *lawn,* which sounds almost like *Lord,* reminds one of the green fields and English country life that we associate with Tennyson.[1]

[1] David Daiches, *A Study of Literature for Readers and Critics,* p. 44.

The *epigram* is a condensed, pithy statement, like that of the young man in Wilde's *Lady Windemere's Fan:* "I can resist everything except temptation." Martial is one of the most famous writers of epigrams:

> I do not love thee, Doctor Fell,
> The reason why I cannot tell;
> But this alone I know full well,
> I do not love thee, Doctor Fell.
> —MARTIAL (ca. A.D. 40–104, Roman poet),
> *Non Amo Te,* tr. by Tom Brown (1663–1704)

And there is always the famous epigram of John Wilmot on Charles II:

> Here lies our Sovereign Lord the King,
> Whose word no man relies on,
> Who never said a foolish thing,
> Nor ever did a wise one.
> —JOHN WILMOT, EARL OF ROCHESTER
> (1648–1680, English courtier and poet),
> *Epitaph on Charles II* (ca. 1675) .

A *parody* is an imitation of a piece of writing, usually a very well-known work. The parody imitates the model very closely but turns the serious sense of the original into ridicule.

Lewis Carroll was a great writer of parodies. He made nonsense of *How Doth the Little Busy Bee.*

> How doth the little crocodile
> Improve his shining tail,
> And pour the waters of the Nile
> On every golden scale!
> —LEWIS CARROLL (1832–1898, English
> mathematician and writer),
> *Alice in Wonderland*

And *Twinkle, Twinkle, Little Star* becomes:

> Twinkle, twinkle, little bat!
> How I wonder what you're at!
> Up above the world you fly,
> Like a tea-tray in the sky.[2]

[2] From David Daiches, *A Study of Literature for Readers and Critics,* p. 205.

THE NATURE OF THE TRAGIC

Tragedy implies an unhappy or unfortunate ending to a series of events; usually it means death. But it is not just any kind of death; if an old man of eighty dies after an illness of months or years, his death is not called tragic. Tragedy implies a sudden reversal in prospects, a drop from a high estate to a low one. In the great tragedies the hero is usually one of royal, or at least noble, blood, so as to make the change in his position all the more apparent. Lear is king, Hamlet is prince, Agamemnon is king and leader of all the Greek armies in the Trojan War. Moreover, he is not just any king or prince; he is an exceptionally fine man. Othello came from "men of royal siege," and he is cherished by all the people of Venice. Macbeth is no average general; he is an unusual person in bravery, courage, devotion; he is "brave Macbeth," "Valour's minion." The tragic hero is always a person of merit, usually of outstanding merit. We admire and respect him for virtues that are above the ordinary. When, therefore, we see his fall, there is something catastrophic about it. We cannot believe that a person so great or fine could come to such an end.

Yet at the same time the hero's fall seems inevitable. In high tragedy the ending must be a necessary consequence from the events and the hero's character.

The *necessity* for the hero's death is clearly defined and distinguished in the two great types of tragedy, the Greek and Shakespearean. With the Greeks, the necessity was primarily religious in character. The hero does something that is against the law and so he must suffer. In the play called by her name, Antigone heard the decree of the ruler, Creon, that her brother should not be buried. This decree pronounced a horrible sentence, since according to the Greek religion the funeral rites determined the welfare of the dead in the next world. Therefore she refused to obey the decree, and buried her brother. By doing so she violated the law and incurred death.

With Shakespeare, the necessity is found not in the law of religion, but in character; because the hero is the kind of person he is, he must fail. Othello sins innocently, but the reason is in the man. His personality, his background, his idealism, his ignorance of Venice, even the secrecy and hurry of the wedding make the murder of Desdemona inevitable. The real cause of the tragedy is in Othello.

But even though the hero fails, tragedy is never fatalistic or pessimistic, nor does it leave one with a sense of frustration. We know that the hero has failed, we realize that he had to fail, but there is not any sense of despair or desolation. We feel even more strongly the essential values of life: love, justice, truth, goodness. In *Othello,* Iago is the only one of the strong characters left alive when the play is over, but we do not admire him as a clever schemer; we hate him with all the power we have, and we love and admire even more the goodness we saw in the lives of Othello, Desdemona, and Emilia. When Antigone tells her sister she has planned to bury her brother and asks for her help, Ismene objects: it is against the law, they are but women, it is no use to attempt the impossible. But Antigone goes right on,

> I'll neither urge thee, nor, if now thou'dst help
> My doing, should I thank thee for thine aid.
> Do thou after thy kind; thy choice is made;
> I'll bury him; doing this, so let me die.
>
> *   *   *
>
> But leave me, and the folly that is mine,
> This worst to suffer—not the worst—since still
> A worse remains, no noble death to die.
>
> —SOPHOCLES (495–406 B.C., Greek dramatist),
> *Antigone,* 74–77, 102–104 (ca. 442 B.C.), tr. by Robert
> Whitelaw

Antigone is killed as she knew she would be, but there is no question but that she has played the nobler part, and that it is better to die for what is right than to live knowing that wrong is being done.

In tragedy we know that the hero will not be saved, he cannot be saved. There is no possibility of a happy ending. And at the same time we know that the values with which these men were identified are not lost, and we feel triumphant in that assurance. Tragedy leaves one in a state not only of grief and sorrow but of positive exaltation. It is a strange combination, and if we add the fact that in tragedy these emotions are felt keenly, we have the reason why tragedy is counted the greatest of all literary forms. The pain of tragedy is great, so great it can hardly be endured. And the heroes of tragedy suffer. Othello, Antigone, Oedipus, and Lear are great because they suffer. "It is by our power to suffer, above all," says Edith Hamilton, "that we are of more value than the sparrows." [3] And because we have the power to

[3] Edith Hamilton, *The Greek Way to Western Civilization,* p. 130.

suffer, we can feel both the pain of the hero and the joy and exaltation that follow.

Tragedy is thus almost an exact opposite of comedy. Comedy is intellectual; tragedy is emotional. Comedy depends on the unexpected, the incongruous; tragedy demands a sense of inevitability. Comedy lives in a world without values where there are no consequences, tragedy in a real world where every deed brings its consequences, and values are triumphant.

TRAGEDY IN THE PRESENT DAY

Tragedy as written by the Greeks and by Shakespeare is generally recognized as the highest phase of literary art, but it is not common today. Aside from the pat assertion that the greatest examples of art are not found easily or in abundance, there are several reasons to which we may call attention.

One has to do with the sense of inevitability in the fall of the tragic hero. With the rise of our concern for all men we do not care to recognize that man is responsible. Today we are apt to see man as the pathetic victim, the worm that crawls on the pavement for a half hour in the sunlight and then is squashed under the heel of some person or thing. It is not his fault, he is the helpless sufferer. Because of this attitude toward man, there has grown up a new type of play which is often called the serious drama, and which tries to fix the blame for man's inadequacy. The fault is that of labor or capital, as in Galsworthy's *Strife;* or it is religion and society which force a woman to live with a diseased man and bring diseased children into the world, as in Ibsen's *Ghosts.* It is anything and everything except a man's responsibility for his own soul.

Another cause of our lack of tragedy is the confusion of values and consequent negative view of life. Before the failure of the hero we tend to feel cynical or frustrated. The different viewpoints can be seen in comparing two novels, *Madame Bovary* and *Anna Karenina.* The former leaves one without hope or philosophy. There is little in Emma Bovary or in any of the other characters that one can admire; this is the way it is, a sorry mess. The latter novel, *Anna Karenina,* has more nearly the tragic point of view. There is much that is wrong, but the good is still good.

A third influence on our judgment may be mentioned, though it is a question as to how much emphasis it deserves—the cheap solution, the idea that all will come out all right anyway. We associate this attitude with Hollywood, but the movie is not the only medium that reflects it.

COMEDY AND TRAGEDY IN THE OTHER ARTS

Literature can deal with the intellectual more completely and more exactly than the other arts because its medium is the language of the intellect, the language of philosophy; therefore, the comic finds itself at home in literature more than in any of the other arts. This does not mean, however, that there is no comedy in music and the visual arts. In the visual arts there are paintings of comic situations. In these, however, the problem of interpretation is ever present. The scene or the character that is intended as comic may not seem comic once it is painted; the picture intended to be tragic may seem comic, as we saw in Brueghel's *Parable of the Blind*. For pictures or statues of happy people having a good time there is no difficulty of interpretation, but neither is there anything comic found in them.

There is a great deal of comedy in program music and in vocal music, but the comedy lies primarily in the story or in the words, not in the music. The music of Haydn is friendly and genial, and we are tempted to call it witty because of the way one theme or one voice repeats and answers another, but it is not really comic. A superb example is the Rondo from the Sonata in E minor. We laugh aloud when listening to it, but it is a laugh of pleasure, of joy and excitement from following the garrulous repetitions; the music is not itself comic.

The tragic, like the comic, is primarily in the realm of literature, though it, too, is found in the other arts. Music can and does portray tragic conflict and the resolution of that conflict. Most of Beethoven's sonatas and symphonies show conflict, and one feels the exultation of the ending. But, as always, music is disembodied unless it is associated with a story. Wagner's music dramas are superb examples of the way music may interpret and resolve the conflict of a story.

Painting and sculpture are limited by the fact that they can present only a single moment of time. Hence they can show either the struggle or the peace attained after the struggle is ended, but they cannot show both. The so-called *Medusa Ludovisi* (Figure 174) from the Terme Museum at Rome shows the struggle but not the peace that follows.

The painting of the *Resurrection* by Piero della Francesca (Figure 175) shows the solution. It is as nearly tragic as can be found in the visual arts. On the face of the Christ one can tell of the suffering and the horror of the time in hell, the sympathy that he had felt for those whom he met, and his final victory over death. Painting and sculpture at their greatest show the elements of the conflict after the conflict is ended, when the warring elements are no longer in collision but at peace.

FOR FURTHER EXPLORATION

1. Test the statement about the kinship of tragedy and comedy by using the same situation for both comedy and tragedy.

2. Think of ten cinema actors; do you find each one is easily identified with one of the four fundamental types of tragedy and comedy?

Fig. 174. *Medusa Ludovisi* (or *Sleeping Fury*), copy of a late Hellenistic original. (Pentelic marble. Size: about 14½ inches. Rome, Terme Museum. Photograph by Alinari.)

Fig. 175. Piero della Francesca (ca. 1410–1492), Italian painter. *The Resurrection of Christ* (1460). (Fresco. Figures life size. Borgo San Sepolcro, Palazzo del Comune. Photograph by Alinari.)

3. Can you think of any examples of comedy that cannot be resolved into the perception of the unexpected?

4. Analyze ten instances of comedy for the types of comedy represented.

5. Analyze one of Shakespeare's comedies for the different types of comedy involved.

6. Do the same for one of Molière's plays.

7. Collect examples of (*a*) jokes of different countries, (*b*) jokes of different states, (*c*) jokes of different people.

8. Collect ten malapropisms from *The Rivals*.

9. Write a parody.

10. Rewrite any of the great tragedies as a news item for a daily paper.

11. Study a modern tragedy, a Greek tragedy, and a Shakespearean tragedy for the forces involved in the conflict.

CHAPTER 17

JUDGMENT

POETRY

I, too, dislike it: there are things that are important beyond all this fiddle.
  Reading it, however, with a perfect contempt for it, one discovers in
  it after all, a place for the genuine.
          Hands that can grasp, eyes
        that can dilate, hair that can rise
              if it must, these things are important not because a

high-sounding interpretation can be put upon them but because they are
  useful. When they become so derivative as to become unintelligible,
  the same thing may be said for all of us, that we
        do not admire what
      we cannot understand: the bat
            holding on upside down or in quest of something to

eat, elephants pushing, a wild horse taking a roll, a tireless wolf under
  a tree, the immovable critic twitching his skin like a horse that feels
                                    a flea, the base-
    ball fan, the statistician—
          nor is it valid
        to discriminate against 'business documents and

school-books'; all these phenomena are important. One must make a
                                          distinction

however: when dragged into prominence by half poets, the result is
                                                                    not poetry,
nor till the poets among us can be
        'literalists of
        the imagination'—above
            insolence and triviality and can present

for inspection, imaginary gardens with real toads in them, shall
                                                                    we have
    it. In the meantime, if you demand on the one hand,
    the raw material of poetry in
        all its rawness and
        that which is on the other hand
            genuine, then you are interested in poetry.
                —MARIANNE MOORE (1887——, American poet)[1]

THE PROBLEM OF JUDGMENT

Judgment asks the last question about a work of art: how good is
it? Is it truly great or is it trivial? Will it be cherished for ages or will
it be forgotten in a decade?

If we have pursued the analysis of art according to the plan of
this book, we have consciously or unconsciously been making judgments of individual qualities in specific works of art, and to that extent
have been answering the questions of judgment. Not that our analysis
has said "This is good," or "That is bad," but through the better
understanding that comes from analysis we have learned to know
details, and as a result we have instinctively judged them interesting
or dull, superficial or significant. What remains now is to assemble
such partial judgments into a comprehensive evaluation. To the questions already discussed, however, we must add others which deal with
judgment alone. They are:

1. Honesty. Is the work sincere?
2. Scope. How much has the artist attempted?
3. Level of meaning. Is the work superficial or deep?
4. Truth. Has the artist shown the essential truth of his subject?
5. Magnitude. How great is it?

[1] From *Poems*, by Marianne Moore. Copyright 1935 by Marianne Moore. Used
by permission of The Macmillan Company, New York.

SINCERITY

One of the important demands in making a judgment has to do with the sincerity of the artist or, as we say more often, the honesty of his work. We want a work of art to be a serious expression of the author's thoughts and ideas. As Marianne Moore says, we want the genuine, and we do not care for those things "so derivative as to become unintelligible," or those other phenomena "dragged into prominence by half poets" or other half artists. We want in a work of art an honest, genuine piece of work.

Honesty is extremely difficult to judge; judging sincerity in art is like judging sincerity in people. Which of our friends are sincere? Which can we trust to give us their honest opinions? What do our friends really think? It is impossible to have any final or fixed judgment of sincerity, but it is nevertheless a matter of the greatest importance. Once we suspect a man or an artist is not being sincere, we judge his work inferior. The *Laocoön* (Figure 32), for instance, seems theatrical; for all its vividness it is hardly sincere; there is a deliberate striving for effect. Is the cathedral of Milan (Figure 176) quite honest? Is there too much decoration "like a wedding cake"?

Fig. 176. Cathedral at Milan (mostly 1386–1522; West Façade seventeenth to nineteenth centuries; most of the pinnacles nineteenth century). (White marble. Length: about 490 feet; width: about 200 feet. Milan. Photograph, courtesy of Italian State Tourist Office.)

SENTIMENTALITY

The form in which insincerity is most often found in art is sentimentality. Sentimentality may be defined as an insincere emotion; it is
interest in the effect of an action rather than in the action itself. Sentimentality is not to be confused with sentiment, which is a genuine
feeling. We are all sentimental when we are young; we love to think
how good and noble we are and how we are not appreciated, how
sorry our parents will be when we die and they recognize us as the
wonderful people we really are. This is essentially the point of view
in the little poem by Christina Rossetti.

> When I am dead, my dearest,
>   Sing no sad songs for me;
> Plant thou no roses at my head,
>   Nor shady cypress-tree:
> Be the green grass above me
>   With showers and dewdrops wet;
> And if thou wilt, remember,
>   And if thou wilt, forget.
>
> I shall not see the shadows,
>   I shall not feel the rain;
> I shall not hear the nightingale
>   Sing on, as if in pain:
> And dreaming through the twilight
>   That doth not rise nor set,
> Haply I may remember,
>   And haply may forget.
>   —CHRISTINA ROSSETTI (1830–1894, English poet
>   of Italian parentage),
>   Song (1862)

Miss Rossetti is interested in the effect of her death, and she is enjoying the melancholy prospects of being in the grave. It is essentially a
romantic pose, but it is a pose nevertheless.

Similarly, in the "Good Night" from the first canto of *Childe
Harold's Pilgrimage,* Byron is not so much lonely and deserted as he is
enjoying the thought of being lonely and deserted.

> And now I'm in the world alone,
>   Upon the wide, wide sea;

> But why should I for others groan,
>   When none will sigh for me?
> Perchance my dog will whine in vain,
>   Till fed by stranger hands;
> But long ere I come back again
>   He'd tear me where he stands.
>   —LORD BYRON (1788–1824, English poet),
>   *Childe Harold's Pilgrimage,* Canto I (1812)

For comparison, read the lyric *She Walks in Beauty,* where Byron has his mind on the woman, not on himself; in other words, he is not sentimental.

> She walks in beauty, like the night
>   Of cloudless climes and starry skies;
> And all that's best of dark and bright
>   Meet in her aspect and her eyes:
> Thus mellow'd to that tender light
>   Which heaven to gaudy day denies.
>   —*She Walks in Beauty* (1814)

It is harder to be sincere about oneself than about other people but, in his later years, Byron was sincere even about himself.

> And I have loved thee, Ocean! and my joy
> Of youthful sports was on thy breast to be
> Borne, like thy bubbles, onward. From a boy
> I wanton'd with thy breakers—they to me
> Were a delight; and if the freshening sea
> Made them a terror—'twas a pleasing fear,
> For I was as it were a child of thee,
> And trusted to thy billows far and near,
> And laid my hand upon thy mane—as I do here.
>   —*Childe Harold's Pilgrimage,* Canto IV (1818)

The examples of the sentimental given so far have been from literature, but sentimentality is found in all the arts. We are especially conscious of it in music, though we cannot explain how we know it any better than we can in literature. Beethoven's Sonata in C minor has in it something of self-pity, something of the spirit that finds itself an abused and sorrowful object; in short, something of sentimentality. This character is evidenced by the title by which it is usually known, the *Pathétique,* "pathetic." In comparison, Beethoven's Symphony in

C minor is entirely lacking in sentimentality; it is open, frank, direct. It shows suffering but it does not enjoy the suffering.

Painting, like literature and music, is an open field for the sentimental; and sweet, sentimental creatures are almost as common in painting as in life. In the *Virgin of Consolation* by Bouguereau (Figure 177) the figures are artificially posed; the Virgin, the mother on her knee, and the child lying at her feet are all designed primarily to produce a certain effect. There is no truth; it is not genuine. If this is compared with any of the great paintings of the Madonna, the difference is clear; in Giotto's *Madonna Enthroned* (Figure 178), for

FIG. 177. Adolphe William Bouguereau (1825–1905), French painter. *Virgin of Consolation* (1877). (Oil on canvas. Size: about 14 feet by 11 feet 3 inches. Paris, Luxembourg. Photograph, Braun, Inc.)

FIG. 178. Giotto (1266–1336), Italian painter. *Madonna Enthroned* (ca. 1304).
(Tempera on wood. Height: 10 feet 8½ inches. Florence, Uffizi Gallery. Photograph by Anderson.)

example, the artist is expressing an emotion he feels—he is not striving to show one that he does not feel.

SCOPE

Another question to ask of a work of art has to do with its scope. How much is the artist trying to do? What has he attempted? A single daffodil may be just as beautiful as the Grand Canyon, and will probably be more perfect, but there is something of greatness in the Grand Canyon that we do not find in a daffodil.

Consider two works by Brahms. The *Lullaby* we love to sing: "Hushabye and goodnight, with roses bedight" is beautiful. But compare it with the magnificent last movement of Brahms's First Symphony. The *Lullaby* remains true and fine but it lacks the breadth of design of the symphony. Each is supreme of its kind, but Brahms has attempted more in the symphony than in the *Lullaby*.

Or take the subject of war. Hardy has a short poem in which a peasant is thinking back on his experiences when he was in the army.

> 'Had he and I but met
> By some old ancient inn,
> We should have sat us down to wet
> Right many a nipperkin!
>
> 'But ranged as infantry,
> And staring face to face,
> I shot at him as he at me,
> And killed him in his place.
>
> 'I shot him dead because—
> Because he was my foe,
> Just so: my foe of course he was;
> That's clear enough; although
>
> 'He thought he'd 'list, perhaps,
> Off-hand like—just as I—
> Was out of work—had sold his traps—
> No other reason why.
>
> 'Yes, quaint and curious war is!
> You shoot a fellow down

You'd treat if met where any bar is,
Or help to half-a-crown!
—THOMAS HARDY (1840–1928, English novelist,
short-story writer, and poet),
The Man He Killed, 1902 [2]

Tolstoi's novel *War and Peace* comes to conclusions that are not radically different from Hardy's poem so far as the real value and meaning of war is concerned, but its scope is much greater. Tolstoi makes us see the horrors of war year in and year out, the hopes, dreads, uncertainties, and dangers as they are stretched out for years, until it seems man can take no more.

The scope of a work is not the same as the size or length, yet it is true that the very small can arouse great emotions only rarely and with difficulty. A very short poem or a very short piece of music is over before one's emotions have had time to be fully aroused. A very small painting, the carving on a ring, or a statuette presents the same difficulty; it may be precise, exact, even perfect, but it is not the greatest. This does not mean, of course, that a poem or a statue is greater the larger it is; obviously that is nonsense; but it does mean that those works which are on a diminutive scale do not usually reach the greatest heights. The poems of Emily Dickinson have a fierce intensity and a nobility of subject and feeling that are very great, but they do not arouse the greatest emotions; they do not have time enough. The very beautiful little ivory statue known as the *Snake Goddess* (Figure 61) is another case in point; it is too small to arouse great emotions.

Here music and literature, the two time arts, have a great advantage. Literature is practically unlimited in time; a novel may go on for days or months. Music is limited only by the time necessary for performance. This is also one of the advantages of architecture; one walks around and through a building seeing it from every angle on the outside, and then as it appears from the inside. The Gothic cathedral, with its aisles and walks, presents an almost endless number of different views. The Stephens Chapel, designed by Saarinen, is an example of the wide scope to be obtained in a very small building. By repeating the same units over and over, Saarinen obtains a great sense of unity. Yet these motives are so subtly varied that there is never any sense of bore-

[2] From *Collected Poems* by Thomas Hardy. Copyright 1925 by The Macmillan Company. Used by permission of The Macmillan Company.

dom; instead, as in the cathedral, each view gives a different perspective, and each new view adds to the emotional impact of the whole.

LEVELS OF MEANING

One of the reliefs from the Temple of Athena Niké in Athens is known by the title *Niké Loosening Her Sandal* (Figure 179). The goddess rests her entire weight on her right leg; the left leg is raised as she leans over to untie the cord of her sandal. Her costume is of a soft material, which falls in soft folds across her body, curve after curve all falling in the same general lines but with no two exactly alike.

We have already studied a Greek vase which shows two women putting away their clothes (Figure 135). The figures, their clothes, are balanced perfectly, the space is filled but it is not crowded, the bodies of the women are very graceful, and each seems to complement the other though there is little exact repetition. It is not a picture to make

FIG. 179. *Niké Loosening Her Sandal* (end of fifth century B.C.), from Temple of Athena Niké. (Pentelic marble. Height: 3 feet 2 inches. Athens, Acropolis Museum. Photograph, courtesy of Royal Greek Embassy.)

one think or ponder. One is not concerned as to who washed the clothes, where they are being put, or why. As in the Niké, one simply rejoices in the grace of the shapes in the design.

There is the same sense of untroubled enjoyment when one reads a little poem like Yeats's *The Fiddler of Dooney:*

> When I play on my fiddle in Dooney
> Folk dance like a wave of the sea;
> My cousin is priest in Kilvarnet,
> My brother in Mocharabuiee.
>
> I passed my brother and cousin;
> They read in their books of prayer;
> I read in my book of songs
> I bought at the Sligo fair.
>
> When we come at the end of time
> To Peter sitting in state,
> He will smile on the three old spirits,
> But call me first through the gate;
>
> For the good are always the merry,
> Save by an evil chance,
> And the merry love the fiddle,
> And the merry love to dance:
>
> And when the folk there spy me,
> They will all come up to me,
> With 'Here is the fiddler of Dooney!'
> And dance like a wave of the sea.
>> —W. B. YEATS (1865–1939, Irish poet and play-
>> wright),
>> *The Fiddler of Dooney,* 1899 [3]

It is very pleasant. We don't stop to ask if the Catholic church puts the work of the fiddler above that of the priest. We just like it; it makes one's heart dance "like a wave of the sea."

These examples are simple, clear, direct, finished, and perfect. We know them at once and we feel we know them well. There is no hidden meaning. But often a work of art has more than one level of meaning. To start with an obvious instance, let us look at a poem by Robert Frost. It has only two lines:

[3] From *The Collected Poems* of W. B. Yeats. Copyright 1903 by The Macmillan Company; rev. ed., 1956. Used by permission of The Macmillan Company.

> The old dog barks backward without getting up,
> I can remember when he was a pup.
>   —ROBERT FROST (1875——, American poet)[4]

It is a short simple piece like the ones we have just studied, but with a difference. Change the second line to

> He was frisky and lively when he was a pup.

and our poem is like the three first pieces, pleasant, final. But go back to the line as Frost wrote it, "I can remember when he was a pup"; the meaning is changed entirely. It gives sudden realization of the weakness of age, the eagerness of youth, and the shortness of life. In spite of the use of the pronoun *I,* it seems far away and abstract. It fits the title, *The Span of Life.*

We find the same in two short poems by Robert Browning, *Meeting at Night* and *Parting at Morning.* The first is a vivid description of the meeting of two lovers, the eagerness hardly to be borne as the lover makes his way to the house where his loved one is awaiting him. The images are very clear: gray sea, long black land, yellow half-moon large and low, tap on pane, scratch of match, warm sea-scented beach.

> The gray sea and the long black land;
> And the yellow half-moon large and low;
> And the startled little waves that leap
> In fiery ringlets from their sleep,
> As I gain the cove with pushing prow,
> And quench its speed i' the slushy sand.
>
> Then a mile of warm sea-scented beach;
> Three fields to cross till a farm appears;
> A tap at the pane, the quick sharp scratch
> And blue spurt of a lighted match,
> And a voice less loud, through its joys and fears,
> Than the two hearts beating each to each!
>   —ROBERT BROWNING (English poet, 1812–1889),
>   *Meeting at Night*

In the second poem, the *him* in the third line refers to the sun.

> Round the cape of a sudden came the sea,
> And the sun looked over the mountain's rim:

---

[4] From *A Further Range* by Robert Frost. Copyright 1936, by Robert Frost. By permission of Henry Holt and Company, Inc.

> And straight was a path of gold for him,
> And the need of a world of men for me.
>   —ROBERT BROWNING,
>   *Parting at Morning*

Each of the two poems has its own meaning, clear and exact when taken by itself. Each describes a situation. But the meaning changes when they are taken together, and Browning is our authority for considering them together. Together, they say that the "need of a world of men" is a greater, higher appeal than that of "two hearts beating each to each."

Ozymandias is nothing if it is only a description of a ruined monument.

> I met a traveller from an antique land
> Who said: Two vast and trunkless legs of stone
> Stand in the desert. . . . Near them, on the sand,
> Half sunk, a shattered visage lies, whose frown,
> And wrinkled lip, and sneer of cold command,
> Tell that its sculptor well those passions read
> Which yet survive, stamped on these lifeless things,
> The hand that mocked them, and the heart that fed:
> And on the pedestal these words appear:
> "My name is Ozymandias, king of kings:
> Look on my works, ye Mighty, and despair!"
> Nothing beside remains. Round the decay
> Of that colossal wreck, boundless and bare
> The lone and level sands stretch far away.
>   —PERCY BYSSHE SHELLEY (1792–1822, English poet).
>   *Ozymandias* (1817)

In the visual arts, we find differences in the levels of meaning illustrated very neatly in the photograph and the portrait. The photograph rarely goes beyond the first level: it shows what can be seen at any time and by anyone. The portrait shows more. It shows the man inside the face, as it were; looking at it, we know what the man hoped and feared, and to what he was true.

In Rembrandt's *Man in the Gold Helmet* (Figure 180), we see first the beauty of the helmet, its rich chasing; then we notice the rich garments. The exterior details show a man who has apparently all that money and power can bring him. The face is a great contrast to the rich garments. It is tired, stern, kind, a man who has known hard work,

FIG. 180. Rembrandt Harmensz van Rijn (1606–1669), Dutch painter. *Man in the Gold Helmet*. (Oil on canvas. Height: 2 feet 2½ inches. Berlin State Museums. Photograph by Stoedtner.)

who has had to make hard decisions and take the consequences; a man who has had so much wealth it means nothing to him; a man who can be trusted to see truth and deal fairly with it.

In *Early Sunday Morning* (Figure 181), Hopper has given us more than a painting of a street. There is a sense of loneliness that pervades the street, and we are conscious of its meager resources and its spiritual poverty. The scene is an indictment of our civilization.

Fɪɢ. 181. Edward Hopper (1882——), American painter. *Early Sunday Morning* (ca. 1930). (Oil on canvas. Size: 35 inches by 60 inches. New York, Whitney Museum of American Art.)

What El Greco has put into his *View of Toledo* (Figure 182) could never be caught in a photograph. It is a painting of a city, a city where a storm is about to break. But beyond the natural appearance, the scene is ominous and foreboding; it is one of emotional intensity, mystery, and passion.

TRUTH

Emily Dickinson wrote two poems on the hummingbird.[5] The earlier is made up of five four-line stanzas.

[5] From *The Poems of Emily Dickinson*, by Bianchi and Hampson. Copyright 1937 by Martha Dickinson Bianchi. By permission of Little, Brown & Company. For this comparison I am indebted to *The Case for Poetry* by Gwynn, Condee, and Lewis.

Within my garden rides a bird
Upon a single wheel,
Whose spokes a dizzy music make
As 'twere a traveling mill.

He never stops, but slackens
Above the ripest rose,
Partakes without alighting,
And praises as he goes;

Till every spice is tasted,
And then his fairy gig
Reels in remoter atmospheres,
And I rejoin my dog.

And he and I perplex us
If positive 'twere we—
Or bore the garden in the brain
This curiosity?

But he, the best logician,
Refers my duller eye
To just vibrating blossoms—
An exquisite reply!
          —EMILY DICKINSON (1830–1886, American poet),
          Within My Garden Rides a Bird

In the later poem these twenty lines were reduced to eight:

A route of evanescence
With a revolving wheel;
A resonance of emerald,
A rush of cochineal;
And every blossom on the bush
Adjusts its tumbled head,—
The mail from Tunis, probably,
An easy morning's ride.
          —*A Route of Evanescence*

By common consent the second is recognized as the better of the two
poems, not because it is shorter but because it portrays more vividly
what we feel is the *truth* of the hummingbird.

Truth as used here is not truth of fact. It is a fact that the sun is
shining as I write this, and it is a fact that I am sitting at my desk. Nor

Fig. 182. El Greco (1548–1614), Spanish painter. *View of Toledo* (ca. 1610). (Oil on canvas. Height: 48 inches; width: 42¾ inches. New York, courtesy of the Metropolitan Museum of Art; bequest of Mrs. H. O. Havemeyer, 1929. The H. O. Havemeyer Collection.)

is it the truth of science, which is a statement of observed phenomena; it is true that the moon governs the tides.

Truth in Emily Dickinson's poem, as in all art, has to do with the essential nature of the thing. It is what we were talking about earlier when we said that an artist tried to get his work "right"; he does not necessarily want it to be like its subject, but he wants it "right." The second poem on the hummingbird is no more exact in its portrayal of nature, but it is more true to our concept of a hummingbird. And this

Fig. 183. Jean Baptiste Siméon Chardin (1699–1779), French painter. *The Kitchen Maid* (1738). (Oil on canvas. Size: 18⅛ by 14¾ inches. Washington, D.C., National Gallery of Art; Samuel H. Kress Collection.)

must be the kind of truth Marianne Moore was thinking of when she spoke of "imaginary gardens with real toads in them."

This is the truth we find in Chardin's *Kitchen Maid* (Figure 183). The girl, as we can see, has been preparing the vegetables, peeling turnips. It is an easy job but a stupid one, so her mind goes wandering, and for a time the work stops as she gazes off into the unknown. Chardin has pictured her with just the right set of the head and the dreamy faraway look on her face.

The demands of truth extend all the way from the simple, almost trivial, instances just noted in Chardin and Emily Dickinson to the deepest concerns of heart and mind. The Norwegian painter and print maker Munch has made a lithograph called *The Scream* (Figure 184). The critic Arnold Rüdlinger has spoken of it thus: "The lithograph . . . bears an inscription written in the artist's own hand: 'Ich höre das Geschrei der Natur' ('I hear the scream of nature'). What we are shown here is the effect of almost crazy panic a terrifying landscape can produce on a highly strung man." [6]

[6] *History of Modern Painting—Matisse, Munch, Rouault:* Arnold Rüdlinger, Expressionism in Norway, etc. Albert Skira, Geneva, p. 93.

FIG. 184. Edvard Munch (1863–1944), Norwegian painter and print maker. *The Scream* (1895). (Lithograph. On extended loan to the Museum of Modern Art, New York. Photograph, Museum of Modern Art.)

It is truth that makes us feel the "rightness" when Othello hears
Emilia at the door just after he has killed his wife, and realizes what
he has done in one awful moment:

> If she come in, she'll sure speak to my wife.
> My wife! my wife! what wife? I have no wife.
>
> V, ii, 96–7

Abstract art presents a particular problem in this matter of truth,
because in the visual arts we commonly associate the subject with the
emotion received from it. We know just how a person feels when peeling potatoes, for instance. But in abstract art we are asked to judge the
truth of an emotion without being told either the nature of the emotion

Fig. 185. Wassilj Kandinsky (1866–1944), Russian painter. *Improvisation #30*
(Warlike Theme) (1913). (Oil on canvas. Size: 43¼ inches by 43¾ inches.
Chicago, courtesy of Art Institute of Chicago; Arthur Jerome Eddy Memorial
Collection.)

or its source. In his *Improvisation #30* (Figure 185) Kandinsky is expressing a state of the soul, showing its mood graphically; it is purely a spiritual essence he makes clear in the painting.

The problem with pure music is exactly the same as with abstract painting, except that we are more familiar with pure music and are not too surprised to find an emotion, a state of the soul, expressed through music. We have no hesitation in ascribing a definite mood and emotion to Beethoven's Ninth Symphony or Schubert's *Unfinished Symphony*.

MAGNITUDE

Magnitude is concerned with the impact of a work as a whole, whether it be shallow or deep, important or unimportant, great or trivial—in short with the quality of greatness felt in it. By common consent the greatest art is called the *sublime*.

The source of the sublime is always a greatness of power. One feels the sublime in the ocean, in a fierce storm, in a mighty waterfall, whereas there is no sense of greatness in a small pond or a trickling stream in a pleasant meadow. But even greater than the sublimity of physical power is the sublimity of spiritual power, the power of the Mass in B minor by Bach, or the book of Job.

The sublime ordinarily demands a great protagonist in the sense of a person who is noble or powerful; it seems more natural to think of great emotions in great persons—kings, queens, and people in authority—hence the tradition that heroes and heroines be of noble birth. But greatness of rank is not essential; the highest emotions can be found even in the simplest subjects. Professor Bradley quotes this passage from Turgenev as an example of sublimity in so little a thing as a sparrow.

I was on my way home from hunting, and was walking up the garden avenue. My dog was running in front of me.

Suddenly he slackened his pace, and began to steal forward as though he scented game ahead.

I looked along the avenue; and I saw on the ground a young sparrow, its beak edged with yellow, and its head covered with soft brown. It had fallen from the nest (a strong wind was blowing, and shaking the birches of the avenue); and there it sat and never stirred, except to stretch out its little half-grown wings in a helpless flutter.

My dog was slowly approaching it, when suddenly, darting from the tree overhead, an old black-throated sparrow dropped like a stone right before his nose, and, all rumpled and flustered, with a plaintive desperate cry flung itself, once, twice, at his open jaws with their great teeth.

It would save its young one; it screened it with its own body; the tiny frame quivered with terror; the little cries grew wild and hoarse; it sank and died. It had sacrificed itself.

What a huge monster the dog must have seemed to it! And yet it could not stay up there on its safe bough. A power stronger than its own will tore it away.

My dog stood still, and then slunk back disconcerted. Plainly he too, had to recognize that power. I called him to me; and a feeling of reverence came over me as I passed on.

Yes, do not laugh. It was really reverence I felt before that little heroic bird and the passionate outburst of its love.

Love, I thought, is verily stronger than death and the terror of death. By love, only by love, is life sustained and moved.[7]

Below the sublime are various other stages. Professor Bradley, in his essay on "The Sublime," distinguishes five modes of beauty, or degrees of magnitude. They are: pretty, graceful, beautiful, grand, and sublime. The pretty is at the opposite end from the sublime; it is pleasant and agreeable, but it arouses no very high or strong emotions. The other stages grow successively more difficult as they mount the scale. The pretty is the easiest, and the sublime the most difficult. The grand and the sublime both have the quality of greatness; the pretty and the graceful have not. The beautiful may or may not be great.

These terms will become more meaningful if we try to apply them to definite works. Differences can be seen most easily if we contrast two subjects that are alike or two works by the same artist.

The *Humoresque* of Dvořák is pretty or graceful, but the same composer's *New World Symphony* is beautiful or even great. Yeats's poem *The Second Coming* is great or beautiful, whereas his *Fiddler of Dooney* is no more than pretty or graceful.

> Turning and turning in the widening gyre
> The falcon cannot hear the falconer;
> Things fall apart; the center cannot hold;
> Mere anarchy is loosed upon the world,
> The blood-dimmed tide is loosed, and everywhere
> The ceremony of innocence is drowned;

[7] Bradley, *Oxford Lectures on Poetry*, "The Sublime," p. 44, with permission of Macmillan & Co., Ltd., St. Martin's Press, Inc.

The best lack all conviction, while the worst
Are full of passionate intensity.

Surely some revelation is at hand;
Surely the Second Coming is at hand.
The Second Coming! Hardly are those words out
When a vast image out of *Spiritus Mundi*
Troubles my sight somewhere in sands of the desert
A shape with lion body and the head of a man,
A gaze blank and pitiless as the sun,
Is moving its slow thighs, while all about it
Reel shadows of the indignant desert birds.
The darkness drops again; but now I know
That twenty centuries of stony sleep
Were vexed to nightmare by a rocking cradle,
And what rough beast, its hour come round at last,
Slouches towards Bethlehem to be born?
      —W. B. YEATS (1865–1939, Irish poet and playwright),
      The Second Coming, 1921 [8]

Compare two great figure compositions by Michelangelo: the *Pietà* (Figure 186) at St. Peter's in Rome, which was done when Michelangelo was a young man, and his *Entombment* (Figure 187) in the cathedral at Florence, some fifty years later. Both are sincere, both are complete. In the *Pietà,* the Madonna is young, her face sweetly serious, her head bent forward as she tries to comprehend the thing that has happened. One hand is holding the body of Jesus, the other is left free in a youthful gesture. In the *Entombment,* youth has been left behind, and all is serious. The greatest change is in the face of Jesus, for he is now the Christ who has died to save the world. This statue has elements of sublimity, whereas the *Pietà* is at best great or beautiful.

The sublime arouses in one a feeling of astonishment, rapture, and awe. In comparison with its greatness one feels his own littleness but, paradoxically, the attempt to share the sublime makes one greater than he was before. Confronted with the greatness of Socrates in Plato's account we feel petty, and yet our attempt to understand him makes us greater than we were.

Crito, when he heard this, made a sign to the servant; and the servant went in, and remained for some time, and then returned with the jailer

[8] From *The Collected Poems* of W. B. Yeats. Copyright 1903 by The Macmillan Company; rev. ed., 1956. Used by permission of The Macmillan Company.

carrying the cup of poison. Socrates said: "You, my good friend, who are experienced in these matters, shall give me directions how I am to proceed." The man answered: "You have only to walk about until your legs are heavy, and then to lie down, and the poison will act." At the same time he handed the cup to Socrates, who in the easiest and gentlest manner, without the least fear or change of color or feature, looking at the man with all his eyes . . . as his manner was, took the cup and said: "What do you say about making a libation out of this cup to any god? May I, or not?" The man answered: "We only prepare, Socrates, just so much as we deem enough." "I understand," he said: "yet I may and must

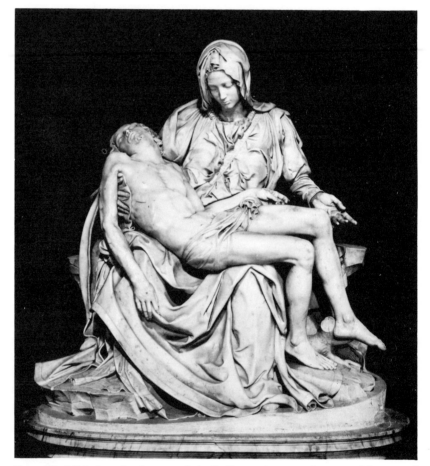

F<small>IG</small>. 186. Michelangelo (1475–1564), Italian painter, sculptor, architect, and poet. *Pietà* (1498–1502). (Marble. Height: about 6 feet 3 inches. Rome, St. Peter's. Photograph by Anderson.)

Fig. 187. Michelangelo. The Entombment (ca. 1550). (Marble. Height: about
7 feet. Florence, Cathedral. Photograph by Anderson.)

pray to the gods to prosper my journey from this to that other world—
may this then, which is my prayer, be granted to me." Then holding the
cup to his lips, quite readily and cheerfully he drank off the poison. And
hitherto most of us had been able to control our sorrow; but now when
we saw him drinking, and saw too that he had finished the draught, we
could no longer forbear, and in spite of myself my own tears were flowing
fast; so that I covered my face and wept over myself, for certainly I was
not weeping over him, but at the thought of my own calamity in having
lost such a companion. Nor was I the first, for Crito, when he found himself unable to restrain his tears, had got up and moved away, and I followed; and at that moment, Apollodorus, who had been weeping all the
time, broke out into a loud cry which made cowards of us all. Socrates
alone retained his calmness. "What is this strange outcry?" he said. "I sent
away the women mainly in order that they might not offend in this way,
for I have heard that a man should die in peace. Be quiet then, and have
patience." When we heard that, we were ashamed, and refrained our
tears; and he walked about until, as he said, his legs began to fail, and
then he lay on his back, according to the directions, and the man who
gave him the poison now and then looked at his feet and legs; and after
a while he pressed his foot hard and asked him if he could feel; and he
said, "No"; and then his leg, and so upwards and upwards, and showed
us that he was cold and stiff. And he felt then himself, and said: "When
the poison reaches the heart, that will be the end." He was beginning to
grow cold about the groin, when he uncovered his face, for he had covered
himself up, and said (they were his last words)—he said: "Crito, I owe a
cock to Asclepius; will you remember to pay the debt?" "The debt shall be
paid," said Crito; "is there anything else?" There was no answer to this
question; but in a minute or two a movement was heard, and the attendants uncovered him; his eyes were set, and Crito closed his eyes and
mouth.

—PLATO (427?–347 B.C., Greek philosopher),
    The Phaedo, tr. by Benjamin Jowett (1817–1893, English scholar)

GROWTH IN JUDGMENT

The judgment each person makes of a work of art is individual and
personal, just as the experience itself was individual and personal. And
since one person is never exactly like any other, his judgment of art will
never be exactly like that of another. Moreover, no person's judgment
of any work of art will remain exactly the same. With each new experience he tends to like it more or less well, to find it more or less reward-

ing. In short, there is never one judgment which can be embalmed and put away as a final evaluation.

Not only does judgment change with each new experience, but it changes as one learns to know the judgments of others. Both history and criticism can help us to see and hear what we have not seen and heard for ourselves, and so our experience becomes richer and deeper.

This is the greatest contribution history and criticism can make to us, but there is a secondary influence which is also of importance. History and criticism can help us in the selection of works we want to become acquainted with. No one can possibly know all the art in the world; he cannot read all the books that are printed or hear all the music that is composed and played in any one year; he can hardly know all the pictures and statues in any one of the great galleries, much less in all of them. Therefore, we use the opinions of others to help us decide what is worth looking at and listening to, to tell what has been thought good and what poor, what has been reckoned great and what mediocre.

This is especially important in the case of those artists who have become known through the ages as the very great: Dante, Homer, Rembrandt, Shakespeare, Phidias, Bach, Beethoven, Michelangelo. They cannot be known easily or at once. Therefore we do not get the immediate satisfaction we get from lesser works; we are perhaps repulsed, and we put them aside. The very great in art, as in everything else, is difficult; almost anything worth doing is difficult; it cannot be attained easily or without hard work. The prophecies of Isaiah and the book of Job in the Old Testament are among the supreme examples of literature, but it is doubtful if anyone can get very great pleasure from them without study. No one can ever appreciate the Mass in B minor or the *Divine Comedy* on a single hearing or a superficial reading; they need concentrated attention. But knowing that they are considered among the world's great masterpieces, we can prepare to give them the necessary study. The person who gives them this study will not necessarily like them; in art, as in life, one must count on a certain number of failures. But no one can know if he will like the great works of art until he has given them the necessary attention.

Fortunately, there is little difference of opinion with regard to the very great. About the lesser works there are many and various judgments; one person prefers this and another that, but as we approach those few masterpieces that can be called supremely great, the differences melt away. Hence we may approach them with greater assurance, understanding that though they demand work, they will bring their reward, and the work will not be in vain. Fortunately, also, the rewards of art, like the rewards of goodness, are open to everyone. Appreciation of art, like virtue, is not reserved for the learned but is free to the honest and sincere.

FOR FURTHER EXPLORATION

1. Compare two artists for the scope of their work.

2. Look up Rodin's statue *The Burghers of Calais* and the description of it in Gsell's book, *The Art of Auguste Rodin* (pp. 85–88).

3. Let each person in the class select a different artist and study the various criticisms that have been made of his work over a period of time. Notice the characteristics that are commented on as well as the degree of praise and blame.

4. Compare a contemporary history of art, music, or literature with one of twenty, fifty, or a hundred years ago. What differences do you find in the subjects stressed?

5. Study Byron's early poems for examples of sentimentality.

6. Choose ten poems, ten paintings, ten pieces of music, ten statues, and ten buildings that you like very much; rank each as pretty, beautiful, etc.

7. Compare three Greek conceptions of Venus: the *Medici Venus,* the *Venus of Melos,* and the *Venus of Cnidus.*

8. Compare any works on the same subject as to their magnitude.

9. Go back over the examples you have studied in this volume to judge their magnitude. Do you agree with the commonly expressed opinion that the late Greek statues are of little real value?

BIBLIOGRAPHY

AESTHETICS AND GENERAL REFERENCE

Adams, Henry: *Mont-Saint-Michel and Chartres,* Houghton Mifflin, Boston, 1925; Doubleday (Anchor), New York.

An introduction to the art of the Middle Ages showing how the ideas of an age are impressed on its art.

Anderson, Maxwell, Rhys Carpenter, and Roy Harris: *The Bases of Artistic Creation,* Rutgers University Press, New Brunswick, N.J., 1942.

To this short volume Anderson contributes an essay on literature, Harris one on music, and Carpenter one on the fine arts. Personal and good.

Art and Artist, University of California Press, Berkeley, Calif., 1956.

A group of sixteen modern artists tell in their own words what they feel about their work.

Barzun, Jacques: *Romanticism and the Modern Ego,* Little, Brown, Boston, 1943.

Beardsley, Monroe C.: *Aesthetics: Problems in the Philosophy of Criticism,* Harcourt, Brace, New York, 1958.

Berenson, Bernhard: *Aesthetics and History in the Visual Arts,* Doubleday (Anchor), New York, 1954.

A very delightful and informal discussion of the principles of art. Mr. Berenson writes as an old man who is not afraid of admitting age or enthusiasm.

Bosanquet, Bernard: *Three Lectures on Aesthetic,* Macmillan, New York, 1915.

Brown, Calvin S.: *Music and Literature: A Comparison of the Arts,* University of Georgia Press, Athens, Ga., 1948.

The value of this book lies primarily in its interpretations of individual works. The author sometimes pulls the strings of his puppets a little too hard in trying to show relations between music and literature, but the discussions are always informative and illuminating.

Croce, Benedetto: *Aesthetic as Science of Expression and General Linguistic,* Noonday Press, New York, 1953.

Dewey, John: *Art as Experience,* Putnam, New York, 1934.

Ducasse, Curt J.: *Art, the Critics and You,* Piest, New York, 1944.
A simple down-to-earth explanation of the relation of philosophy to aesthetics and the bases of criticism.

Fleming, William: *Arts and Ideas,* Holt, New York, 1955.
Historical approach to the humanities.

Ghiselin, Brewster: *The Creative Process: A Symposium,* University of California Press, Berkeley, Calif., 1954.
Descriptions of the creative process by 38 people known for their creative ability. The subjects range from mathematics to painting and dancing.

Hospers, John: *Meaning and Truth in the Arts,* University of North Carolina Press, Chapel Hill, N.C., 1946.

Langer, Susanne K.: *Feeling and Form,* Scribner, New York, 1953.

——: *Philosophy in a New Key,* 3d ed., Penguin, Baltimore, 1957.

——: *Problems of Art: Ten Philosophical Lectures,* Scribner, New York, 1957.
Although given to a variety of audiences, these lectures all have to do with the basic issues of art: "What is created, what is expressed, what is experienced." A simpler statement than Mrs. Langer's other books.

Langfeld, H. S.: *The Aesthetic Attitude,* Harcourt, Brace, New York, 1920.

Longinus: *On the Sublime,* tr. by A. O. Prickard, Clarendon Press, Oxford, 1906.

Maritain, Jacques: *Creative Intuition in Art and Poetry,* Bollingen Series XXXV.I, Pantheon, New York, 1953.

Mundt, Ernest: *Art, Form, and Civilization,* University of California Press, Berkeley, Calif., 1952.
A plea for the "unitary" man who stands midway between art and science and participates in both in a total, unified response.

Munro, Thomas: *The Arts and Their Interrelations,* Liberal Arts Press, New York, 1949.
Philosophical in outlook.

Pepper, Stephen C.: *The Basis of Criticism in the Arts,* Harvard University Press, Cambridge, Mass., 1949.

——: *Principles of Art Appreciation,* Harcourt, Brace, New York, 1949.
Limited almost entirely to the visual arts. Excellent analysis.

Rader, Melvin: *A Modern Book of Aesthetics: An Anthology,* Holt, New York, 1935.

Read, Herbert: *The Meaning of Art,* Penguin, Baltimore, 1949.
Simply stated aesthetics of visual arts. Stimulating.

Sachs, Curt: *The Commonwealth of Art: Style in the Fine Arts, Music and the Dance,* Norton, New York, 1946.
In three parts: I. An Outline of Comparative Art History; II. The Nature of Style; and III. The Fate of Style. Learned and comprehensive.

Schoen, Max: *Art and Beauty,* Macmillan, New York, 1932.

Seldes, Gilbert: *Seven Lively Arts,* Harper, New York, 1957.

Stace, W. T.: *The Meaning of Beauty,* Cayme Press, London, 1929.

Stein, Leo: *The A. B. C. of Aesthetics,* Boni, New York, 1927.

————: *Appreciation: Painting, Poetry and Prose,* Crown, New York, 1947.
An informal narrative of the author's experiences in the arts.

Sypher, Wylie: *Four Stages of Renaissance Style,* Doubleday (Anchor), New York, 1955.

Vivas, Eliseo, and Murray Krieger: *The Problems of Aesthetics: A Book of Readings,* Rinehart, New York, 1953.

Weitz, Morris: *Problems in Aesthetics: An Introductory Book of Readings,* Macmillan, New York, 1959.

Wellek, René: "Aesthetics and Criticisms," Lecture III in *The Philosophy of Kant and Our Modern World,* Liberal Arts Press, New York, 1957.
Four lectures delivered at Yale University commemorating the 150th Anniversary of the death of Immanuel Kant.

LITERATURE AND THEATER

Bacon, Wallace A., and Robert S. Breen: *Literature as Experience,* McGraw-Hill, New York, 1959.

Baugh, Albert C., ed.: *A Literary History of England,* Appleton-Century-Crofts, New York, 1958.
Encyclopedic in scope.

Beardsley, Monroe, Robert Daniel, and Glenn Leggett: *Theme and Form,* Prentice-Hall, Englewood Cliffs, N.J., 1956.
An excellent anthology.

Benét, William Rose, ed.: *The Reader's Encyclopedia,* Crowell, New York, 1948.
This book not only gives résumés of literary works and biographies of authors but also contains common allusions and references.

Blackmur, R. P.: *Form and Value in Modern Poetry,* Doubleday (Anchor), New York, 1957.
Essays from *Language as Gesture,* 1952.

Bradley, A. C.: *Shakespearean Tragedy,* Macmillan, London, 1904.

————: *Oxford Lectures on Poetry,* 2d ed., Macmillan, London, 1909.

Brooks, Cleanth, Jr.: *The Well Wrought Urn,* Harcourt, Brace (Harvest), New York, 1947.

————, and R. P. Warren: *Understanding Poetry,* rev. ed., Holt, New York, 1950.
An anthology for college students. Analysis and theory focused on the detailed study of individual works.

————, J. T. Purser, and R. P. Warren: *An Approach to Literature,* 3d ed., Appleton, New York, 1952.

Butcher, S. H.: *Aristotle's Theory of Poetry and Fine Art,* 4th ed., Macmillan, London, 1920.
With a critical text and translation of *The Poetics.* An excellent discussion of the fundamental principles of poetry and of all literature, using Aristotle's essay as the point of departure.

Cheney, Sheldon: *The Theatre: Three Thousand Years of Drama, Acting, and Stagecraft,* Tudor Publishing Co., New York, 1935.
The standard text.

Cherry, Colin: *On Human Communication,* Wiley, New York, 1957.
Discussion of signs, denotations, meaning.

Coleridge, Samuel Taylor: *Biographica Literaria,* 1817. 2 vol. ed. by J. Shaw-cross, Clarendon Press, Oxford, 1907.

Daiches, David: *A Study of Literature for Readers and Critics,* Cornell University Press, Ithaca, N.Y., 1948.
A clear, honest, sensible study of literature, with special emphasis on the novel.

———: *Critical Approaches to Literature,* Prentice-Hall, Englewood Cliffs, N.J., 1956.

Day-Lewis, Cecil: *The Poetic Image,* Oxford, New York, 1948.

Deutsch, Babette: *Poetry in Our Time,* Holt, New York, 1952.
Good, clear, precise evaluations of twentieth century poetry.

———: *Poetry Handbook: A Dictionary of Terms,* Funk and Wagnalls, New York, 1957.

Eliot, T. S.: *What Is a Classic?* Faber, London, 1945.

———: *Poetry and Drama,* Harvard University Press, Cambridge, Mass., 1951.

———: *On Poetry and Poets,* New York, Farrar, Straus, Cudahy, 1957.

Empson, William: *Seven Types of Ambiguity,* 2d ed. rev., Chatto and Windus, London, 1947.

Ferguson, Francis: *The Idea of a Theatre,* Doubleday (Anchor), New York, 1953.

Forster, E. M.: *Aspects of the Novel,* Harcourt, Brace, New York, 1927.

Fowler, H. W.: *A Dictionary of Modern English Usage,* Clarendon Press, Oxford, 1927.

Frankenberg, Lloyd: *Pleasure Dome: On Reading Modern Poetry,* Houghton Mifflin, Boston, 1949.
Excellent chapters on James Stephens, T. S. Eliot, Marianne Moore, E. E. Cummings, and Wallace Stevens.

Gassner, J.: *A Treasury of the Theatre,* rev. ed., Simon and Schuster, New York, 1951.
World drama.

Gayley, C. M.: *Classic Myths in English Literature and in Art,* Ginn, Boston, 1911.

Guérard, Albert: *Preface to World Literature,* Holt, New York, 1940.
In three parts: (1) Explorations and Definitions: folklore, taste, prose, poetry; (2) Tendencies: classic, romantic, realistic, symbolic; Genres: lyric, epic, dramatic; Periods; and (3) Problems in World Literature: the social approach to the study of literature.

Gwynn, Frederick, Ralph W. Condee, and Arthur O. Lewis, Jr.: *The Case for Poetry,* Prentice-Hall, Englewood Cliffs, N.J., 1954.
Many of the poems in this anthology are accompanied by critiques or case studies.

Hamilton, Clayton: *The Theory of the Theatre and Other Principles of Dramatic Criticism,* with a foreword by Burns Mantle, Holt, New York, 1939. Consolidated edition including *The Theory of the Theatre, Studies in Stagecraft, Problems of the Playwright,* and *Seen on the Stage.*

Hamilton, Edith: *The Greek Way to Western Civilization,* New American Library (Mentor), New York, 1948.

This book contains material published in 1930 under the title *The Greek Way,* with additional material published in 1942 in *The Great Age of Greek Literature.* Most of the chapters are devoted to Greek authors, but there are chapters on general subjects such as the Greek mind and Greek religion. An outstanding book, clear and vivid.

Hart, J. D.: *Oxford Companion to American Literature,* 3d ed., Oxford, New York, 1956.

Harvey, P.: *Oxford Companion to English Literature,* 3d ed., Clarendon Press, Oxford, 1946.

One of the best books for ready reference. The material is arranged as in an encyclopedia.

————: *Oxford Companion to Classical Literature,* Clarendon Press, Oxford, 1946.

Hayakawa, S. I.: *Language in Thought and Action,* Harcourt, Brace, New York, 1949.

Hewitt, Barnard: *Theatre U. S. A.,* McGraw-Hill, New York, 1959.

Jesperson, Otto: *Growth and Structure of the English Language,* 9th ed., Doubleday (Anchor), New York, 1955.

Kenner, Hugh: *The Art of Poetry,* Rinehart, New York, 1959.

Kreuzer, James R.: *Elements of Poetry,* Macmillan, New York, 1955.

Krutch, Joseph Wood: *The Modern Temper,* Harcourt, Brace (Harvest), New York, 1929.

Leavis, F. R.: *The Great Tradition: A Study of the English Novel,* Doubleday (Anchor), New York, 1954.

Legouis, E., and L. Cazamian: *A History of English Literature, 630–1914,* tr. by H. D. Irvine and W. D. MacInnes, 2 vols., London, 1926–1927. Rev. ed., Macmillan, New York, 1957.

McCollom, William G.: *Tragedy,* Macmillan, New York, 1957.

Meredith, George: *The Ideas of Comedy and the Uses of the Comic Spirit,* 1877.

Miles, Josephine: *The Poem: A Critical Anthology,* Prentice-Hall, Englewood Cliffs, N.J., 1959.

Murray, Gilbert: *The Classical Tradition in Poetry,* Harvard University Press, Cambridge, Mass., 1927; Vintage books, 1957.

Nicoll, Allardyce: *The Theory of Drama,* Crowell, New York, 1931.

————: *British Drama: An Historical Survey,* 4th ed., Barnes and Noble, New York. 1957.

————: *The Development of the Theatre: A Study of Theatrical Art from the Beginnings to the Present Day,* 4th ed., rev. and enl., Harrap, London, 1958.

O'Connor, William: *Sense and Sensibility in Modern Poetry,* University of Chicago Press, Chicago, 1948.

Perrine, Laurence: *Sound and Sense: An Introduction to Poetry,* Harcourt, Brace, New York, 1956.

Quiller-Couch, Arthur: *On the Art of Writing,* Putnam, New York, 1916, Chap. 12, "On Style."

Ransom, John Crowe: *The New Criticism,* New Directions, New York, 1941.

Sampson, George: *The Concise Cambridge History of English Literature,* Macmillan, New York, 1941.

A condensation of the fourteen-volume *Cambridge History of English Literature.*

Sapir, Edward: *Language,* Harcourt, Brace, New York, 1921; Harvest, 1949.

Sewall, Richard B.: *The Vision of Tragedy,* Yale University Press, New Haven, Conn., 1959.

Shipley, Joseph T., ed.: *Dictionary of World Literature,* 2d ed., Philosophical Library, New York, 1943.

Skelton, Robin: *The Poetic Pattern,* University of California Press, Berkeley, Calif., 1956.

Spurgeon, Caroline: *Shakespeare's Imagery,* Cambridge University Press, New York, 1935; Beacon, 1958.

Stallman, R. W., ed.: *Critiques and Essays in Criticism, 1920–1948,* Ronald, New York, 1949.

A useful introduction to the more important criticism of recent years.

Strickland, F. Cowles: *The Technique of Acting,* McGraw-Hill, New York, 1956.

Tate, Allen: *On the Limits of Poetry: Selected Essays, 1928–1948,* Swallow Press, New York, 1948.

Thrall, William Flint, and Addison Hibbard: *A Handbook to Literature,* Odyssey, New York, 1936.

A very useful dictionary of literary terms.

Wellek, René, and Austin Warren: *Theory of Literature,* 2d ed., Harcourt, Brace, New York, 1956.

In this short volume the authors give a synopsis of each of the fields involved in the study of literary theory, including the nature and function of literature, the extrinsic study (biography, psychology, society), and the intrinsic study (meter, style, genres, etc.). The treatment of each item is clear and comprehensive, though necessarily brief.

Wimsatt, W. K., Jr.: *The Verbal Icon: Studies in the Meaning of Poetry,* Noonday Press, New York, 1958.

―――― and Cleanth Brooks: *Literary Criticism: A Short History,* Knopf, New York, 1957.

Wordsworth, William: *Preface to Lyrical Ballads,* 1800.

MUSIC

Abraham, Gerald: *Design in Music,* Oxford, New York, 1949.

Apel, Willi: *Harvard Dictionary of Music,* Harvard University Press, Cambridge, Mass., 1944.

Limited to musical subjects. No biographies are included.

Bernstein, Martin: *An Introduction to Music,* 2d ed., Prentice-Hall, Englewood Cliffs, N.J., 1951.

The author treats concisely and yet adequately, in a lively and readable manner, the whole field of music from the simple fundamentals of rhythm and melody to the grandeur of Beethoven's symphonies. Interesting and informative studies of the major composers from Bach to Sibelius are combined with detailed analyses of typical works.

Boatwright, Howard: *Introduction to the Theory of Music.* Norton, New York, 1956.

In two parts: I. Intervals and Rhythms, II. Scales and Melody. Useful "experiments" to give practice in applying the principles. Simple, clear, direct. Recognizes melody as tune and not only as a subdivision of harmony.

Bockman, Guy A. and William J. Starr: *Scored for Listening,* Harcourt, Brace, New York, 1959.

Brockway, Wallace, and Herbert Weinstock: *The Opera: A History of Its Creation and Performance, 1600–1941,* Simon and Schuster, New York, 1941.

Burrows, Raymond, and Bessie Carroll Redmond: *Symphony Themes,* compiled with special editorial assistance by George Szell, Simon and Schuster, New York, 1942.

The themes of a hundred symphonies, with no comment. The volume gives also a bibliography of scores.

Chase, Gilbert: *America's Music From the Pilgrims to the Present,* McGraw-Hill, New York, 1955.

Cooper, Grosvenor: *Learning to Listen: A Handbook for Music.* (Prepared with the Humanities staff of the College at the University of Chicago.) University of Chicago Press, Chicago, 1957.

An earnest attempt to present music as a listener's art without technical abracadabra.

Copland, Aaron: *Music and Imagination,* Harvard University Press, Cambridge, Mass., 1953.

Charles Eliot Norton Lectures at Harvard University for 1951–1952. Intelligent and intelligible lectures on the two general topics: (1) Music and the Imaginative Mind and (2) Musical Imagination and the Contemporary Scene.

————: *What to Listen for in Music,* rev. ed., McGraw-Hill, New York, 1957.

This edition contains new chapters on Contemporary Music and Film Music. An interesting and easily read book.

Dent, Edward J.: *Opera,* Penguin, Baltimore, 1940.

Ewen, David, ed.: *From Bach to Stravinsky: The History of Music by Its Foremost Critics,* Norton, New York, 1933.

Each chapter is by a recognized authority.

Ferguson, Donald N.: *A History of Musical Thought,* Crofts, New York, 1935.

Finney, Theodore M.: *A History of Music,* rev. ed., Harcourt, Brace, New York, 1947.

A simple and clear statement of the development of music. The author does not attempt to analyze individual compositions, or to relate the lives of composers except as these have influenced their work. He does, however, state clearly the main features of an artist's work and style, and how these are related to the other work of his time. (Other good histories are those of Nef and Ferguson.)

Forsyth, Cecil: *Orchestration,* 2d ed., Macmillan, New York, 1942.

Foss, Hubert J., ed.: *The Heritage of Music,* 2 vols., Oxford, New York, 1927. Each volume contains twelve studies, by notable musical writers of today. Not biography or criticism, but a summing up of the place a composer holds in musical tradition and his past and present influence. The essays written by Tovey, Gray, and Terry are especially illuminating.

Gehrkens, Karl W.: *The Fundamentals of Music,* Oliver Ditson, Boston, 1924. The first year of a study course in music understanding prepared for the National Federation of Music Clubs. Very simple and easy for the musical amateur.

Gray, Cecil: *A Survey of Contemporary Music,* 2d ed., Oxford, New York, 1927. A critical survey of Strauss, Delius, Elgar, Debussy, Ravel, Stravinsky, Scriabine, Schönberg, Bartók, and Sibelius. Short, dated, but good.

————: *The History of Music,* 2d ed., rev., Knopf, New York, 1935. This is neither an elementary textbook primarily designed for educational purposes, nor a scientific and technical book for the highly trained musician, but a book for the average intelligent music lover, the general cultured reader. The contents include a study of music from the chants of the fifteenth century to the ballets of Stravinsky. There are no musical examples. The book not only treats the development of music but induces in the reader a more receptive and responsive attitude toward the great masterpieces of the past.

Grout, Donald Jay: *A Short History of Opera,* 2 vols., Columbia University Press, New York, 1947.

Grove, George: *Beethoven and His Nine Symphonies,* Novello, London, 1896.

Hadow, Sir W. H., ed.: *The Oxford History of Music,* 6 vols., 2d ed., Oxford, New York, 1929.

Hill, Ralph: *The Symphony,* Penguin, Baltimore, 1949. Brief descriptions of the major symphonies from Haydn to Bax. Some have musical illustrations.

Hindemith, Paul: *The Craft of Musical Composition,* Part I. The Theoretical Part. Associated Music Publishers, New York, 1942. A new theory of the derivation of the tones of the chromatic scale as a basis for all melodic and harmonic principles. Not for the beginner.

————: *A Composer's World: Horizons and Limitations,* Harvard University Press, Cambridge, Mass., 1952.

Howard, John Tasker, and James Lyons: *Modern Music: A Popular Guide to Greater Musical Enjoyment,* rev. ed., New American Library (Mentor), New York, 1957. Excellent work, first published in 1942 as *This Modern Music.*

Kitson, C. H.: *Rudiments of Music,* Oxford, New York, 1927. A small volume which gives the rudiments simply and clearly.

Lang, Paul Henry: *Music in Western Civilization,* Norton, New York, 1941.
From the ancient Greeks through Debussy.

Lavignac, Albert: *Music and Musicians,* tr. by William Marchant, 4th ed., rev. and ed., with an appendix on music in America and the present state of the art of music, by H. E. Krehbiel, Holt, New York, 1899.
The five chapters are entitled (1) "A Study of Musical Sound," (2) "The Materials of Sound," (3) "Grammar of Music," (4) "Esthetics," (5) "History of the Art of Music." The treatment is clear and comprehensive. A valuable book that has not been superseded.

Leibowitz, Rene: *Schoenberg and His School,* tr. by Dika Newlin, Philosophical Library, New York, 1949.
The subtitle gives the subject as "the contemporary stage of the language of music."

McKinney, Howard D., and W. R. Anderson: *Discovering Music: A Course in Music Appreciation,* 3d ed., American Book, New York, 1952.
Useful as a textbook for the student who has had no formal musical training, because the subject matter has been arranged in a manner suitable for presentation in class. Suggestions for further reading are at the end of each chapter along with a list of suggested recordings. At the end of the book is a glossary of musical terms.

Machlis, Joseph, *The Enjoyment of Music,* Norton, New York, 1955.
This book is an outgrowth of the introductory course in Music at Queens College of the City of New York. A good text in the hands of an experienced and capable teacher. It is best in its short introductions, usually with themes of the compositions discussed. Good list of records and bibliography.

Meyer, Leonard B.: *Emotion and Meaning in Music,* University of Chicago Press, Chicago, 1956.
Music in terms of its expectations: what we expect determines what we hear. Good.

Morris, R. O.: *The Structure of Music: An Outline for Students,* Oxford, New York, 1935.
Short and clear explanations of the forms of music.

Murphy, Howard A.: *Form in Music for the Listener,* 2d ed., rev., Radio Corporation of America, Camden, N.J., 1948.
The author reduces to a minimum the technical language of music. Good analyses and bibliographies.

Newman, Ernest: *Stories of the Great Operas and Their Composers,* Garden City, New York, 1935.
Three volumes in one: Vol. I, *Wagner;* Vol. II, *Mozart to Thomas;* Vol. III, *Verdi to Puccini.*
For each opera included, the story is told in detail, with many excerpts from the music. The best book for the study of opera.

————: *The Wagner Operas,* Knopf, New York, 1949.

Parry, C. Hubert H.: *The Evolution of the Art of Music,* Appleton, New York, 1906.

————: *Style in Musical Art,* Macmillan, London, 1924.

Piston, Walter: *Harmony,* rev. ed., Norton, New York, 1948.
Not for the beginner. Serious and complete.

Pole, William: *The Philosophy of Music,* 6th ed., Harcourt, Brace, New York, 1924.
In three parts: I. Material of music; II. Elementary arrangement of the material; III. Structure of music.

Ratner, Leonard G.: *Music, The Listener's Art,* McGraw-Hill, New York, 1957.
One of the few books really written for the listener.

Redfield, J.: *Music: A Science and an Art,* Knopf, New York, 1928.

Rufer, Josef: *Composition with Twelve Tones. Macmillan,* New York, 1954.

Salazar, Adolfo: *Music in Our Time: Trends in Music Since the Romantic Era,* tr. by Isabel Pope. Norton, New York, 1946.

Schoen, Max: *The Understanding of Music,* Harper, New York, 1945.

Scholes, Percy A.: *Listener's Guide to Music,* with a concertgoer's glossary and an introduction by Sir W. Henry Hadow, 10th ed., Oxford, New York, 1942.
Musical notation, form, the orchestra, and something about schools. Only about a hundred pages, this little book gives the essentials of musical theory in a clear but compact form.

——: *Oxford Companion to Music,* 9th ed., rev. Oxford, New York, 1950.
Short and usually clear discussions of terms, composers, and compositions. Extremely useful for quick reference.

Simon, Henry, and Abraham Veinus: *The Pocket Book of Great Operas,* Pocket Books, New York, 1949.
Plots and musical excerpts.

Spaeth, Sigmund: *Great Program Music,* Garden City, New York, 1940.

——: *A Guide to Great Orchestral Music,* Modern Library, New York, 1943.
Probably the best single book for the amateur who knows something of music and wants help in analysis of individual works. The volume covers a very large range of orchestral music and gives melodies of important themes. The appendix contains a register of recorded music with comments on the performance.

——: *A History of Popular Music in America,* Random House, New York, 1948. Like all the author's books, good and very readable.

Stokowski, Olga Samaroff: *The Layman's Music Book,* Norton, New York, 1935.
Based on the Layman's Music Courses given by the author in New York City. The first chapter is excellent for its discussion of the universal interest in and need for music.

Stringham, Edwin John: *Listening to Music Creatively,* Prentice-Hall, Englewood Cliffs, N.J., 1946.

Thomson, Virgil: *State of Music,* Morrow, New York, 1939.
To quote the author's words: "I am here occupied in describing the state of the musical tradition in Western society and telling how it actually works."

——: *The Musical Scene,* Knopf, New York, 1945; and *The Art of Judging Music,* Knopf, New York, 1948.
These two books consist of selected essays and reviews which appeared in

the *New York Herald Tribune* between Oct. 9, 1940, and Aug. 23, 1947. They offer a panoramic view of musical America by one of our outstanding and readable music critics. The essays are arranged under headings such as Orchestras, Recitalists, Composers, Compositions, and Operas. An index facilitates easy reference to specific compositions and performers.

Toch, Ernst: *The Shaping Forces in Music,* Criterion Music Corp., New York, 1948.

Harmony, melody, counterpoint, form. A clear statement of the fundamentals of musical form, and of organic structure as distinguished from skeletal structure.

Tovey, Donald Francis: *Essays in Musical Analysis,* 6 vols., Oxford, New York, 1935–1939.

Generally considered the best work of its kind. The first volume contains an elaborate introduction defining musical terms, followed by illuminating and comprehensive musical criticism of major symphonies. The second volume concludes the treatment of symphonies, and includes variations and orchestral polyphony. The third volume covers concertos; the fourth, illustrative music; the fifth, vocal music; and the sixth, miscellaneous notes, glossary, and index. To the original six volumes a seventh was added in 1945 on chamber music. These essays are a complete collection of the famous program notes which the author wrote over a number of years, mainly for his concerts with the Reid Orchestra in Edinburgh.

———: *Beethoven,* with an editorial preface by Hubert J. Foss, Oxford, New York, 1944.

A study of Beethoven's art under headings such as Rhythm and Movement, Phrasing and Accent, The Larger Tonality, etc.

———: *Musical Articles from the Encyclopaedia Britannica,* with an editorial preface by Hubert J. Foss, Oxford, New York, 1944.

Articles on the "techniques and aesthetics of music." Though designed and written as separate articles, they form a well-built volume.

———: *The Main Stream of Music and Other Essays,* collected with an introduction by Hubert J. Foss, Oxford, New York, 1949.

Eighteen essays which represent the larger part of Tovey's writings not previously made available.

Teaching Materials

Skeleton Scores. A skeleton score shows the melodic line of a composition, with annotations which give indications of form (first theme, development, etc.), timbre, tempo, and dynamics.

The series of *Symphonic Skeleton Scores* is edited and annotated by Violet Katzner (Theodore Presser Company, Bryn Mawr, Pa.). The series at present contains these six symphonies:

Beethoven, Symphony No. 5 in C minor
Brahms, Symphony No. 1 in C minor
Brahms, Symphony No. 3 in F major
Franck, Symphony in D minor
Mozart, Symphony in G minor
Schubert, Symphony in B minor (*Unfinished*)
Tchaikowsky, Symphony No. 4 in F minor
Tchaikowsky, Symphony No. 6 in B minor (*Pathétique*)

Scored for Listening, by Bockmon and Starr (Harcourt, Brace, New York, 1959) contains skeleton scores for many of the compositions referred to in this volume.

Miniature Scores. As the name implies, the miniature score gives the entire score, but in miniature; collections of miniature scores are published by E. F. Kalmus Orchestra Scores, Inc., New York City, and by Penguin, Baltimore.

Librettos. The complete words of operas, often with one or two musical excerpts, can be obtained from The Metropolitan Opera Association or Fred Rullman, Inc., in New York City, and Oliver Ditson Co., Boston.

VISUAL ARTS (INCLUDING CINEMA AND DANCE)

Amberg, George: *Ballet in America,* New American Library (Mentor), New York, 1949.
    Clear and interesting discussion of the present place of ballet in America.
Arnheim, Rudolf: *Art and Visual Perception: A Psychology of the Creative Eye,* University of California Press, Berkeley, Calif., 1954.
    An excellent analysis of what the eye sees and how it is interpreted. The chapter headings include: Balance, Shape, Form, Growth, Space, Light, Color, Movement, Tension, Expression.
Barr, Alfred H., Jr.: *What Is Modern Painting?* Museum of Modern Art, New York, 1943.
———: *Picasso: Fifty Years of His Art,* Museum of Modern Art, New York, 1946.
———, ed.: *Masters of Modern Art,* Museum of Modern Art, New York, 1954.
    This volume is primarily a catalogue of the collections of the Museum of Modern Art.
Beam, Philip C.: *The Language of Art,* Ronald, New York, 1958.
Berenson, Bernhard: *The Italian Painters of the Renaissance,* Phaidon, New York, 1952.
Blake, Vernon: *The Art and Craft of Drawing,* Oxford, New York, 1927.

————: *Relation in Art,* Oxford, New York, 1932.

Brummé, Ludwig: *Contemporary American Sculpture,* with introduction by William Zorach, Crown, New York, 1948.

The author discusses interesting and vital aspects of modern sculpture: the highly simplified treatment of forms derived from the visual arts or conceived without reference to natural objects.

Burckhardt, J. C.: *The Civilization of the Renaissance in Italy,* Phaidon, New York, 1945.

Casson, Stanley: *Some Modern Sculptors,* Oxford, New York, 1928.

————: *XXth Century Sculptors,* Oxford, New York, 1930.

————: *The Technique of Early Greek Sculpture,* Oxford, New York, 1933.

Chase, G. H., and C. R. Post: *A History of Sculpture,* Harper, New York, 1925.

The standard text.

Colman, S.: *Nature's Harmonic Unity,* Putnam, New York, 1912.

Craven, Thomas: *A Treasury of Art Masterpieces,* Simon and Schuster, New York, 1939.

Good selection of great paintings in color.

Davidson, Morris: *An Approach to Modern Painting,* Coward-McCann, New York, 1948.

Doerner, Max: *The Materials of the Artist,* tr. by Eugen Neuhaus, Harcourt, Brace, New York, 1949.

Faulkner, Ray, Edwin Ziegfeld, and Gerald Hill: *Art Today,* 3d ed., Holt, New York, 1956.

The book is divided into three parts which have to do with (1) human needs, (2) organization, (3) materials and processes. A lively presentation.

Fletcher, Bannister: *A History of Architecture on the Comparative Method,* Scribner, New York, 1938.

Indispensable.

Fry, Roger: *Transformations: Critical and Speculative Essays,* Doubleday (Anchor), New York, 1956.

Gardner, Ernest A.: *A Handbook of Greek Sculpture,* 2d ed., Macmillan, New York, 1929.

Definitive.

Gardner, Helen: *Art Through the Ages,* 4th ed., revised by the Department of the History of Art, Yale University, Harcourt, Brace, New York, 1959.

A readable and valuable history. One of the best.

Giedion, S.: *Space, Time and Architecture,* 3d ed., rev., Harvard University Press, Cambridge, Mass., 1954.

Gloag, John: *Guide to Western Architecture,* Grove Press, New York, 1958.

Gombrich, E. H.: *The Story of Art,* Phaidon, New York, 1950.

A clearly written history designed for boys and girls in their teens. The author says that he has followed three rules: (1) not to write about works not shown in the illustrations, (2) to limit himself to real works of art, and (3) to resist the temptation to be original in his selections. The result is a very useful book for people of any age.

Graves, Maitland: *The Art of Color and Design,* 2d ed., McGraw-Hill, New York, 1951.
Simple, clear, exact, excellent.

Grosser, Maurice: *The Painter's Eye,* New American Library (Mentor), New York, 1955.
A meaty and stimulating book. Easy reading.

Hambidge, J.: *Dynamic Symmetry: The Greek Vase,* Brentano's, New York, 1920.
————: *The Parthenon and Other Greek Temples: Their Dynamic Symmetry,* Yale University Press, New Haven, Conn., 1924.

Hamlin, Talbot: *Architecture: An Art for All Men,* Columbia University Press, New York, 1947.

Haskell, Arnold: *Ballet,* rev. and enl., Penguin, Baltimore, 1949.
Intended as "a guide to the appreciation of ballet," this little book serves its purpose admirably, giving historical and aesthetic background, as well as discussion of present-day ballets and dancers.

Herbert, J. A.: *Illuminated Manuscripts,* Putnam, New York, 1911.

Hind, A. M.: *History of Engraving and Etching,* Houghton Mifflin, Boston, 1923.

Hitchcock, Henry-Russell, and Arthur Drexler: *Built in U.S.A.: Post-War Architecture,* Museum of Modern Art, New York, 1953.

Hudnut, Joseph: *Architecture and the Spirit of Man,* Harvard University Press, Cambridge, Mass., 1949.
Part I, On Traditional and Modern Architecture. Part II, On the Architecture of Cities.

Ivins, William M., Jr.: *How Prints Look,* Beacon Press, Boston, 1943.

Johnson, Charles: *The Language of Painting,* Cambridge University Press, London, 1949.
Very clear and concise criticisms of paintings from the official lecturer of the National Gallery, London. Illustrations are taken largely from the National Gallery.

Kimball, S. F., and G. H. Edgell: *A History of Architecture,* Harper, New York, 1918.

Le Corbusier (pseud. of Charles E. Jeanneret-Gris): *Towards a New Architecture,* tr. from the 13th French ed., with an introduction by Frederick Etchells, Payson and Clarke, New York, 1927.
————: *The City of To-Morrow and Its Planning,* tr. from the 8th French ed. of *Urbanisme,* with an introduction by Frederick Etchells, John Rodker, London, 1929.

Lee, Kathryn Dean, and Katharine Tyler Burchwood: *Art, Then and Now,* Appleton-Century-Crofts, New York, 1949.

Leicht, Hermann: *History of the World's Art,* G. Allen, London, 1952.

Loran, Erle: *Cézanne's Composition: Analysis of Cézanne's Form with Diagrams and Photographs of His Motifs,* University of California Press, Berkeley, Calif., 1946.
The paintings are accompanied by photographs of the scenes from which the paintings were made, with detailed analysis of the changes made and the reasons for them. Excellent.

Lowrie, Walter: *Monuments of the Early Church.* Pantheon. New York, 1917.

Lutz, E. G.: *Practical Engraving and Etching,* Scribner, New York, 1933.

Mâle, Emile: *Religious Art from the Twelfth to the Eighteenth Century,* Noonday Press, New York, 1958.

Malraux, André: *The Voices of Silence,* tr. by Stuart Gilbert. Doubleday, New York, 1953.

Manvell, Roger: *Film,* rev. ed., Penguin, Baltimore, 1946.
An excellent book. Part I discusses the film as a new art form, and Part II, the influence of the film on present-day society.

———: *The Film and the Public,* Penguin, Baltimore, 1955.

Mather, Frank Jewett, Jr.: *A History of Italian Painting,* Viking, New York, 1924.

Mayer, Ralph: *Artist's Handbook of Materials and Techniques,* Viking, New York, 1957.

Morey, Charles Rufus: *Mediaeval Art,* Norton, New York, 1942.

Mumford, Lewis: *The Culture of Cities,* Harcourt, Brace, New York, 1938.
Sociological studies in which city planning is stressed.

———: *City Development,* Harcourt, Brace, New York, 1945.

———: *Sticks and Stones,* 2d ed., Dover, New York, 1955.

Munsterberg, Hugo: *Twentieth Century Painting,* Philosophical Library, New York, 1951.

Myers, Bernard S.: *Art and Civilization,* McGraw-Hill, New York, 1957.

———: *Understanding the Arts,* Holt, New York, 1958.

———: *Modern Art in the Making,* 2d ed., McGraw-Hill, New York, 1959.
The present volume undertakes to set forth for both student and layman the "why" of modern painting as well as the "how," with examination of stylistic changes and historical sequence.

Nelson, George, and Henry Wright: *Tomorrow's House,* Simon and Schuster, New York, 1945.
A very practical book, by the editors of *The Architectural Forum,* on the various parts of a house as designed to meet their separate functions.

New Art in America: Fifty Painters of the 20th Century. Essays by John I. H. Baur, editor, Lloyd Goodrich, Dorothy C. Miller, James Thrall Soby, Frederick S. Wight, Praeger, New York, 1957.

Newton, Eric: *European Painting and Sculpture,* 3d ed., Penguin, Baltimore, 1945.

Nicoll, Allardyce: *Film and Theatre,* Crowell, New York, 1936.

Ozenfant: *Foundations of Modern Art,* first French ed., 1928; new American ed., augmented 1952. Dover, New York, 1952.

Panofsky, Erwin: *Meaning in the Visual Arts,* Doubleday (Anchor), New York, 1955.

Peter, John: *Masters of Modern Architecture,* Braziller, New York, 1958.

Pevsner, Nikolaus: *European Architecture,* 5th ed., Penguin, Baltimore, 1958.

Pfuhl, Ernest: *Masterpieces of Greek Drawing and Painting,* Macmillan, New York, 1956.
Reprint of '26 volume.

Pijoan, Joseph: *An Outline History of Art,* 3 vols., Harper, New York, 1927–1928.

Pope, Arthur: *The Language of Drawing and Painting,* Harvard University Press, Cambridge, Mass., 1949.

Raphael, Max: *Prehistoric Cave Paintings,* tr. by Norbert Guterman. The Bollingen Series IV. Pantheon, New York, 1945.
   Excellent pictures.

Rathbun, Mary Chalmers, and Bartlett H. Hayes, Jr.: *Layman's Guide to Modern Art: Painting for a Scientific Age,* Oxford, New York, 1949.
   One hundred reproductions, each with a few words of simple explanation. Many of the illustrations of modern art are accompanied by more conservative paintings which illustrate the same principles.

Read, Herbert: *The Meaning of Art,* Penguin, Baltimore, 1949.

Rewald, John: *Post-Impressionism: From Van Gogh to Gauguin,* Museum of Modern Art, New York, n.d.
   Van Gogh, Gauguin, Seurat, Redon, and others.

Richards, J. M.: *An Introduction to Modern Architecture,* Penguin, Baltimore, 1956.
   A *must* for any student of modern architecture. Clear, comprehensive, sensible. A very readable account of modern architecture from a sympathetic but conservative point of view.

Richter, Gisela M. A.: *The Sculpture and Sculptors of the Ancient Greeks,* Yale University Press, New Haven, Conn., 1930.

Ritchie, Andrew C.: *Sculpture of the Twentieth Century,* Museum of Modern Art, New York, n.d.
   Analysis of modern sculpture in its relation to the various modern schools. Clear and exact.

Robb, David M., and J. J. Garrison: *Art in the Western World,* 3d ed., Harper, New York, 1953.
   As the title indicates, this history limits itself to Western art. The content is organized in three sections: architecture, sculpture, painting. This treatment means a lack in the over-all picture of an age but greater concentration on each of the arts. Deservedly popular.

Rothschild, Lincoln: *Sculpture through the Ages,* with a foreword by Paul Manship, McGraw-Hill, New York, 1942.
   One hundred twenty-three full-page plates, each with a short description.

Sachs, Curt: *World History of the Dance,* tr. by Bessie Schönberg, Norton, New York, 1937.
   In two parts: the first has to do with movements, themes and types, forms and choreography, and music; the second gives a brief history of the dance.

Schaefer-Simmern, Henry: *Sculpture in Europe Today,* University of California Press, Berkeley, Calif., 1955.
   One hundred twenty-eight plates with biographical notes of the artists.

Scott, Geoffrey: *The Architecture of Humanism,* Doubleday (Anchor), New York, 1954.
   The standard volume on the value of form and order of the Renaissance.

Seuphor, Michel: *Dictionary of Abstract Painting,* Tudor Publishing Co., New York, 1957.

Sewall, John Ives: *A History of Western Art,* Holt, New York, 1953.
Definite, clear, intelligent.

Shapley, Fern Rusk, and John Shapley: *Comparisons in Art: A Companion to the National Gallery of Art, Washington,* Phaidon, New York, 1957.

Speed, H.: *Practice and Science of Drawing,* Lippincott, Philadelphia, 1913.

Taylor, Joshua C.: *Learning to Look: A Handbook for the Visual Arts,* prepared with the Humanities Staff of the College at the University of Chicago. University of Chicago Press, Chicago, 1957.
A brief but clear book. The first half deals with the analysis of a work of art, the second with its medium and the techniques for making it.

Teague, Walter Dorwin: *Design This Day,* Harcourt, Brace, New York, 1940.

Upjohn, Everard M., Paul S. Wingert, and Jane Gaston Mahler: *History of World Art,* 2d ed., Oxford, New York, 1958.
One of the best one-volume histories available now.

Valentiner, W. R.: *Origins of Modern Sculpture,* Wittenborn, New York, 1946.
An aesthetic of sculpture, as well as a clear presentation of the sources from which modern sculpture has drawn its inspiration. Good illustrations.

Venturi, Lionello: *Painting and Painters: How to Look at a Picture, from Giotto to Chagall,* Scribner, New York, 1945.
Not as elementary as the subtitle would suggest. Good discussions of the bases of the study of art.

Weitenkampf, Frank: *How to Appreciate Prints,* rev. ed., Scribner, New York, 1932.

Weller, Allen S.: "The Image of Man in Contemporary Art," in *Contemporary American Painting and Sculpture,* University of Illinois Press, Urbana, Ill., 1959.

Wilenski, R. H.: *French Painting,* Branford, Boston, 1931.

Wölfflin, H.: *Principles of Art History,* tr. from the 7th German ed. by M. D. Hottinger, Holt, New York, 1949.
Wölfflin is interested in the way we see rather than in chronological development.

Wright, Frank Lloyd: *The Natural House,* Horizon Press, New York, 1954.

———: *An American Architecture,* ed. by Edgar Kaufman, Jr., Horizon Press, New York, 1955.

———: *The Story of the Tower: The Tree that Escaped the Crowded Forest,* Horizon Press, New York, 1956.
The story of the building of the Price Tower in Bartlesville, Oklahoma.

———: *The Living City,* Horizon Press, New York, 1958.

Zevi, Bruno: *Architecture as Space,* tr. by Milton Gendel, Horizon Press, New York, 1957.
Internal and external space. The interplay of volumes. Space as a concept through the ages right up to the present time. Excellent illustrations.

ILLUSTRATIONS OF ART SUBJECTS

Unesco World Art Series (N. Y. Graphic Society)

The following volumes have been issued: Spain, India, Egypt, Australia, Yugoslavia, Norway, Iran, Ceylon.

Skira

Albert Skira of Geneva has brought out a number of books of art with excellent illustrations in color. Some deal with a single artist, some with a movement or a period.

Phaidon Press

A series of volumes brought out by the Oxford University Press, New York, exceptionally high in quality. Each volume is devoted to a single artist, or more rarely a period or group of artists.

University Prints (Cambridge, Mass.)

Photographs of the major art works of the world. The price (only a few cents) makes reproductions easily available.

Artext Prints (Westport, Conn.)

A large collection of colored prints, very inexpensive.

Teaching Portfolios (Museum of Modern Art, New York)

Large illustrations suitable for mounting on a wall, one on *Modern Sculpture,* one on *Textures,* one on *Structure and Space in Contemporary Architecture.*

Three Smaller Series

Form and Color (Harper, New York)
Hyperion (Duell, Sloan, & Pearce, New York)
Iris (Oxford, New York)

Form and Color devotes a volume to many reproductions of a single masterpiece. *Hyperion* is a collection of modern painters, one artist to a volume. Some volumes are excellent. *Iris* is an excellent set of very thin volumes devoted to subjects of restricted interest, e.g., *Art of the Far East, French Cathedral Windows, Persian Painting.*

INDEX

Page references in **boldface** type indicate illustrations and quotations.